# THE FAMILY HANDYMAN PRO TIPS

Editor in Chief: Ken Collier
Books Editor: Gary Wentz
Designer: Diana Boger
Cover Design: Vern Johnson
Contributing Copy Editors: Judy Arginteanu, Donna Bierbach
Indexing: Stephanie Reymann

The Reader's Digest Association, Inc.
President & Chief Executive Officer: Robert E. Guth
Vice President, Group Publisher: Russell S. Ellis

Warning: All do-it-yourself activities involve a degree of risk. Skills, materials, tools, and site conditions vary widely. Although the editors have made every effort to ensure accuracy, the reader remains responsible for the selection and use of tools, materials, and methods. Always obey local codes and laws, follow manufacturer's operating instructions, and observe safety precautions.

ISBN 978-1-62145-105-1

Address any comments to:
Books Editor
2915 Commers Drive, Suite 700
Eagan, MN 55121

To order additional copies, visit shopthefamilyhandyman.com

For more Reader's Digest products and information, visit our Web site at rd.com.
For more about The Family Handyman magazine, visit familyhandyman.com.

Printed in the United States of America.
1 3 5 7 9 10 8 6 4 2

# Contents

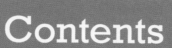

## 1 CABINETS, COUNTERTOPS AND SHELVES

## 2 FLOORING AND CARPETING

## 3 REMODELING AND CONSTRUCTION

## 4 CONCRETE AND MASONRY

# 5 LAWN AND GARDEN

# 6 ELECTRICAL

# 7 SAVING ENERGY

# 8 PLUMBING

## 9 TILING

## 10 PAINTING AND DECORATING

## 11 DECKS AND TREE HOUSES

## 12 CARS, TRUCKS, MOTORCYCLES AND RVS

## 13 GARAGES

## 14 WOODWORKING

## 15 TOOLS, MATERIALS AND SUPPLIES

## 16 DOORS, WINDOWS, BASEBOARD AND TRIM

# THE FAMILY
# Handyman

## More ways to get DIY jobs done right

**The Family Handyman Magazine** is North America's top DIY home improvement magazine, with new projects, repairs and tips in every issue. Subscribe and save at FamilyHandyman.com.

**The Family Handyman** for **iPad®** gives you each issue of the magazine, plus videos and bonus content. Get it on the App Store.

**FamilyHandyman.com** gives you instant access to thousands of projects, techniques and expert fixes. And it's all free!

We have **books** too! From storage projects to energy saving, get the tips and step-by-step advice you need at shopthefamilyhandyman.com.

Sign up for **FREE newsletters** at familyhandyman.com/freenewsletter. Get DIY tips, projects, expert repairs and more delivered to your inbox every week.

**The Family Handyman eBooks** cover a huge range of DIY topics, from tool tips and repairs to painting and flooring. Get them for your Nook, Kindle, iPad at familyhandyman.com/ebooks.

Whether you're an experienced DIYer or just getting started, we put know-how at your fingertips.

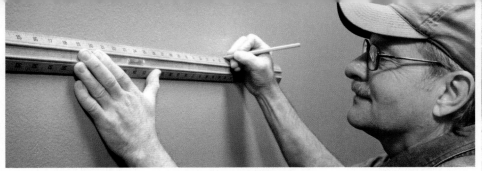

# Chapter One

# CABINETS, COUNTERTOPS AND SHELVES

# Installing cabinets

Kitchen cabinets aren't cheap, and while you shouldn't be afraid to install them, you don't want to screw them up, either. We asked Jerome Worm, an experienced installer, to show you what it takes to install basic box cabinets successfully. His tips can save you time and help you avoid costly mistakes on your next installation.

**MEET THE PRO**

**Jerome Worm** has installed cabinets in hundreds of kitchens. These days, he can hang them in his sleep. Here are some of his best tips.

## Mark up the wall first

Every good cabinet installation starts with a good layout. Jerome calls it "blueprinting" the wall. Here's how to do it: Measure from the highest point in the floor (see "Raise the Cabinets for Flooring," p. 13), and draw a level line marking the top of the base cabinets. Measure up 19-1/2 in. from that line and draw another line for the bottom of the upper cabinets. Label the location of the cabinets and appliances on the wall. Draw a vertical line to line up the edge of the first cabinet to be installed. Finally, mark the stud locations.

**TOP OF HINGE**

24 30 LEFT SINK

## Remove the doors and drawers

Removing shelves, doors and drawers makes installation easier and prevents damage. Mark the location of the doors on painter's tape, and make a pencil mark at the top of the hinges so you have a good starting point when you reinstall them. Remember that many upper cabinets have no designated top or bottom. They can be hung either direction depending on which way you want the doors to swing. So decide that before you mark the hinges.

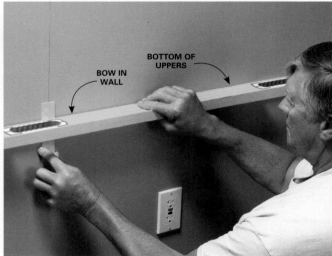

**BOW IN WALL**

**BOTTOM OF UPPERS**

## Shim extreme bows

Most of the time you can shim the cabinets as you go, but if there's an extreme bow in the wall (more than 3/8 in.), shim it out before you hang the cabinet. If you don't, you may accidentally pull the back off the cabinet while fastening it into place. Hold a level across the wall, and slide a shim up from the bottom (go in from the top when you're doing the top side) until it's snug. Then pin or tape it into place.

**LEDGER BOARD**

## Start with the upper cabinets

It's easier to hang the uppers when you're not leaning way over the base cabinets. Rest the uppers on a ledger board—it'll ensure a nice, straight alignment and eliminate the frustration of holding the cabinets in place while screwing them to the wall.

## Clamp, drill and fasten

When connecting two cabinets to each other, line up the face frames and clamp them together. Both cabinets should be fastened to the wall at this point, but you may have to loosen one cabinet or the other to get the frames to line up perfectly. Jerome prefers hand-screw clamps because they don't flex, and less flex means a tighter grip. Predrill a 1/8-in. hole before screwing them together with a 2-1/2-in. screw. Choose the less noticeable cabinet of the two for drilling and placing the screw head.

## Use a block of wood for scribing

Find the largest distance between the outside of the cabinet and the wall. Take that measurement and make a pencil mark on your filler strip (measure right to left in this case). Clamp the filler onto the cabinet flush with the inside of the vertical rail. Measure from the wall to your pencil mark, and make a scribing block that size. Use your block to trace a pencil line down the filler strip. Masking tape on the filler strip helps the pencil line show up better and protects the finish from the saw table.

FILLER STRIP

SCRIBING BLOCK

## Mark the stud locations on upper cabinets

Jerome prefers to predrill the screw holes from the inside of the cabinet so the drill bit doesn't "blow out" the wood on the inside where it can be seen. Do this by marking the stud locations on the inside of the cabinet and drilling pilot holes. Start by finding the distance from the wall or adjacent cabinet to the center of the next stud. For 1/2-in.-thick cabinet walls, subtract 7/8 in. from that measurement, and measure that distance from the inside of the cabinet. Make a pencil mark on both the top and the bottom nailing strip. The outside of the cabinet walls are not flush with the rest of the cabinet; that 7/8 in. represents the thickness of the cabinet wall and the distance the walls are recessed.

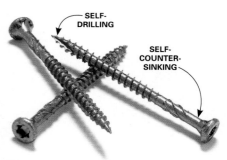

SELF-DRILLING

SELF-COUNTER-SINKING

## Use good screws

Jerome prefers GRK's R4 self-countersinking screw, which he calls "the Cadillac of screws" (available at home centers or online). You'll pay accordingly, but why scrimp on screws when you're spending thousands of dollars on cabinets? Whatever you do, don't use drywall screws—they'll just snap off and you'll end up with an extra hole.

## Fasten the back, then shim

Line up the base cabinets with the level line on the wall. Fasten the back of the cabinets to that line. Once the backs of the cabinets are level, use shims to level the sides. Take your time on this step—nobody likes to have eggs roll off a slanted countertop.

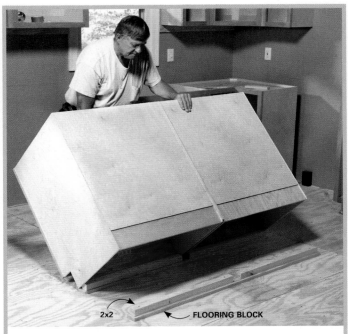

2x2    ← **FLOORING BLOCK**

## Use 2x2s to secure cabinets to the floor

Cabinets that make up islands and peninsulas need to be secured to the floor. Join the island cabinets and set them in place. Trace an outline of the cabinets on the floor. Screw 2x2s to the floor 1/2 in. on the inside of the line to account for the thickness of the cabinets. Anchor the island cabinets to the 2x2s with screws. If needed, place flooring blocks under the 2x2s (see "Raise the cabinets for flooring," p. 13).

## Cut oversize holes

Cutting exact size holes for water lines and drainpipes might impress your spouse or customer, but such precision is likely to result in unnecessary headaches for you. Cutting larger holes makes it easier to slide the cabinet into place and provides wiggle room for minor adjustments. No one's going to notice the oversize holes once the cabinet is filled with dish soaps, scrubbers and recycling bins.

FLOORING BLOCK

GAP FOR FLOORING

## Raise the cabinets for flooring

If the kitchen flooring is going to be hardwood or tile, and you're installing it after the cabinets, you'll have to raise the cabinets off the floor or the dishwasher won't fit under the countertop. Use blocks to represent the finished floor height, and add those distances to the guide line for the base cabinet tops. Hold the blocks back a bit from the front so the flooring can tuck underneath. Your flooring guys will love you for this.

## What's the best lube for squeaky drawers?

When using lubricants indoors, a bad smell is only one of the issues to consider, says Dr. Larry Beaver, a research expert at the company that makes Liquid Wrench products. "Some products can leave graphite stains, sticky residues that attract dust and dirt, and can even drip onto flooring or cabinet interiors."

For lubing drawer slides, door hinges, overhead fans, and other sticky or squeaky things inside the house without causing stains or odor, Beaver recommends using a dry lubricant that contains PFTE (commonly known as Teflon). "It dries fast and leaves a durable, light-colored lubricating film right where you spray it."

Three common brands are Liquid Wrench Dry Lubricant, DuPont Teflon and Blaster Dry Lube, which are available at many home centers and hardware stores.

**MEET THE PRO**

**Dr. Larry Beaver** is the vice president of technology at Radiator Specialty Co. in Charlotte, NC. In this position, he oversees the product research and development, regulatory and environmental functions for all divisions of the manufacturing company, including GUNK and Liquid Wrench brands.

## Get more storage space— without remodeling

Lower cabinets offer the biggest storage spaces in most kitchens. But according to kitchen designers, the back half of this space is usually wasted—it's packed with long-forgotten junk or left unused because stored items are out of view and hard to reach. Rollout bins let you see and use the whole space.

# Installing cabinet hardware

There's more to installing kitchen hardware than drilling holes and screwing on knobs and pulls. Whether you're installing hardware on brand-new cabinets or replacing the hardware in a 100-year-old kitchen, think before you drill. Cabinets are expensive, and they look a whole lot better without extra holes. We asked our cabinet expert, Jerome Worm, for some tips on how he installs the "jewelry of the kitchen." Having installed thousands of pulls and knobs, he has assembled quite a toolbox of tricks.

TOP OF RAIL

RAIL

STILE

## Use the door rail as a guide

The location of knobs and pulls isn't written in stone, but there are some standard practices. One good rule of thumb is to line up a knob with the top of the bottom door rail. If you're installing door pulls, line up the bottom of the pull with the top of the door rail. Always center them on the door stile.

## Temporarily attach the hardware

Ultimately, the person paying for the hardware has the final word on where the knobs and pulls are to be installed. If Jerome's customers don't like his suggestions, he sticks a piece of reusable putty adhesive to the hardware and lets them put it wherever they want. He marks that spot with a pencil and installs the rest of the hardware accordingly. Reusable putty adhesive is sold at home centers.

ADHESIVE PUTTY

## Templates make the job easier

If you have more than a few knobs or pulls to install, use a template. A template makes the job go faster, increases uniformity and reduces the chance for mistakes. Installation templates are available at a home centers.

If you install a lot of hardware, buy a pro version like the one Jerome is using in the photo on p. 14. That's an EZ-JIG EZ1000 (available online). It's adjustable and has steel grommets where you insert the drill bit.

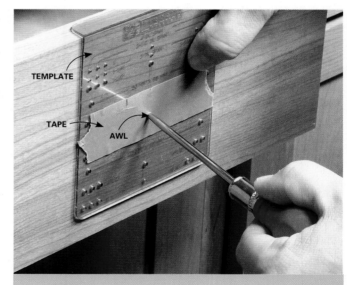

TEMPLATE

TAPE

AWL

## Cover unused holes with tape

Store-bought templates and well-used homemade templates have a bunch of holes you won't use on every job. Avoid using the wrong hole by sticking masking tape over the jig and poking through only the holes you need. Instead of using a pencil to mark the location of the hole on the cabinet, use an awl. That way your drill bit won't skate off in the wrong direction when you drill the hole.

## Hide old holes with back plates

If you're switching from a pull to a knob or you'd prefer to select pulls with a different hole pattern, you can cover the old holes or hide damaged surfaces with back plates. Home centers don't have a huge selection, so consider buying yours online. You'll find hundreds to choose from.

OLD HOLE

BACK PLATE

OLD HOLE

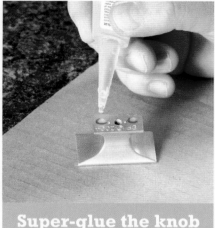

## Super-glue the knob

Oblong and rectangular knobs that fasten with a single screw are notorious for twisting over time. Thread sealant will keep a screw from coming loose from the knob, but it won't necessarily stop the knob from twisting. Jerome avoids callbacks by adding a drop of super glue to the back of these types of knobs before he installs them.

TEMPLATE

## Make a simple drawer template

If you don't have a template, make one. This simple template consists of two pieces of wood and takes only a few minutes to make. This same template can be used for almost any size door and most hardware sizes.

TWO-SIDED TEMPLATE

## Two-sided templates prevent tear-out

If you're having problems with the wood on the back side of the cabinet doors tearing out every time you drill a hole, make a two-sided template. Make sure the spacer wood is close to the same size as the cabinet doors. The tighter the fit, the less chance of tear-out.

## Don't install hardware in front of the sink

The false drawer directly in front of the sink may look naked without any hardware, but it's not very comfortable getting poked by a knob in your midsection every time you lean over the sink.

## Mix putty to match

If back plates won't cover the old holes, use putty to fill them. The wood grain on cabinet doors and fronts usually varies in color, so take one of the doors to a hardware store or home center, and buy three different colors of putty. Buy one that matches the darkest grain, one that matches the lightest grain and one halfway between. Use the three to mix a custom color to fill the holes.

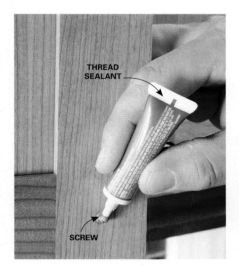

THREAD SEALANT

SCREW

## Use thread sealant to keep the screws tight

Every time the screw in a knob works itself loose, the owners of those cabinets are going to think unflattering thoughts about whoever put them in. Keep your customers happy—add a dab of removeable thread sealant to every screw you install. Loctite is one brand.

## Take old hardware to the store

Not every pull is the same size, and not every cabinet door/drawer is the same thickness. If you have the old hardware with you at the store, you'll be able to tell the size of the pulls you need as well as the length of screws required.

HIGHER THAN CENTER

## Install hardware higher on the lowest drawer

Most drawer pulls are centered on the drawer fronts, but if the cabinet you're working on has two or three drawers the same size and one larger one at the bottom, install the bottom knob (or pull) higher than the center of that drawer front. Install it so all the knobs on the cabinet are spaced evenly. This configuration is pleasing to the eye—and you don't have to bend over as far to open the bottom drawer.

## Space-saving electrical detail

Continuous electrical strips with outlets spaced every 12 in. are positioned along the back lower edge of these wall cabinets. A valance built into the cabinets helps hide the strips—and the undercabinet lighting—from view, and the close spacing provides power for small appliances wherever they're used.

OUTLETS

# Wire shelving made easier

Wire shelving is popular because of its price, flexibility and ease of installation. Wire shelving can be designed to meet almost any need at a fraction of the cost of a custom built-in system. And while installing wire shelving isn't quite a no-brainer, you don't need to be a master carpenter or own a fully equipped cabinet shop to get it done. We picked the brain of a pro for these tips to help you on your next installation.

## MEET THE PRO

Over the past 15 years, **Tim Bischke** has hung wire shelves in thousands of closets. His jobs have ranged from simple one-shelf reach-in closets to elaborate walk-in wardrobe sanctuaries. When you've hung that many shelves, you can't help but know what you're doing.

## Buy extra pieces

Even if you're just planning to build one closet shelf, have extra parts on hand. It takes a lot less time to return a few wall clips than it does to stop working to make a special trip to the store for just one. And plans change, so if you or your customer decide to add a section of shelving, you'll be prepared.

**CLOSET GAUGE**

**HEAVY GAUGE**

## Leave the heavy stuff for the garage

Tim primarily works with standard wire shelving sold at home centers. Most manufacturers make a heavier-duty product for garage storage, but Tim feels that the regular stuff is plenty strong for the average bedroom, pantry or hall closet. However, if your customer's closet is going to store a bowling ball collection, you may want to consider upgrading.

**BUBBLE STICK**

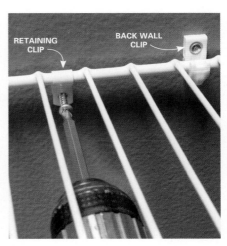

**RETAINING CLIP**

**BACK WALL CLIP**

## Avoid upheaval

Back wall clips are designed to support the shelf, but if there are a bunch of clothes hanging on the front of the shelf with nothing on top to weigh them down, the back of the shelf can lift. To keep the shelf in place, Tim installs a retaining clip in a stud near the middle of the shelf. One clip toward the middle of an 8-ft. shelf is plenty.

## Lay it out with a bubble stick

Tim uses a bubble stick rather than a level. A bubble stick is like a ruler and a level rolled into one. Holding a level against the wall with one hand can be frustrating. Levels are rigid, and they pivot out of place when resting on a stud that's bowed out a bit. A bubble stick has a little flex, so it can ride the imperfections of the wall yet still deliver a straight line. You can get one online.

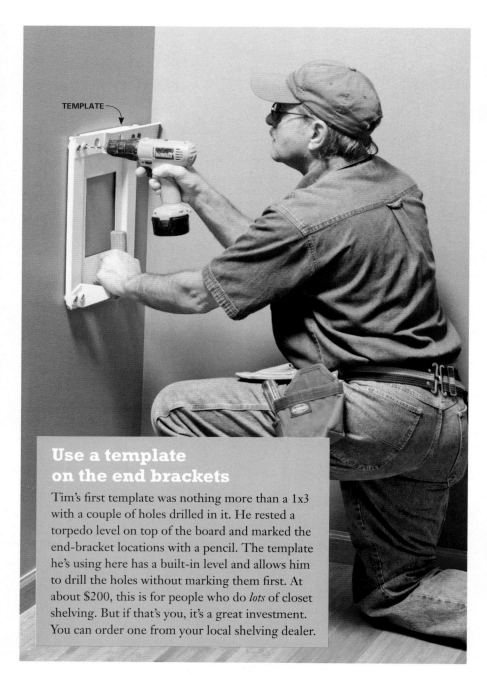

## Use a template on the end brackets

Tim's first template was nothing more than a 1x3 with a couple of holes drilled in it. He rested a torpedo level on top of the board and marked the end-bracket locations with a pencil. The template he's using here has a built-in level and allows him to drill the holes without marking them first. At about $200, this is for people who do *lots* of closet shelving. But if that's you, it's a great investment. You can order one from your local shelving dealer.

TEMPLATE

## A bolt cutter works best

Cut your shelving with a bolt cutter. It's quick and easy, and it makes a clean cut. To make room for the cutter, Tim uses his feet to hold the shelving off the ground.

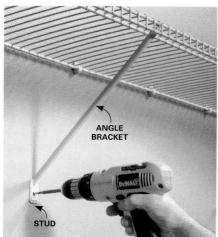

ANGLE BRACKET

STUD

## Space the angle brackets evenly

Tim considers aesthetics when installing his angle brackets. If a shelf only needs one bracket, he'll find the stud closest to the center. If two or three brackets are required, he'll try to space them evenly, making sure that at least one bracket toward the center is hitting a stud.

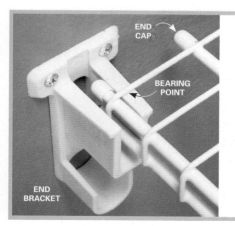

END CAP

BEARING POINT

END BRACKET

## Measure an inch short

When cutting the shelf, measure wall to wall, and subtract an inch. This allows for the thickness of the end brackets plus a little wiggle room. It's the top, thinner wire that actually supports the shelf, and one wire per end is enough. Cutting exact lengths will only earn you wall scratches and a trip back to the cutting station.

## Pegboard prevents tipping

When Tim installs wire shelving in pantries, he likes to cap the top of the shelves with white 1/4-in. pegboard. This stops the skinnier items from tipping over. He uses white zip ties to hold the pegboard in place. Find 4 x 8-ft. sheets at home centers.

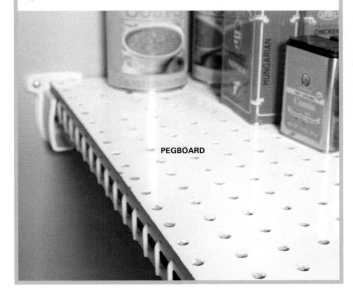

PEGBOARD

CORNER HANGING BAR

BAR HANGER SUPPORT

## Hanger sliding freedom

One common complaint about wire shelving is that it restricts the movement of the hangers because the hangers are stuck between the shelves. That's why Tim always offers the upgrade of a hanger rod. Most manufacturers make some version of one. A hanger rod allows clothes to slide from one end of the closet to the other, even past an inside corner. This upgrade will add about 30 percent to the cost of the materials on a standard shelf design. Make sure the type of shelving you buy will work with the hanging rod hardware you plan to use.

## Back wall clips don't need to hit studs

It may go against your every instinct, but hitting a stud when you're installing the back wall clips slows the process down and isn't necessary. After marking their locations, Tim drills a 1/4-in. hole and pops the preloaded pushpin in with a push tool. He loves his push tool. It has a little indentation in the tip that won't slip off the pin when it's being set in the drywall. The occasional wall clips that do land on studs need to be fastened with a screw instead of a pin. You can order a push tool from your local shelving dealer.

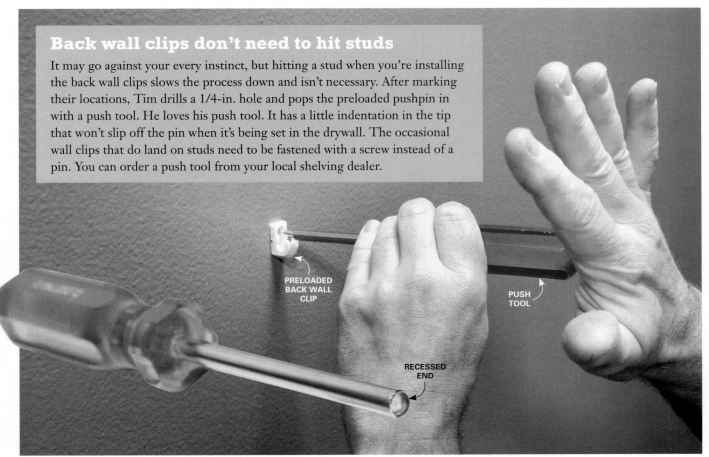

PRELOADED BACK WALL CLIP

PUSH TOOL

RECESSED END

# The perfect countertop

On any given day, your kitchen countertop may wind up playing the roles of cutting board, hot pad, office desk, food prep surface, snack bar and headquarters for hindquarters. You need a surface that's durable, attractive and easy to get along with. It's worth weighing the options carefully when you're remodeling. Top-notch tops are installed by pros only, but they have a look and feel no other material can match.

## When you're choosing countertops, note these guidelines

- Expect to spend 10 to 15 percent of your kitchen remodeling budget on countertops and installation. If you spend disproportionately more or less, you may wind up with tops that don't fit the look and feel of the rest of your kitchen.
- Solid surface and engineered stone countertops (see p. 23) are very uniform and homogenous; what you see in the showroom is what you'll get in your kitchen. Some people like this predictability. But if you want something more natural looking, consider granite.

- Consider installing more than one type or color of top. Serious cooks may want to include a section of wood for chopping; bakers may want to include a section of marble for rolling dough. Using a different-color top on an island than you use in the rest of the kitchen can help differentiate workspaces and add interest.
- Colors and trends come and go, but most of these super-durable countertops stay in place for 15 to 20 years or more. Think twice before specifying that bright blue top.

Here's a look at the pros and cons of three popular high-end options: solid surface, engineered stone and granite.

## Solid surface: a zillion options

These tops—sold under brand names such as Corian, Avonite, Fountainhead and Swanstone—are made from acrylic and polyester blends. One company alone offers its product line in more than 110 colors and textures, and with dozens of edge profiles available, the possibilities are endless. Solid surface tops are nonporous, making them excellent for food preparation and difficult to stain. They can be formed into nearly any shape and size, sinks can be undermounted, and joined sections, when installed correctly, appear seamless. These tops are durable, and if they're burned or scratched, the damage can usually be sanded and buffed out by a certified installer. Avoid placing hot pans directly on the surface; intense heat can pop seams and discolor surfaces.

Expect to spend $45 to $85 per square foot installed (about $90 to $160 per linear foot of countertop). Manufacturers typically warranty their product for 10 years.

## Engineered stone: the best of two worlds

Engineered stone tops (sold under various brand names) combine the beauty of natural stone with the functional benefits of solid surface materials. They're composed of a blend of about 95 percent crushed natural stone—usually quartz—and 5 percent synthetic resins to bind the stone. Tops can be tinted in a wide variety of colors. They're nonporous and resistant to both stains and scratches. Sinks can be undermounted and a wide range of edging options are available. Like genuine stone, they have an extremely hard surface, which is excellent for durability but also slippery and cold to the touch.

Costs range from about $65 to $150 per square foot installed, and most carry a 10-year warranty.

## Granite:
## rock solid and natural

Twenty years ago, granite countertops were a rarity; today, because of greater availability and an increased number of fabricators, granite tops are more common and affordable. Granite is available in a variety of colors, sinks can be under-mounted and a variety of edgings can be crafted. Since each piece is unique, you may want to visit the fabricator to select the exact slabs for your kitchen. Seams are slightly more evident in granite, and hot grease can stain unsealed tops, but overall, granite requires very little maintenance. Expect to spend $75 to $150 per square foot installed.

Soapstone and marble tops are also available through most granite top fabrica-tors. Both products are softer, require more upkeep and are more susceptible to stains and scratches. But if you're willing to commit to more maintenance, they're viable, unique-looking alternatives.

## Pros only, please

Besides a high-end look and great durability, solid surface, engi-neered stone and granite tops have something else in common: All must be professionally installed. Manufacturers of the first two products will not warranty their tops unless they're installed by certified pros who have undergone extensive training.

Almost all granite tops are installed professionally, since fabrication and installation require specialized tools and skills. It's simply not worth it for a do-it-yourselfer to invest the time and dollars required, especially for a project that's usually a once-in-a-lifetime affair. If you want to roll up your sleeves, pick up a paint-brush or hammer, but leave these tops to the pros.

# Shortcuts to better built-ins

Sometimes you can speed up, simplify and still build a masterpiece. In the following pages, a veteran cabinetmaker spills some of his best secrets for cutting labor and hassles without sacrificing quality.

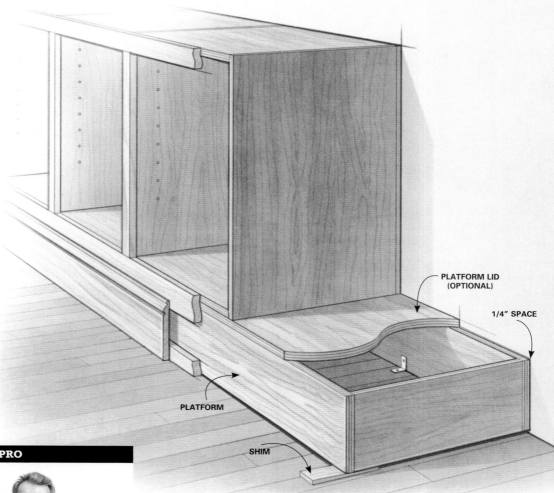

**PLATFORM LID (OPTIONAL)**

**1/4" SPACE**

**PLATFORM**

**SHIM**

**MEET THE PRO**

**Ken Geisen** has been a cabinetmaker in North Branch, MN, for 20 years.

## Set cabinets on a platform

Most lower cabinets include a base or toe-kick that raises them off the floor. But Ken doesn't build them that way. Instead, he builds a plywood platform that acts as the base for an entire row of cabinets. The platform can be undersized to allow for a toe space or full size for a more traditional look (shown here).

This approach has a couple of major advantages. First, cabinet construction is simpler. The cabinets are just boxes; no extended sides to form a base, no toe-kick cutouts. Second, installation is faster. Leveling one platform is a lot easier than positioning each cabinet individually. Ken sets the box 1/4 in. from walls to allow for wavy or out-of-plumb walls.

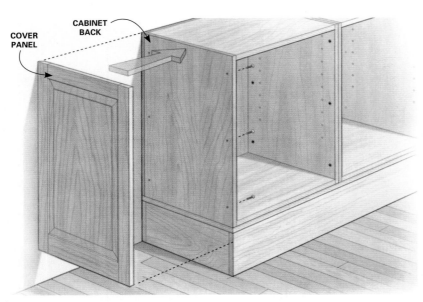

## Quick, classic side panels

When the side of a cabinet box will be exposed, you have to hide the cabinet back edge somehow. The usual method is to rabbet the side and recess the back. But Ken gets a richer look with less hassle. He simply glues and nails the back to the cabinet box and hides the exposed plywood with a frame and panel for a classic look. And since the cover panel is a separate part, it's easy to scribe it to the wall before fastening it to the cabinet.

## Secret screws for shelves

Lots of designs have upper shelf units that rest on lower cabinets. Here's Ken's trick for fastening the shelf units to the cabinet top so that the screws are hidden: He sets the cabinet top on the lower cabinets, and scribes it and sands it to fit the wall. But he doesn't screw it in place yet. Instead, he positions the shelf units on the top and carefully slides the top forward just far enough so that he can drive screws into the shelf sides and dividers. After sliding the top back into place, he screws the top to the cabinets from below and screws the shelf units to the wall.

## Use prefinished plywood (sometimes)

With its tough, flawless clearcoat, prefinished plywood eliminates finishing hassles. But Ken uses it only for "no-show" parts like cabinet boxes and shelves. Finishing other parts to match the color and sheen of the factory-finished plywood is just too difficult.

Finding prefinished plywood can be difficult. Your best bet is a lumberyard that caters to cabinet-makers (search online for "cabinet making supplies" followed by the name of your city). Expect to pay about $40 to $120 per 4 x 8-ft. sheet, depending on the thickness, grade and species.

## Break down face frames

Pocket screws are a standard joinery method, but Ken has a nonstandard approach. He assembles face frames with pocket screws, but without glue. He sands the frames, labels the back of each part and then disassembles them for easier finishing. Transport is easier too: Ken can pack a mile of face-frame parts into his van and carry them into the house without banging up walls. The cabinet boxes need less TLC too, since they're frameless during transport. Once on-site, Ken reassembles the frames with pocket screws and glue. For pocket joinery, Ken uses a Kreg Jig (sold at home centers).

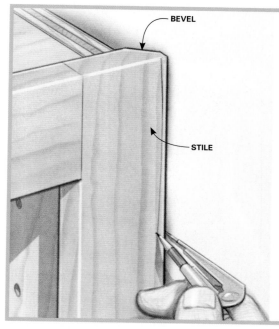

BEVEL

STILE

## Back-bevel wall stiles

Before scribing stiles that will meet walls, bevel the back edge on your table saw. That way, you'll have less wood to belt-sand off when you shape the edge to the contour of the wall. Ken cuts a 45-degree bevel about 1/2 in. deep, so he has only 1/4 in. of wood remaining.

## Thicker backs save time

Most cabinetmakers use 1/4-in. plywood for cabinet backs. But Ken prefers 1/2-in. material. The thicker plywood usually adds less than $5 to the cost of each box and eliminates the need for a hanging strip or "nailer" at the back of the cabinet. That means quicker construction and a cleaner interior look. Best of all, it allows you to drive a screw through the back anywhere, not just at the nailer.

She's spent 13 years sanding hardwood and teaching others to do it themselves.

## Does DIY make cents?

DIY floor refinishing typically costs about a third or a fourth of what you'd pay to hire a pro. On average, especially on jobs that are larger than 500 sq. ft., my DIY customers save $1,000 by doing it themselves. Not bad for a weekend of work. Keep in mind that pro costs vary a lot, so it's worth making a few calls to check on pro rates in your area.

## Good-bye, base shoe

If a room has quarter-round molding (aka "base shoe") at the bottom of baseboards, I usually pry it off and reinstall it later. Here's why: Edge sanding slightly lowers the floor and leaves the baseboard standing on a little plateau. You think you won't notice this, but you will. Edge sanding also scuffs up the base shoe, which means touch-up work later.

Removing the base shoe sidesteps both problems. Label the base shoe as you remove it to avoid confusion when you reinstall it. Exception: If the base shoe is bonded to the baseboard by decades of paint buildup, I leave it in place. If you have newer baseboards and no quarter-round, leave it in place, but expect lots of the aforementioned touch-ups.

## Pet stains are forever

Water stains usually disappear after a couple of passes of the sander. But stains caused by pet urine often penetrate so deep into the wood that you just can't sand them out. Bleach formulated for wood floors may be worth a try, but in my experience the results are mediocre at best, and at worst, the wood is left pitted and blotched.

Often, the only solution is to replace the wood—or finish over the stain and think of it as a permanent memorial to a beloved pet.

How do you tell water from pee? Pet stains are darker (deep gray, almost black around the edges) and often look like a map of Indonesia, with big and small islands covering a large area.

## Prep the room

Some of the prep work is obvious, like removing all the furniture and covering doorways with plastic. Here are some steps DIYers often don't think of:

- Cover or plug air grilles to keep dust out of ducts. Turn off the HVAC system at the thermostat; less air movement means less dust traveling around your house.
- Remove all window coverings and any art on the walls (unless you want to clean them later).
- Remove doors that open into the room. You can't completely sand under doors, even by opening and closing them.
- Raise low-hanging light fixtures; just tie two links of the chain together with wire. Otherwise, you're guaranteed to bump your head. Repeatedly.
- Nail down any loose boards with finish nails.
- When you're sanding, nail heads will rip the sanding belt (which costs you money) or gouge the sanding drum (which costs you more money). So countersink all nails by at least 1/8 in.

## Scrape out corners

When the sanding is done, use a paint scraper to attack spots that the machines can't reach. A sharp scraper will leave a super-smooth glazed surface that won't take finish the same as the surrounding wood. So rough up scraped areas with 80- or 100-grit paper.

## Rental tips

You'll need two rental machines: a drum sander to sand most of the floor and an edger to sand along baseboards. Here are some tips:

- Rent from a flooring specialty shop rather than a general rental store. You'll get expertise at no extra expense.
- Measure the room. Knowing the square footage will help the crew at the rental store estimate how many sanding belts and discs you'll need.
- Prep before you rent. The prep work will take longer than you think. Don't waste money by picking up the sanders before you're ready to use them.
- Get a drum sander that uses a continuous belt or sleeve, not one that requires you to wrap a strip of abrasive around the drum. That's tedious and often leads to chatter marks on the floor.
- Think twice before you rent a flat-pad sander (aka "orbital" or "square-buff" sander). Sure, they're easier to use, but they're just not aggressive enough to bite into finishes or hardwoods.

### One critical feature

Choose a sander that has a lever to raise and lower the sanding drum. That makes graceful stops and starts easier—and reduces gouging.

### Nix the stripper

DIYers often think that paint stripper is a good way to get rid of the finish before sanding. But don't waste your time. Sanding is faster. And cheaper.

### Detect nails

Drag a metal snow shovel across the floor (upside down). When it hits a nail, you'll hear it.

## Pick a starting grit

It takes coarse abrasive to cut through a finish and into hardwood. But determining just how coarse isn't easy for a DIYer. So I recommend a trial-and-error process: Start with 36-grit. If that doesn't completely remove the finish in one pass, step down to 24-grit. If 24-grit doesn't remove at least three-quarters of the finish in one pass, go to 16-grit. Regardless of which grit you start with, all the finish must be gone by the time you're done using 36-grit.

### Change belts often

I sell sanding belts, so this might sound self-serving. But trust me. Using dull belts is a strategy you'll regret. Here's the problem: After the floor finish is gone, you can't see whether the sander is doing its job, so you keep sanding. The machine is raising dust and everything seems fine. But the dull paper isn't cutting deep enough to remove the scratches left by the previous grit. And you may not discover this until you put a finish on the floor. A dull edging disc is even worse, since it won't remove the ugly cross-grain scratches left by the previous disc.

Even if paper feels sharp, it may be beyond its prime. So the best way to judge is by square footage covered. The belts I sell cover about 250 sq. ft., and edger discs are spent after about 20 sq. ft. That varies, so ask at the rental store.

## Screen the floor

After you've finished with the sanders, the floor will look so good that you'll be tempted to skip this step. But don't. "Screening" blends the edge-sanded perimeter with the drum-sanded field and polishes away sanding scratches. You can do it with a rented buffing machine or with a sanding pole (like the one used for sanding drywall). Either way, the abrasive to use is 120- or 150-grit sanding screen (again, just like the stuff used on drywall).

## Edger education

The edger is basically a sanding disc mounted on a big, powerful motor. A simple tool, but not so simple to use. Here are some tips to help you master the edger and minimize the inevitable swirls left by the spinning disc:

- Follow up each phase of drum sanding with edging. After you've drum-sanded at 36-grit, for example, edge with 36-grit.
- Place a nylon pad under the sandpaper. This cushion minimizes gouges and deep swirls. Get pads at the rental store.
- Replace the sandpaper when it's dull. Dull paper won't remove swirls left by the previous grit.
- At the end of the job, lay a flashlight on the floor to highlight any leftover swirls. Then hand-sand them out with 80- or 100-grit paper.
- A warning to woodworkers: You'll be tempted to edge with your belt sander, but even the biggest belt sander can't cut half as fast as an edger. You'll also be tempted to polish out swirls with a random orbit sander. But beware: That can overpolish the wood so it won't take finish the same as the surrounding wood. Hand-sanding is safer.

## Clean up between grits

Sweep or vacuum the floor before you move up to the next grit. Even the best abrasives throw off a few granules while sanding. And a 36-grit granule caught under a 60-grit belt will leave an ugly gash in the floor. Wrap the vacuum nozzle with tape to avoid marring the floor.

## Don't skip grits

The initial coarse grits remove the finish and flatten the wood. But that's not enough. You need to progress through every grit to polish off the scratches left by the previous grit. On most of my jobs, the sequence is 24-36-60-80 for coarse-grained wood like oak. Scratches are more visible on fine-grained wood like birch or maple, so I go to 100-grit.

# Laminate floor tips

**MEET THE PRO**

**Jay Heise** grew up in the flooring business (his parents have owned a flooring store since he was a kid). He started at the bottom, meaning he's installed acres of laminate flooring and knows every pitfall and shortcut in the book. He's since moved into the front office. Lucky for us, Jay agreed to strap on his knee pads to show us a trick or two. Here are his pearls of wisdom.

## Shear—don't cut

Cutting laminate with a miter saw is a noisy and dusty affair. And walking back and forth to your miter saw isn't very efficient. Why not cut the planks with a laminate shear—quietly and cleanly—right where they're going to be installed?

Laminate shears cost anywhere from $60 to $1,000. The lower-end models are available at most home centers. Higher-end models are found at flooring specialty stores or online. Search online for "laminate floor shears."

## Grind down the highs, fill in the lows

Laminate floor systems don't function well on uneven surfaces. Before starting any flooring work, inspect the subfloor. Crawl around with a straightedge to find any areas that are more than 1/8 in. high or low. Subfloor seams are the usual suspects.

A belt sander sporting a coarse-grit belt will knock down seams pretty fast, but you may have to rent a commercial floor sander to grind down severe peaks.

A dip in the floor will cause a soft, spongy section in the laminate floor. Most dips can be taken care of with a trowel and vinyl floor patch. Buy a fast-drying variety if you want to start laying the floor the same day.

"Avoid self-leveling floor compounds, especially on older homes," Jay says. "An out-of-level floor could take a whole truckload of self-leveling compound to flatten out the floor. And oh, yeah—this is the time to screw the plywood to the joists anywhere there's a squeak."

## Use the proper tape

All underlayment seams need to be taped. It's tempting to use whatever tape you find in the pickup, but don't do it. Some packing tapes and house-wrap tapes are too rigid and may cause an annoying crinkling noise when they're stepped on. Use the tape that's recommended by the underlayment manufacturer, or buy an underlayment that has built-in seam tape.

Jay recommends installing underlayment perpendicular to the way the planks will be installed. The underlayment will be less likely to "bubble" as you lay the flooring. And he suggests installing only a few rows of underlayment at a time to avoid tearing it up with your boots.

## Rip down the starter row if you must

It's tempting to find the longest, straightest wall and start slapping down planks. The problem is that when you get to the opposite wall, you may end up ripping down a sliver-thin row of flooring. That won't look good and is tough to install.

Plan ahead by snapping together a section of four or five pieces, put it against one wall and make a pencil line on the outside of the connected piece, then slide the section toward the opposite wall, lining it up with the pencil line. Walk your way across the room like this to determine whether you should start with a ripped row and how wide it should be.

Jay says, "It's not an exact science, but it's a quick way to get a good idea of how wide that last row is going to be without doing a bunch of math."

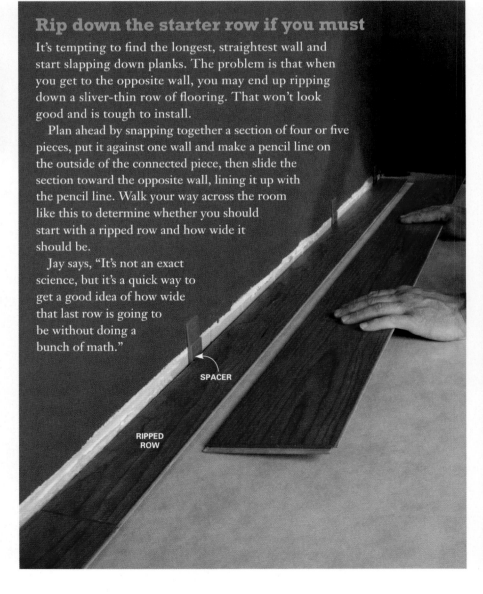

SPACER

RIPPED ROW

## Snap in a whole row at once

If you read the instructions on most laminate flooring (that's a big "if," I know), the pieces are supposed to be snapped in consecutively. Some flooring (usually the cheap stuff) is almost impossible to install that way without damaging the planks. If you're having problems, snap the butt ends of a whole row together, then snap it in as if it were one long piece.

TRANSITION STRIP

## Use transition strips under doors

If you're installing flooring that continues through a doorway, you'll be better off leaving a gap (rather than snapping together the flooring) to receive a transition strip between rows. Position the gap directly under the door so the transition strip will make visual sense. A transition strip lets you treat each room as a separate project. This allows for greater flexibility on your layout.

10'

10' 6"

## Is the room square?

When figuring out the size of your starter row, you also have to make sure the walls are parallel. You may find yourself installing laminate in a room that is 6 in. narrower at one end than at the other. That means you'll have to rip a severely tapered last row and it'll look ugly.

Unless one side of the room will be forever covered with furniture, you're better off splitting the difference and tapering both the first and the last rows so neither side will be so noticeable.

## Beware of heavy furniture

Laminate floors expand and contract with variations in humidity and temperature. So before starting any laminate job, pay attention to the furniture in the room. Heavy furniture like a pool table or a fully loaded bookshelf can pin down the laminate, causing it to either push up as it expands or separate as it contracts. The trouble really starts when you have two heavy pieces of furniture directly across from each other, which traps the floor. You'll have to either lose one of the furniture pieces or go with a different flooring material to avoid trouble. How much weight will trap a floor? A good rule of thumb is that a typical laminate floor can still move properly under a fully stocked refrigerator.

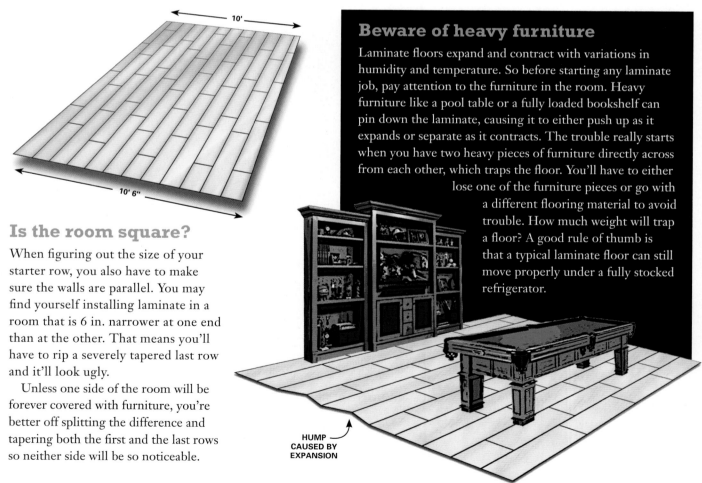

HUMP CAUSED BY EXPANSION

## Buy gel-filled knee pads

The hard-shell knee pads you wear for roofing and landscaping are not the knee pads you should wear to install a floor. There's no question about it: Flooring is hard on the knees, and the wrong knee pads will scratch laminate floors. Flooring installation calls for pads that have a cloth, foam or soft rubber material on the business end. "Gel-filled pads are probably the most comfortable, because the gel helps distribute the weight," Jay says.

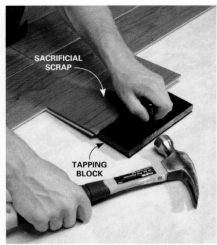

## Tap on a sacrificial piece

Occasionally it'll be necessary to tap a plank into place or snug together an uncooperative one. Yes, you should use a tapping block, but to avoid damaging your brand-new floor, snap in a sacrificial scrap, and tap on that to prevent wrecking the edge of the new flooring.

## Ending at doorways

Often, there's no avoiding ending up at a doorway. When that happens, it's a bit tricky because you have to slide the flooring under both jambs. Here's how to handle it.

**Start where there are the most doors.** Flooring around doorways is one of the thorniest issues you'll deal with. Simplify it by starting on the wall that has the most doorways. Of course, you'll still have to undercut jambs and trim, but it's a lot easier starting at a doorway than ending up at one.

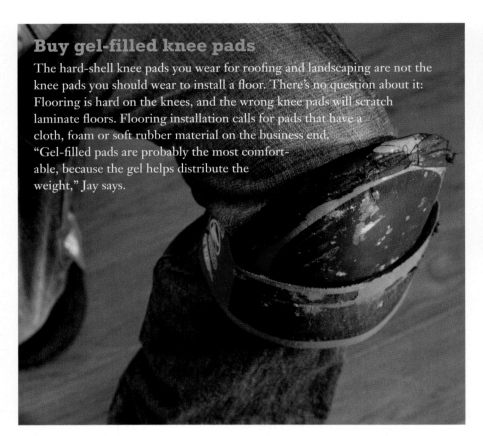

**1 LIFT TO FIT**
Plan on a seam in the middle of the doorway. Notch and cut the first piece to fit and then slide it completely under the jamb. Notch the second piece so it'll be just short of the door stop when it's in place. Lift the flooring to get it around the corner and under the casing, then snap it in.

**2 SLIDE BOTH PIECES OVER**
Once the two pieces are connected, slide them both over just far enough so that both jambs cover the flooring ends.

# Pull the wrinkles out of your carpet

Wall-to-wall carpets sometimes develop loose, wrinkled areas, usually due to installation problems. If you ignore the wrinkles, they'll wear and become permanent eyesores—even if you stretch them later. You don't have to hire a carpet layer—fix it yourself with rental tools and our instructions. Rent a power stretcher and knee kicker at an equipment rental store. Then buy a carpet knife (not a utility knife) at any home center.

You'll be stretching from the center of the carpet and pulling it at an angle into a corner. So move any furniture that'll be in the path of the stretch. Loosen the carpet in the corner (Photo 1). Next, set up the power stretcher at an angle across the room. Set the tooth depth on the power stretcher based on the carpet pile depth (Photo 2).

Operate the power stretcher with the lever and capture the excess carpet in the tack strip as you stretch. Use the knee kicker on both sides of the locked power stretcher to help lock the carpet into the tacks. Once the wrinkles are out and the carpet is secure in the tack strip, cut off the excess (Photo 4).

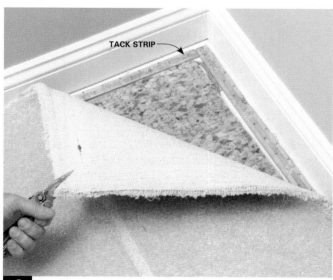

TACK STRIP

## 1 Pull the carpet free.

Grab the carpet right next to the baseboard and pull it straight up. Then loosen the rest of the carpet along the wall.

## 2 Dial in the correct tooth depth.

Adjust the tooth depth by loosening or tightening the screws on the spacer bar. Set the bar so the teeth grab just the carpet pile, not the jute backing or pad (the pad is stapled to the floor and shouldn't be stretched).

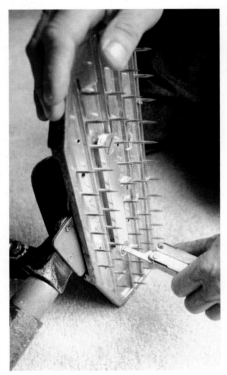

## 3 Sink and stretch.

Set the teeth into the carpet near the wall and push down on the stretcher handle. Then lock the stretched carpet into place by jamming it behind the tack strip with a putty or linoleum knife.

## 4 Trim off excess carpet.

Fold the excess carpet so the backing is facing up. Then cut it off with the carpet knife.

## Smooth talk about wrinkles

Professional carpet installer Steve Hoover explained how carpet gets wrinkled. "Carpet has to acclimate to interior conditions before it's installed. That's especially important if the carpet has been in a cold truck or exposed to high humidity. If it's installed while it's still cold or humid, you're going to have wrinkling problems later on," he says.

Improper stretching during installation is another cause. "Some installers lay the pad and carpet and secure it with just the knee kicker. Since the carpet was never really stretched, it's going to wrinkle after it's seen some traffic. If the carpet wasn't stretched during installation, it's going to wrinkle later," he adds.

Steve's advice? Make sure the installers allow enough time for the carpet to acclimate and insist that they actually stretch it with a power stretcher during installation.

# How to save a flooded carpet

**Q** My basement flooded and I've got wet carpet. Is it possible to save it?

**A** You'll have to go by these rules: If the floodwater was clean (broken pipe, burst washing machine supply hose or a foundation leak), you can probably save the carpet (the pad is iffy). But you've got to act fast. If the carpet isn't dry within 72 hours, it'll start to grow mold. However, if the floodwater was dirty (sewer backup or washing machine drain water), you need to call in the pros (see "Call in the Pros" on p. 40).

We'll assume the basement was flooded with clean water, the water is now shut off and the cost of the carpet is less than your insurance deductible (or that you simply want to do it yourself to avoid a claim). Before you set one boot on that squishy carpet, heed this warning: You must turn off the power to the basement. If you're

CARPET CLEANER

Rent a commercial extractor or a carpet cleaner to suck out as much moisture as possible. Move slowly and do several passes in different directions.

## MEET THE PRO

Flood cleanup consultant **Pete Duncanson** is director of training at Servicemaster.

COMMERCIAL DEHUMIDIFIER

COMMERCIAL AIR MOVER FAN

Rent a commercial dehumidifier and air mover fan ASAP. Position the machines on opposite sides of the room to pick up and remove most of the moisture.

## Save your stuff

Most people leave their valuable items in the basement while they dry out the carpet. Big mistake. The longer your items sit in the basement, the more moisture they'll soak up. And that means mold. So get them out of the basement fast!

- Move all electronic gear upstairs (high humidity can corrode electronic components).
- Take photos and artwork off the walls and move them to a dry location.
- Place valuable wet books in your freezer until the "freeze-drying" effect removes all the water from the pages.
- If you can't move furniture out of the basement, place aluminum foil under the legs.

not positive which breakers power the basement receptacles, flip the main circuit breaker in the garage panel. If your electrical panel is in the basement, call an electrician to turn off the power.

Next, remove any extension cords and power strips from the floor and unplug or switch off all electrical appliances (washer, dryer, HVAC). Ask the electrician (if you hired one) to repower the upstairs (to keep the fridge going) and inspect the basement receptacles to determine whether it's safe to repower them. If not, you'll have to buy several GFCI-equipped extension cords and run power from upstairs receptacles.

Then it's time to extract the water from the carpet. Don't waste your time with a wet/dry shop vacuum—it simply doesn't have enough power. Instead, rent an extractor (if available) or carpet cleaner, an air mover fan or two, and a large commercial dehumidifier. Rent the largest dehumidifier available. The big ones can remove up to 30 gallons per day, compared with 4 gallons for the largest home units.

Extraction is 1,200 times more effective than dehumidification. You'll want to move the extractor slowly across the carpet to suck up as much water as possible. Don't rush this step! Once the water is out, peel back the carpeting (watch out for those rusted sharp nails on the tackless stripping) and remove the wet pad. Cut the pad into strips, roll it up and haul it outside. If the weather is hot, dry and sunny, you can try drying it yourself by rolling it out on your driveway. If that works, you can reinstall it by taping it back together. Just be aware that new carpet pad is cheap, so don't waste a lot of time trying to dry the old stuff.

Lay the carpet back on the floor and fire up the air movers and rental dehumidifier. Keep the basement temperature at or below 75 degrees F. You might think hotter is better because it will dry everything faster. But a higher temp will accelerate

bacterial growth and turn your basement into a petri dish.

While the carpet is drying, check the condition of the wall insulation. If you don't have insulation and you dry out the basement quickly, you don't have to replace the drywall. But if the insulation is wet, it's gotta go (wet insulation cannot be saved). Snap a chalk line, cut the drywall with a recip saw and toss the wet stuff. Replace the insulation and install new drywall.

Finally, if your appliances or furnace was under water, call in appliance and HVAC specialists before plugging any of them back in.

## Call in the pros

If you had a sewer backup, washing machine drainwater spill or river flood, you need professional help. Pros are the only ones with the proper equipment to get your basement dry and disinfected in the shortest possible time.

To find a certified water restoration professional, search online for "water damage restoration." Look for IICRC (Institute of Inspection, Cleaning and Restoration Certification) credentials in the ad (Servicemaster is one company that is fully certified). Or search for IICRC online.

Be aware that pros can give you a rough price estimate (the average cost of a basement cleanup is $2,500), but the final cost depends on how long it takes them to dry out your basement. There are just too many variables beyond their control (inside and outside temperature and humidity levels) to give you a set price up front. Be wary of any company that gives you a set price over the phone.

# What's the best carpet for traffic zones?

As you browse for carpet at a home center or flooring store, don't ignore the label on the back of the sample. That's where you'll find the "yarn content," which, for the vast majority of carpet, is nylon or polyester. For high-traffic areas like hallways or busy family rooms, nylon is the best choice by far, according to flooring authority Scott Lesnick. It's just plain tougher and less likely to become crushed and matted. For medium- to low-traffic zones, save yourself some cash and go with polyester, which costs 10 to 20 percent less.

**MEET THE PRO**

**Scott Lesnick** knows carpet right down to the chemistry. For 26 years, he's been with Shaw Industries, the world's largest carpet manufacturer.

# The lowdown on buying carpet

Shopping for carpet is a lot like shopping for a car. It involves a huge financial investment; all the different styles, colors and brands can make your head spin; and you often end up dealing with high-pressure salespeople. The experience can be so overwhelming that it's tempting to shop with only a basic color and style in mind and rely on salespeople for recommendations.

Don't. Carpeting is one of the largest investments you'll make in your home. By doing some basic homework, comparison shopping and working with a reputable retailer, you'll be able to buy carpeting that fits your needs—and gives you confidence that you're getting a quality product for a good price.

This article will give you a basic background in carpet styles and quality, and discuss the primary things to think about when you're shopping for new carpeting. We'll give you tips on what to look for as well as what to look out for. We're going to concentrate on synthetic fibers in this article. Natural fibers like wool are gorgeous, but they're out of most people's price range.

**Bend the carpet sample backward. If you can see the backing easily, it's a low-density (lower quality) carpet that will crush more easily.**

## Carpet styles

**Saxony** (also called velvet or plush) is a cut pile that works well in formal dining rooms, living rooms and bedrooms. It shows footprints and vacuum marks and is not a good choice for high-traffic areas and active kids. The basic grade lasts about five years.

**Textured** cut pile has more than one color of yarn and varying tuft heights. Its two-toned appearance hides dirt and reduces footprints and vacuum marks, making it a better choice for active lifestyles. It's similar to Saxony in life expectancy and cost.

**Frieze** ("fri-zay") is the most durable and most expensive of the three cut-pile styles. Its tightly twisted tufts give the surface a nubby texture that covers footprints. It wears better than Saxony and textured, can be used in heavy traffic areas and can last 20 years or more if well maintained.

**Sculptured,** or cut-and-loop, made with looped and non-looped tufts, is economical and durable. The varied shading hides dirt well, but the seams can be more visible. Price and durability increase with higher face-weight yarns.

**Looped** or **Berber** is popular for its elegant appearance. Berbers with smaller loops wear better than large-looped Berbers, which mat down quickly and are harder to clean. Not good if you have small children or pets (toys and claws) because they snag and run easily and are tough to repair.

## Where to buy carpet

Visit several retailers, including local, family-owned businesses that survive on customer referrals. Choose the one that will give you the best service, price and guarantee. Be aware that "basic installation specials" often include hundreds of dollars in extra fees for basic installation items like steps, furniture moving, and carpet and pad removal. Carpet retailers located in a mall or other high-rent locations tend to have higher overhead that is passed on to you in higher prices.

## Choose the right type of carpet fiber for your needs

**Nylon** outperforms all other fibers in durability, resilience and easy maintenance. This is a good choice if you want your carpet to last a decade or longer, for high-traffic areas, and in homes with kids and pets. Higher-quality nylon fibers are "branded," and the carpet label will use terms like "100% Mohawk Nylon" or "100% Stainmaster Tactesse." Lower-quality, "unbranded" nylon fibers are listed simply as "100% nylon." The strongest and softest type (and most expensive) is 6.6 nylon.

**Triexta** (brands include Smart-Strand and Sorona) is a newly classified fiber derived partly from corn sugar. It has excellent, permanent anti-stain properties (nylon must be treated with stain protectors over its life span). It also has good resilience, but it's too soon to tell whether it will match the durability of nylon in high-traffic areas. Because of its superior stain resistance, this is a good choice if you have young kids or pets. This is one of the more expensive fibers.

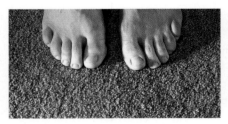

**Polyester** (also called PET) is stain resistant, very soft and luxurious underfoot, and is available in deep and vibrant colors. However it's harder to clean, tends to shed and isn't as durable as nylon. It's best used in low-traffic areas (like bedrooms) and in households without kids or pets. A nice, cushy choice if you like to exercise on the carpet.

**Olefin** (polypropylene) is an attractive, inexpensive fiber that's strong and resists fading, but it's not as resilient as nylon. It's most often made into a looped Berber with a nubby weave that conceals dirt. It has good stain, static and mildew resistance. Olefin carpeting is often selected for high-traffic "clean" areas such as family rooms and play areas.

## In a nutshell

- Do your research, and make sure a salesperson doesn't make the decisions for you.
- Base your carpet and pad decisions on your lifestyle, household occupants (kids and/ or pets) and traffic levels. Also consider the desired life span, maintenance requirements, and the looks and price of the carpet.
- Common sales gimmicks such as "free pad with carpet purchase" can get you cheap pad that can wreck your carpet.
- Take the carpet samples you've selected to at least three stores and compare prices of similar products.
- Get every item in your carpet bid priced individually. This will make it easier to compare bids.

## Buy the right pad

The quality of carpet pad is determined by density, not thickness. The right pad will extend the life of your carpet. The wrong pad can cut the life of your carpet in half. A good-quality pad will be 3/8 to 1/2 in. thick and have a density/weight rating of at least 6 lbs. (the residential standard). In most cases, cheap, low-density pad will only last a few years before it needs to be replaced. For high-traffic areas, get a thinner pad with a density of 8 lbs. or more. Some carpet manufacturers require a specific type of pad in order to maintain your carpet warranty (such as when the carpet is laid over heated floors). Check the carpet warranty before you buy padding.

## The signs of a quality carpet

A salesperson might tell you that a certain carpet is a good deal, but don't rely on his or her word alone. Check the label, handle the carpet and ask the salesperson about these signs of quality.

**At least a 34- to 40-oz. face weight.** This is the number of ounces of fiber per square yard. The range is generally from 20 to 80, and the higher the number, the heavier and more resilient the carpet.

**A tuft twist of 5 or higher.** Twist is the number of times the tufts are twisted together in a 1-in. length. The higher the number, the more durable the carpet.

**A density rating of 2,000 or more.** Density is determined by the thickness of the fibers and how tightly packed they are. The thicker and heavier they are, the better quality the carpet and the less susceptible to crushing. Bend the carpet sample backward. If you can see the backing easily, it's a low-density (lower-quality) carpet.

**Is it BCF or staple fiber construction?** Carpet fibers can be either bulked continuous filament (BCF) or "staple." Staple fibers shed more than BCF fibers. This doesn't affect the long-term quality of the carpet, but it does mean you'll have to vacuum more often until the initial shedding stops (which can take up to a year), and it can also be an issue for allergy sufferers.

**At least a 10-year "texture retention" warranty.** This covers how well the fibers return to their original shape after being walked on. Although manufacturers tout their 15- and 25-year warranties, salespeople caution that warranties are seldom honored except in cases of obvious product defects.

## How to get the best deal (and avoid being ripped off)

Salespeople have a tendency to "overmeasure" your carpet needs. This means you pay for carpet and pad you don't use. Get several estimates, compare the yardage numbers, and consider paying an independent carpet installer (see below) to measure your home.

"JUST LEAVE EVERYTHING TO ME!"

A lot of carpet problems stem from poor installation. Bad seaming, a too-thin pad and inadequate stretching can make a carpet look terrible within a few years. If you or a friend knows a great carpet installer, use that person instead of one provided by the carpet dealer. The installer will measure your house, tell you exactly how much carpet and pad to get, recommend a quality dealer, and pick up the carpet and deliver it on installation day. You can save yourself some money on the installation by removing the old carpet and pad yourself. Ask your installer how much you'll save to see if it's worthwhile.

Get at least three estimates. Tell every salesperson that you'll be getting several estimates, and don't discuss details about other carpet bids you've received.

Have each carpet estimate include a flooring diagram that shows measurements and seam locations.

Get an individual price quote for each aspect of the job, including carpet, pad, delivery, installation, transition metal pieces, furniture moving, stairs, and old carpet and pad removal and disposal. It's easy to be overcharged if you just get an overall price for the job.

Make sure you're home on installation day. Get a sample of the carpet and pad you've ordered and compare them with the carpet and pad that show up on the truck. In some instances, retailers deliver a lower quality pad or carpet than you've paid for.

# Chapter Three

# REMODELING AND CONSTRUCTION

# Smart remodeling

Two of the most common complaints thrown at remodelers are the mess they make and the time it takes to finish the job. And even though remodeling projects are by their very nature unpredictable and messy, most jobs can be run more efficiently.

It's hard to work efficiently, though, if your job site is in shambles, you don't have the proper tools on hand or you're making lots of unnecessary trips to the store for materials. The trick is to work smarter, not harder. The following tips can help save you time and money—and most important— your reputation.

## Make a list

Remodeling is a fluid process. Unexpected situations arise daily. Whether you use a block of wood, a piece of cardboard or a notebook, always have a pencil and something to write on so you can keep track of the materials, tools and supplies you'll need to bring the next day.

## Lay down a protective path

It's impossible to demo a wall or bust up a floor without making a mess, but that doesn't mean you need to track that mess all over the rest of the house. The next time you have to tear out some carpet, cut several long strips and use them as pathways to protect the flooring in other areas of the house. Make sure to flip the carpet upside down so the abrasive backing won't scratch the finish on wood floors. Canvas drop cloths are still the best method for protecting stair treads. Buy 4 x 15-ft. drop cloth at home centers.

DROP CLOTH

SALVAGED CARPET

## Bring plenty of garbage cans

Two stacked garbage cans don't take up much more room in the back of a truck than one, so why not bring at least two? Put them wherever the mess is being made—like next to the miter saw to drop in cutoffs. Think twice about buying the giant heavy-duty cans. For the same money, you're best off with sturdy medium-size cans that are easier to carry. Garbage bags work fine for stuffing in old insulation but little else.

## Save those buckets

Buckets are a remodeler's best friend. They work great for mixing, hauling heavy debris, storing water, dragging tools in and out, organizing fasteners, setting stuff on, bailing water, sitting on. There's a reason home centers sell empty ones. Never, ever throw away a usable bucket!

## Order early

It seems that every job needs to be finished yesterday, but don't even think about getting started until you know that *all* the materials will be there when you need them. Make sure you get a definite delivery confirmation on your flooring, cabinets, windows, doors and any other materials needed to complete the job. Starting a project a week late is better than waiting around for cabinets while the kitchen is torn apart and the homeowners are living in a motel.

## Throw together a junk station

As soon as the major demo is completed, make yourself a junk station. Bring extra sawhorses, and throw a couple of boards or a piece of plywood on them. It's smart to have a central location for your tools, fasteners, batteries and chargers, radio, beverages and whatever else it takes to get the job done. Having items scattered all over the job-site floor makes cleanup harder, and wandering around looking for the stuff you need is a waste of time.

## Bring extra fasteners

Dedicate a toolbox just for fasteners. You may think you'll need only two different-size screws to finish your job, but it rarely works out that way. And keep a variety of bits along with the fasteners; that way you'll always have the right bit with the right screw.

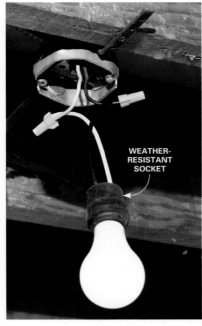

WEATHER-RESISTANT SOCKET

## Install temporary lighting

Lighting is one of the last items to be installed on most remodeling projects, but it's hard to do a good job when you're working in the dark. Plug-in work lights take up precious outlets and are always being tripped on or moved around. As soon as you have power to the lighting receptacles, consider installing temporary lighting. Home centers sell them as "Weather-Resistant Sockets." Wiring them is as simple as turning a couple of wire nuts.

## Clear the room—completely!

So there's no place to store the pool table, treadmill or Grandma's baby grand—well, find a place! Working around furniture and other obstacles is a monster pain in the backside during major remodels—it just doesn't work. Moving a piece of furniture back and forth from one side of the room to the other is time-consuming. Rent a storage locker.

## Organize tools by the job

Knowing exactly which tools you'll need for every job is next to impossible. Organize your toolboxes and storage bins according to the work that needs to be done: a box for plumbing tools, electrical, drywall, etc. No doubt this will lead to owning more than one of the same tool. But you won't believe how much time you'll save having all the proper tools on hand.

## Smaller compressors for smaller jobs

If you only have a few studs to nail in or a few pieces of base shoe to install, why on earth would you haul that giant, heavy compressor around? Mini compressors are a must for smart remodeling. They're light and inexpensive and easy to carry right to the area you're working in. You can get a 1-gallon, 1-hp compressor at home centers.

MINI COMPRESSOR

# Working with steel studs

How would you like to be able to frame a perfectly straight wall each and every time? Using studs that won't split or crack, and so light that you could carry 20 of them at once? If this sounds good to you, consider using steel studs for your next project. When you add in steel's other benefits—it won't burn or rot or get eaten by insects—we're confident that these tips from our pro will make you think about steel.

**MEET THE PRO**

**Joe Welle** has put up miles and miles of steel stud walls, but these days you'll find him supervising multimillion-dollar projects for a national construction company.

## Don't lay track over a door opening

There are two basic steel framing components: studs and tracks. The track functions as the top and bottom plates. Lay out your walls and openings just as you would with wood, but when you install the bottom plate, don't run the track across the door openings. You can't use your recip saw to cut the opening out later, as you can with wood. Concrete screws (Tapcon is one brand) work well to attach the track to concrete.

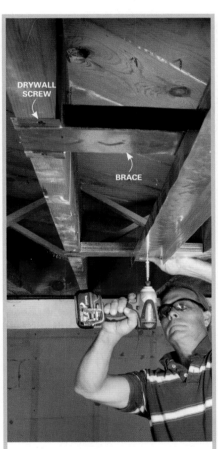

## To cut, snip both sides, then score

Most home centers sell circular and chop saw blades designed for cutting studs, but Joe prefers a quieter and less messy approach. He cuts both sides with snips and scores a line on the back. After bending the stud back and forth a few times, he ends up with a burr-free cut. No need for hearing protection and no metal shavings sticking to your boots. Caution: Steel studs and tracks are sharp. Joe is a pro—you should wear gloves.

## Use the track for blocking

Top plates that run parallel to joists often need to be fastened to braces. You could use wood, but Joe prefers to use scrap pieces of track instead. Just cut the sides of the track and fold them out. Then fasten the track to the underside of the joist with drywall screws.

## Use a stud to locate the top plate

Unlike wood, steel studs are reliably straight. Cut one stud to size and use that, along with a level, to mark the location of the top plate at both ends, and snap a line to guide placement. Don't worry about cutting your studs to fit perfectly. It's completely unnecessary. This is a great advantage if you're working on an uneven floor. You can cut steel studs about 1/4 in. shorter than the actual measurement.

## Lay out studs from the back of inside corners

Drywall is hung a little differently on steel framing. Drywall sheets don't butt up to each other at inside corners. One of the sheets will be slid all the way to the back of an inside corner (see "Leave the Last Stud Loose at Inside Corners" on p. 51). So when you lay out the stud locations, slide your tape measure all the way to the back of the track. Joe clamps his tape into place with a spring clamp. He clamps it several inches away from the end to avoid damaging the tang (steel tab).

SCRAP TRACK

## Protect your cords and yourself

Accidentally stepping on an extension cord that's draped over a sharp track is a perfect way to cut your cord. To avoid potentially shocking developments, Joe takes a scrap chunk of track, flips it upside down and puts it under the cord.

DOOR HEADER

## Install track as a header

Use a section of track as a header on those interior openings that aren't load bearing. Cut the track 3 or 4 in. wider than the opening, cut the sides and use a rafter square as a guide to bend them back. Have the open side of the track face up so you can slide in the cripple studs if you need them.

KERF IN CABINET BLOCKING

## Cut a kerf in the blocking

Like doors, cabinets and other heavy objects need extra support. You can use plywood or 2x4s, but make sure you cut a kerf in them to accept the lip on the inside of the stud. If you don't, that lip of the stud will press against the support board and twist the stud, creating a bow in the wall.

DOOR BUCK

## Use wood bucks to hang a door

It's a hassle to hang a door directly onto steel studs. Instead, frame the openings 3 in. wider and 1-1/2 in. higher, and use drywall screws to fasten 2x4 bucks on the inside of the steel opening, then hang your door from the wood bucks. The bucks are also there for nailing on the casing. Slide a plastic shim under each side 2x4 if the wood is going to be in direct contact with a concrete floor.

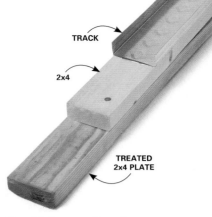

TRACK

2x4

TREATED
2x4 PLATE

## Build up the bottom plate

Base trim can still be installed with trim screws. If you don't like the look of the screw heads, you can install two layers of 2x4 plates instead of steel track. With 3 in. of wood under the track, you'll be able to nail all the base trim just as you would a wood-framed wall. Over concrete, make sure you use treated wood for the bottom plate.

PAN-HEAD

CONCRETE

FINE-THREADED
DRYWALL

## Choose the right screws

Don't use drywall screws to screw your studs together—they're not designed for that. Pan-head framing screws work best. Concrete screws work great to attach the bottom track to the floor. And be sure you use fine-threaded drywall screws to hang the drywall.

## Finding steel studs

Drywall supply companies furnish lumberyards and home centers with steel studs. So if you're having trouble finding them, go directly to the source.

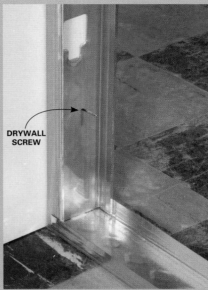

GAP FOR
DRYWALL

LOOSE
STUD

DRYWALL
SCREW

## Leave the last stud loose at inside corners

The proper way to drywall an inside corner is to slide the first sheet all the way into the inside corner and then fasten the last stud on the wall adjacent to the drywall. To do this, you'll need to leave that last stud loose until the drywall goes up. This method may seem a little goofy, but it requires fewer studs and it results in an extremely stable joint. When laying out the tracks, make sure you leave a gap for the drywall to slide in.

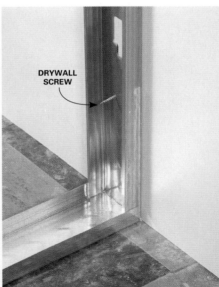

LOOSE
STUD

GAP FOR
DRYWALL

DRYWALL
SCREW

## Leave the last stud loose at 'T' intersections, too

Similar to handling inside corners, leave the last stud loose on the wall that makes up the stem of a "T" intersection. After the drywall is hung, that last stud on the intersecting wall will be fastened to the drywall. Once again, this method requires fewer studs and results in a rock-solid joint that's almost guaranteed not to crack the drywall mud. Leave the top and bottom tracks short to allow room for the drywall to slide behind.

# Fiber cement board

**MEET THE PRO**

**Jaime Venzor** has been in the siding business for more than 15 years. He started out installing mostly vinyl, but now 80 percent of his work is fiber cement. He earned his good reputation with his customers by doing things the right way, and he earned our thanks by sharing some of his knowledge with us. So read on and learn what Jaime thinks are the most important tips.

15-GAUGE TRIM GUN

OUTSIDE CORNER

## Hold the starter 1/4 in. down

Find your most beat-up pieces of siding and rip them down into 1-1/4-in. starter strips. These strips, installed at the bottom, will make your first row of siding angle out to match the rest of the rows. Snap a line 1 in. above the bottom of the wall sheathing as a guide. Install these fragile starter strips with a 15-gauge trim gun. Snap another line for the bottom row of siding, positioning it so it will hang down an additional 1/4 in. from the starter.

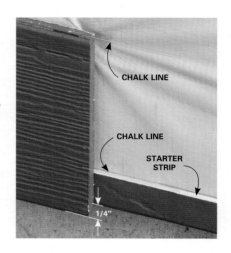

CHALK LINE

CHALK LINE

STARTER STRIP

1/4"

## Preassemble the corners

It's a lot easier to preassemble corners on a flat surface. Jaime uses 2-1/4-in. galvanized nails in his 15-gauge trim gun. He uses the same size nails to install the corners on the wall. Don't use a framing gun or try to hand-nail the corners together; that's a good way to break the trim boards. Also, the trim nails look better where nails will be exposed, especially on a prefinished corner board. So if you don't have a 15-gauge trim gun, what a perfect "opportunity" to go buy one.

## Remove the plastic last

Prefinished fiber cement boards come with a protective plastic coating. To protect the paint from getting scratched during installation, leave the plastic on and make your cuts right through it. Peel away the plastic after the board has been fastened to the wall.

## Flash the butt joints

Caulking butt joints is unnecessary, and some manufacturers prohibit it. However, you should flash behind the joints. You can use metal, house wrap or any other approved WRB (weather-resistant barrier), but Jaime prefers to use 30-lb. felt paper. It's easy to work with and cheap, and it isn't noticeable if a seam happens to open up a little. Tack it to the wall so it doesn't get knocked out of place when you install the second piece of siding.

30-LB. FELT

## Nailing basics

Fiber cement siding can be hand-nailed, but because it's so much harder and more brittle than wood, you have to predrill holes near any edge. You can save yourself a bunch of time by using a pneumatic coil siding nail gun. Unfortunately, a siding gun will set you back twice as much as a 15-gauge trim gun, and it's only half as versatile, so if installing fiber cement isn't your full-time gig, you may want to rent one (about $110 a week). Every manufacturer has specific nailing guidelines, but here are some basic rules:

- Use 6d galvanized or stainless siding nails and install them no more than 16 in. apart.

- Nail lengths should be chosen so they penetrate a minimum of 1-1/4 in. into the solid wood (wood sheathings like OSB and plywood count toward the 1-1/4 in., but "soft" sheathings like fiber board and foam don't).
- Don't drive nails into the siding at an angle.
- Fastener heads should be snugged up against the siding, not driven into the surface.
- The end of each plank making up a butt joint needs to be fastened to a stud.
- Nail butt joints last. That way you can tweak the ends of each plank so the bottom edges line up perfectly.

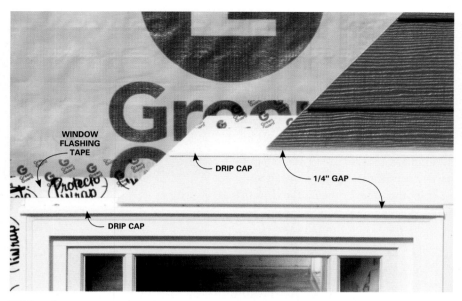

WINDOW FLASHING TAPE

DRIP CAP

1/4" GAP

DRIP CAP

## Windows need drip cap and a gap on top

Whether or not you're installing trim boards around your windows, you'll need to install a drip cap over the window. You'll also need to leave a 1/4-in. gap (no caulking) between the top of the window and the plank or trim board directly above it. This is to allow any water that may have gotten behind the siding to weep out. Tape the drip cap to the wall, but don't tape all the way to the bottom of the drip cap because it will be visible through the 1/4-in. gap. The top trim board will also need its own drip cap and 1/4-in. gap. Treat the tops of doors the same way.

## Painted vs. primed

We decided to use a prefinished product in this story, but the other way to go is simple primed siding. That material is primed and ready for you to paint. Here are some facts to consider when making your decision.

**The advantages of primed:** Primed products cost 50 percent less than prefinished products. On-site painting looks better up close because the touch-up paint and caulked areas aren't as noticeable. Primed products are easier and less expensive to install.

**The advantages of prefinished:** The color on a prefinished product won't fade nearly as fast. Some finishes come with a 15-year warranty. But the best part of using a prefinished product is that after installation, you're done and not faced with painting an entire house.

## Cut the planks with a circular saw

Tons of fiber cement cutting gadgets are available, but most jobs can be handled with just a steady eye and a standard circular saw fitted with a fiber cement blade. If you plan to hang a lot of fiber cement, though, you'll want a chop saw with a proper blade that will allow you to cut several pieces at once. You can buy fiber cement blades sized to fit any saw style or size at most home centers. When you're cutting this stuff, a dust mask is the bare minimum protection, and this is not a casual warning: The silica dust generated by cutting fiber cement can be bad news for your health!

## Vinyl mounting blocks work best

Most fiber cement manufacturers make mounting blocks for lights, electrical receptacles, A/C lines, PVC venting, etc. Jaime prefers to use the vinyl mounting blocks typically used with vinyl siding. They're cheaper and easy to install, and you can cut the proper-size hole in a plastic mounting block with a utility knife or a snips. With fiber cement blocks, you have to use a jigsaw or a hole saw.

Mounting blocks are available in more than 25 colors, but you can order paintable blocks if you want an exact match with your siding or trim.

VINYL MOUNTING BLOCK

## It's a two-man job without siding gauges

Fiber cement siding is heavy and breaks if it's bent too much. Installing this stuff by yourself is tough, but it's possible with the aid of siding gauges. These tools not only create the proper reveal (the part of the siding that shows) between rows but also actually hold the planks in place while you nail. Even if you do just one fiber cement job, siding gauges are worth the money. A pair of quality gauges costs about $85 online, but cheaper versions are available. Most gauges are adjustable to accommodate reveals from 5 to 8 in.

## Paint, prime or caulk all cut edges

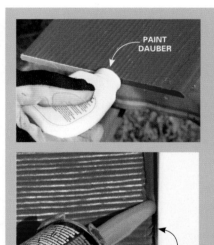

PAINT DAUBER

1/4" GAP

Every time you cut a plank, you create an exposed surface that has no primer or paint to protect it from the elements. If a cut edge is going to butt up against a corner post or trim board, it gets caulked. If the cut edge is part of a butt joint in the middle of the wall, it needs to be painted (try to use factory edges on all butt joints). Planks that have been cut to fit over windows and doors also need paint. Order paint kits and caulking to match both the trim and the siding colors. Your siding supplier should have access to both.

## Dont skip the kick-out flashing

Kick-out flashing is essential for preventing water from running down a roof and behind the siding on an adjacent wall. You'll fail your inspection if the inspector doesn't see it on your job. It's a pain to work around, but it helps if you don't nail the flashing tight until you have your siding cut to size. It's much easier to get a proper fit for a plank if you can shift the flashing beneath it.

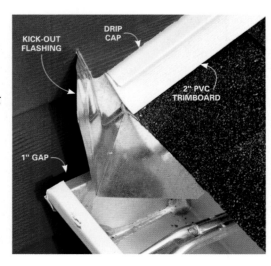

KICK-OUT FLASHING

DRIP CAP

2" PVC TRIMBOARD

1" GAP

## The lowdown on clearances

Fiber cement siding is not bulletproof—it will deteriorate if exposed to water for a long time. It's imperative that you honor the proper spacing between the siding and the roof surfaces, and between the siding and the horizontal surfaces, such as the ground or cement slabs and decks. Check with your specific manufacturer before you start. Here are some general guidelines.

**Leave:**

- 1/8 in. to 1/4 in. between siding and trim.
- 1/4 in. between siding and horizontal flashing.
- 1 in. between the gutter and an adjacent wall.
- 2 in. between siding and roofing, decks, patios, driveways, steps and walkways. (Using PVC trim boards is a good way to accomplish these clearances.)
- 6 in. between the siding and the ground.

# Construction tips

## Renting a Dumpster

Trash bins, aka "Dumpsters," aren't cheap. And there are plenty of ways to make mistakes with their rental and use. We pooled our experiences to bring you these six money-saving tips:

- Search for a local hauler either on the Internet or in the Yellow Pages. Most of the top Dumpster listings on Internet searches are actually just brokers who may charge a few hundred dollars extra. So scroll down until you find an actual local trash bin supplier.
- Telling the hauler what you'll be putting in the bin may help you get the size you need. For example, the staff will know that you'll need a 15-yard bin to dispose of 20 squares of shingles.
- Negotiate a longer rental period up front if you know you'll need extra time. It's cheaper to extend the rental time than to rent a new bin to finish the job.
- Get the bin properly placed. Figure out where you want the bin, allowing enough room for the swing door to open fully. Then mark your driveway so the driver knows exactly where to place it if you won't be there when it arrives. Provide wood blocks to protect your driveway if they're not included with the rental.
- Don't let it become the neighborhood trash bin. You'll be amazed at how many "good" neighbors will dump trash in it without your permission. So tell them you're renting a bin and ask if they want to share the cost. That way, they'll be on the lookout for nonpaying "dumpers," too.
- Cover it with a tarp if you won't be using it for a few days. That'll keep snow and rogue "dumpers" out.

### Dumpster diving

Some people wouldn't be caught dead poking around in a Dumpster, but we think it's one of the great satisfactions of the DIY life. With the right skills and tools, you can turn that broken office chair, that crushed TV stand, that *whatever* into something useful, if not exactly beautiful. The fashionable term is "upcycling," but we call it just plain DIY: being creative, saving money, fixing stuff and making something out of nothing. Ain't that the greatest?

## Mark's favorite laser level

If a long, straight line is what you're after, nothing beats a rotary laser level. As a general contractor, I've used mine for hanging cabinets, setting pole barn poles, straightening walls, setting fence posts, leveling floors, hanging suspended ceilings, installing chair rail, leveling footings, stacking block and laying out retaining walls.

My laser level is self-leveling. I just set it up on the wall bracket or tripod and it's ready to go. It can spin 360 degrees, creating a continuous line around the room, or—get this!—it can make one dot on the wall that can be moved to wherever I want using the remote control. There is a beeping locator that can be mounted on a story pole, which works great for leveling floors. This laser can be set on its side to beam a plumb line as well. Sometimes I invent projects just to play with it!

The more accurate the level, the more it will cost you. I got the one shown about five years ago. Today, a similar device costs about $900 or more. There are many less expensive models available. I love my laser level and can't imagine life without it.

—*Mark Petersen, contributing editor*

LOCATOR

18V BATTERY

REMOTE

STORY POLE

# House-wrap smarts

Let's face it—installing house wrap is not a lot of fun, but with today's emphasis on energy efficiency, it's here to stay.

In recent years, there have been several changes in the building codes that apply to house-wrap installation (none of which makes it any easier to put up), and building inspectors have been rigorously enforcing these new codes. Here are a bunch of installation tips and techniques to speed up your installation and help keep the inspector off your back.

**TACK**

## Tack, straighten, fasten

When starting a new row, don't fasten the whole vertical length of the wrap right away. Get the roll into position and attach a few fasteners in the center of the paper. This will allow you to roll out several feet and still be able to adjust the roll up and down without creating wrinkles. Wrinkles not only look sloppy but can also trap water.

## Talk to your subs

If you're the general contractor, make sure there's an extra roll of house wrap at the job site for the framers, electricians and any other sub who's going to be attaching objects to the wall. (Include instructions for installing it!) Soffit stringers, trim boards and electrical meters all need house wrap behind them.

## Don't cut out window openings!

The way we used to deal with window openings was to roll right over them, cut them out, then move on down the wall. It was quick, but there's a much better way.

After the opening is covered, make one cut with your knife straight up and down in the center. Next, cut the house wrap flush at the top and bottom of the opening, creating two flaps. Wrap the flaps inside the building, past the jack stud, before cutting off the excess. At the top, slice several inches up and away at an angle, and hold the flap up with a piece of tape (it will be folded back down and taped after the window is installed).

The opening is now ready for pan flashing and a window. This method will meet the requirements of most window manufacturers, and best of all, the inspector will be happy.

## Avoid cheap house wrap—or plan on expensive callbacks

"Perm rate" is the rate at which house wrap allows water vapor to pass through it. Bargain house wraps often have low perm rates and they should be avoided. In cold climates, this is especially true for older homes with little or no moisture barriers. Moisture will escape through the wall cavity and sheathing, and if the house wrap doesn't allow it to pass through fast enough, it will condense and accumulate in the form of frost and ice. When the ice thaws, you'll end up with wet sheathing and/or wall cavities—not good.

Bargain house wraps have perm ratings in the 8 to 12 range. Instead, choose a quality house wrap like Tyvek, with a perm rating of 54.

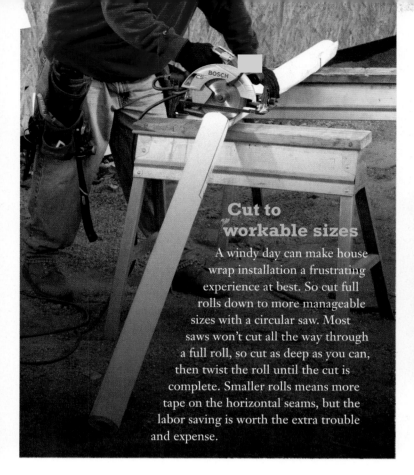

## Cut to workable sizes

A windy day can make house wrap installation a frustrating experience at best. So cut full rolls down to more manageable sizes with a circular saw. Most saws won't cut all the way through a full roll, so cut as deep as you can, then twist the roll until the cut is complete. Smaller rolls means more tape on the horizontal seams, but the labor saving is worth the extra trouble and expense.

## Overlap 6 in. or more

Overlap all seams at least 6 in. And make sure to think like you're shingling. Work from the bottom up so that higher rows overlap lower ones.

## No more staples, gentlemen

The good old days of using a hammer tacker to install house wrap are gone forever. Today, most house wrap manufacturers require their product to be installed with cap nails or cap staples. This change definitely slows down the process, but on the upside, capped fasteners hold house wrap to the wall up to 25 times better than staples. Using them will assure you of a good night's sleep on those windy nights knowing the house wrap you installed last week is not blowing all over the neighborhood.

**CAPPED FASTENER**

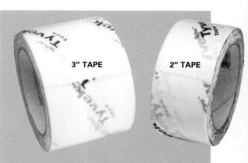

3" TAPE    2" TAPE

## Cap staple hammer

Yes, you can hand-nail capped fasteners, but it'll take you forever. Pick up a cap staple hammer instead. It works like a hammer tacker, only it sinks capped nails instead of staples. There is a learning curve to using the Stinger, and the caps and staples aren't cheap, but it beats the heck out of hand-nailing cap nails.

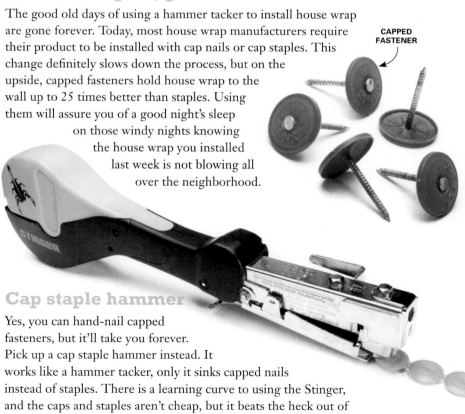

## Save time— buy 3-in. tape

Years ago, only vertical seams required tape, but no longer. Now every seam must be taped, and most manufacturers recommend that a minimum of 1 in. of the tape be sealed to each side of the seam—that's hard to accomplish using 2-in. tape! Instead, buy 3-in. rolls. If your house wrap supplier doesn't stock 3-in. tape, it should be able to order it. If not, like practically everything else, it's available online.

## Prime wood siding

Water tends to condense on house wrap, much more so than it would if there was just wood sheathing behind the siding. That water will penetrate wood siding and lift off the finish. So it's more important than ever to prime the back side of wood siding before it's installed.

## Every wall penetration needs tape

It's not only seams that need taping—everything that penetrates a wall needs it, too! Regular house wrap tape is usually sufficient.

Here's how to deal with a pipe. Cut out around it as closely as you can, then make two angled cuts up and away from the top of the pipe. Tape the flap up to keep it out of the way and then starting at the bottom, tape the pipe to the wall. Finally, fold down the flap and tape it up.

## Patch large holes and tears

Inevitably you'll have to deal with a tear in your beautiful handiwork. Small holes and tears can be repaired with tape, but larger ones require a patch. Here's how to do it. Make a horizontal slice in the house wrap just above the damaged area and slide in a patch, making sure to cover the hole by 2 in. in every direction. Tape up the seams and get back to making money.

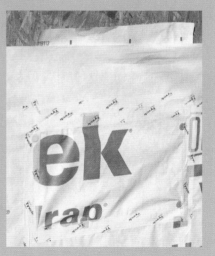

## Use flexible flashing on existing windows and doors

If you're installing house wrap around existing windows and doors, most building inspectors require those windows and doors to be sealed directly to the house wrap. This means you have to roll a butyl-style tape up onto the edge of the brick mold or window itself. This can be a tedious operation, especially if you're working with a super-sticky tape. Here's a suggestion: Don't peel off the window tape backing all at once; do just one section at a time.

## Leave a chunk in the middle

House wrap is easy enough to cut with a sharp utility knife, but cutting a smaller piece off the roll can be a pain. Cutting the first half always goes slick, but when you get to the last little bit, it tends to crumple up. You can avoid this by starting in the middle and cutting one half, then the other. Leave a small section of wrap intact, and cut off the other half. Then simply tear the piece away from the roll.

# Wall and ceiling solutions

### Plaster wall cover-up

Some walls are so bad that the best fix is to tear them out and install new drywall. Wall liner is the next-best fix. It's basically extra-thick, paintable wallpaper that acts as a big patch over the whole wall. Some versions are smooth; some have a textured or patterned surface. Fill cracks and holes with joint compound, prime the patches and then hang the liner just like wallpaper. Rolls of wall liner are sold at home centers, paint stores and online.

### Mini texture gun

I've had some good results using texture from aerosol spray cans—and some disasters. The texture blasts out fast and heavy. One wrong move and you've got an overtextured mess.

This little hand-pump gun is much easier to control. It spits out just a little texture with each blast. So you can spray on a light texture, then add more until it looks right. Still, it's best to practice on some cardboard first. Also have a bucket and sponge handy in case you need to wipe away a misfire and start over. I got good results matching orange peel, splatter and knockdown textures, but lousy results with popcorn ceiling texture (see tip at left). The gun is available at some home centers or search online for "texture touch-up gun." This kit comes with texture packets, but watered-down joint compound works fine too.

—*Gary Wentz, senior editor*

### Texture in a jar

For small repairs on popcorn ceilings, dab on this stuff. Start with a light application, let it dry and add more if needed. With some careful brush work, you can perfectly match the surrounding texture. If you don't find it at a home center, search online for "popcorn ceiling patch."

# Hanging drywall

Hanging drywall is not all that complicated, but there is a right and a wrong way to do it. Here are some tips to save time and money, make taping easier and earn the confidence of your customer.

## Cut outside corners flush with the framing

It's tempting to cut the first piece of an outside corner flush with the framing and run the perpendicular piece flush with the first. Don't do it! If you run the first piece just a little too long, the second piece will flare out. If you cut the second piece a bit too long, it will have to be shaved down to accommodate the corner bead. A good-quality metal corner bead will cover a gap and hold up as well as a perfectly flush corner—without the fuss.

CORNER BEAD WILL COVER

CUT SIDES WITH SAW

### Hang it, then cut it

You can save time and be guaranteed a perfect fit if you cut out the door opening after you hang the sheet. Once the sheet is up, score the back of the piece, pull the scrap forward and finish it off by cutting the paper on the front side.

## Inside corners: Measure exact, then subtract

When you're working in a smaller area like a closet and have to cut a piece that's going to fit between two perpendicular walls, don't try to cut exactly. Precision is a worthy goal, but you're not building a piano. All the inside corners are going to receive mud and tape anyway. If the piece is too big and you try to force it into place (which you will do), besides scraping up the drywall on an adjacent wall, you're more than likely going to damage the piece you're trying to install.

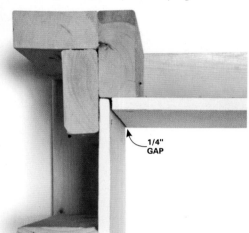

1/4" GAP

## Master the basics

Even pros sometimes forget a few of the basics of good drywall installation. Here are some that we think are important to know:

■ Think ahead when you deliver the drywall. For example, don't bury the sheets for the ceiling behind the ones for the walls. Stack all the sheets so the finished side is facing out. Place the drywall throughout the job site where it is most handy and won't be in the way. Order 12-ft.-long sheets whenever possible. Order 54-in.-wide sheets for 9-ft. walls. Consider having your drywall delivered;

it costs a little more but saves your back.

■ Most manufacturers now offer a stiffer, 1/2-in. drywall that can be used on ceilings in certain situations. Half-inch is considerably easier to hang than 5/8-in., but make sure the drywall you use conforms to the fire code in your area.

■ If you use a chalk line to mark your pieces before you cut them, use blue chalk. Red, orange or any other color is likely to bleed through the finish.

■ If you write down measurements or mark the stud lines with a pencil, do it very, very

lightly. Even modest pressure on drywall with a pencil will show up on your finished walls.

■ In our neck of the woods, screws need to be spaced no more than 12 in. on ceilings and 16 in. on walls. Nails require 8-in. spacing on ceilings and 7-in. on walls. Technically, the fastening schedule code is whatever the manufacturer requires. That information can usually be found online.

■ Don't overtighten the screws. If a screw breaks the paper, its holding power has been compromised. And don't undertighten the screws, or your

taper will curse your name while finishing your job.

■ Leave about a 1/2-in. gap between the drywall and the floor. You don't want drywall to wick up moisture from concrete or from an inevitable spill in an upper-level room. In addition, a gap at the floor makes it easier for carpet to be tucked under the trim.

■ On a long wall, it's not always possible to steer clear of seams located directly over a window or door, but a seam that's in line with the horizontal edge of a window or door should be avoided at all costs. It's sure to crack.

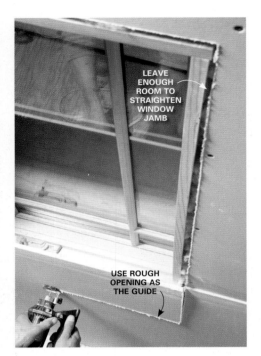

LEAVE ENOUGH ROOM TO STRAIGHTEN WINDOW JAMB

USE ROUGH OPENING AS THE GUIDE

## Don't hang drywall too close to jambs

Window and door jambs are not always straight. Often, the jamb has to be adjusted when you install the casing. This can't be done if the drywall is cut too close to the jamb. When you're using a spiral saw, guide it with the wood that makes up the rough opening, not the window jamb itself.

NEEDS TO BE TAPED

SPIRAL SAW BIT BURN-THROUGH

## Use heavy boxes and watch out for the wires

If you have any control over which electrical boxes are going to be used on the job, buy the ones made from hard plastic. A spiral saw can cut right through boxes made from soft plastic (usually blue) sending the saw off on an unfortunate path.

Make sure wires are tucked in far enough so the spiral saw won't cut them. Fishing new wire can be an expensive inconvenience, but cutting a live wire could be worse.

THICKER PLASTIC

## Gaps mean extra work

All tear-outs and gaps that won't be completely covered by a cover plate have to be taped and feathered out—more work. So use your spiral saw carefully (and see the note above about heavy plastic electrical boxes!). If a gap around an electrical box is just filled with mud and the cover plate is overtightened, the mud will crack and crumble out of the gap. The areas around outlets are particularly vulnerable because of the pressure of plugging in and unplugging electrical cords.

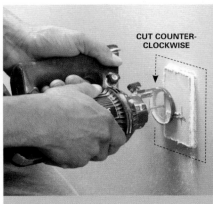

CUT COUNTER-CLOCKWISE

## Spiral saws—a hanger's best friend

Spiral saws save time and money if they're used properly. Here are a few tips for getting the most out of this important drywall tool:

- Make sure you're using a sharp bit, and have extra bits handy because they will break.
- Don't insert the bit too far into the spiral saw. About 1/8 in. of the bit's shank should be exposed. This allows the bit to flex and reduces the chance of breaking.
- Make sure the bit is adjusted to the proper depth. If the bit extends too far, you may cut right through an electrical box or nip a wire inside it. If the bit doesn't extend far enough, the tip of the bit may hop right over an electrical box or recessed light and head off in the wrong direction.
- Cut in the proper direction. Go clockwise when cutting freehand. When cutting around an electrical box or recessed light, move the spiral saw in a counterclockwise direction. The spinning motion of the bit should pull toward the object that's being cut around.
- Never overtighten the drywall or drive screws too close to the cutting area. The pressure will crack and tear the drywall as you're finishing the cut.

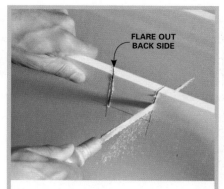

FLARE OUT BACK SIDE

## Back-beveling gives you wiggle room

Even in a world of spiral saws and screw guns, two classic tools—handsaws and keyhole saws—are still essential on any job site. One advantage of hand-sawing is the ability to create a back bevel. This allows for a little more leeway when you're sliding a piece into place, because if you need to trim, you won't have to remove as much material.

STRIP OF 3/8" DRYWALL

1/2" GAP AT FLOOR

## Avoid a large gap at the floor

When you're dealing with a wall that is a few inches over 8 ft., two sheets of 4-ft. drywall will leave you with a large gap at the floor. While most base trim will cover that gap, the tapered edge on the bottom sheet will have to be filled with mud or it will show above the trim line, and that's a lot of extra work (and bending over!) for the taper. Instead of leaving a gap at the bottom, leave a gap in the center of the wall, and fill it with 3/8-in. drywall. The thinner drywall is a snap to tape over smoothly. Your taper will thank you.

## What butt joint?

A butt joint in drywall will result in a raised layer of tape and mud because the edges aren't tapered. A good taper can minimize the ridge over a butt joint, but it's hard to eliminate it altogether. If you're installing drywall by yourself or installing in a space where it's impossible to deliver 12-ft. sheets, butt joints are going to be unavoidable. And if you're dealing with wall sconces or areas where raking light means a truly flat wall is imperative, a butt joint backer may be the answer.

A butt joint backer is basically a 4-ft.-long, 5- or 6-in.-wide board with 1/16-in. to 1/8-in. spacers added along the edges. You can purchase them at a drywall supply store or make your own. You could use an inexpensive 1x6 pine board and either glue or staple strips of ripped-down wood to the outside edges.

Installing the backer is easy. First, install the sheet of drywall, making sure the end doesn't land on a stud. Next, attach the butt joint backer to the back of that piece. Finally, fasten the second piece of drywall to the backer. When installed properly, the butt joint backer will cause the ends of each piece to suck in, resulting in a recess similar to the recess created by two tapered edges.

ATTACH DRYWALL FIRST

ATTACH BACKER TO THE FIRST PIECE OF DRYWALL

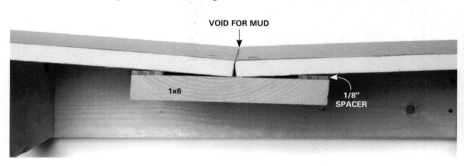

VOID FOR MUD

1x6

1/8" SPACER

**1** APPLY THE FIRST COAT BY HAND
Scoop up a handful of the sealer and wipe it onto the crown. Force the sealant into the cracks and into the crown-to-brick seam.

**2** EVEN OUT THE FIRST COAT
Stroke the wet sealant with a brush to level the high and low spots and create a smooth surface.

## Start at the chimney crown

Masonry chimneys are capped with a mortar "crown" to prevent water from getting behind the bricks and alongside the flue, and into the house. Over time, normal expansion and contraction cycles can cause cracks to form, as shown on p. 67. Sealing the chimney crown with crown sealer, a flexible elastomeric coating, is the best way to stop existing cracks from spreading and prevent new ones.

Choose a clear or overcast day for the project (no rain in the forecast for at least four hours). Prepare the crown by cleaning it with a stiff poly or nylon brush. Fill any large cracks with patching cement or 100 percent silicone caulk (they'll cure even after you apply the crown sealer).

Next, wrap duct tape all around the crown about 1/4 in. below the edge of the crown-to-brick seam. Press the tape into the vertical brick joints. Then tape around each flue liner 1 in. above the crown. Lay canvas (not plastic) tarps around the base of the chimney to protect the shingles from crown sealer drips.

Our chimney repair expert applies crown sealer by hand so he can force it into cracks and get the first coat done faster. If you choose that method, just slip on a disposable glove and apply the sealer (Photo 1). (Search online for "brushable crown repair.") Cover the entire crown and then smooth it with a paintbrush (Photo 2). Wait until the sealer dries tacky to the touch, then apply a second coat with a brush. Clean up with water.

## Seal the bricks

Once the crown sealer feels dry to the touch (30 to 60 minutes), remove the duct tape but leave the roof tarps in place. Then mask off any painted chimney flashings before applying the water repellent. Spray on the repellent (search online for "chimney water repellent") with a low-pressure, garden pump sprayer (Photo 3).

## Finish it off with a chimney cap

A chimney cap keeps water and critters out of your flue and extends flue life. Many codes require a mesh cap, so check before buying. Chimney expert Jim Smart recommends spending extra to get a stainless steel cap (sold at fireplace stores, masonry suppliers or online) because it will last much longer than the galvanized type.

You'll need the outside dimensions of the flue liner to get the right size cap for your chimney. Then install it on the flue liner (Photo 4).

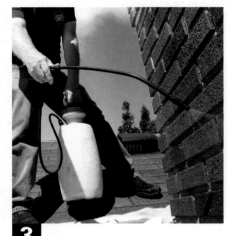

**3** SPRAY THE BRICK WITH WATER REPELLENT
Start at the bottom of the chimney and spray the brick until the excess repellent runs down about 8 in. below the spray line. Work your way up to the top. Apply a second coat within five minutes using the same technique.

**4** INSTALL THE CAP
Set the cap over the flue liner and secure it with screws. Tighten until snug, but no more. Excessive pressure can crack the clay liner.

# What's the best type of bagged concrete to use for a walkway?

"If you want to get your walkway back into service fast," says concrete expert Frank Owens, "your best choice is 'high early strength' concrete." This type of concrete has a higher percentage of cement in the blend so it sets up faster than standard concrete mix. You can walk on it within 10 to 12 hours, compared with several days.

It also generates more heat than standard bagged concrete mix, which means you can tackle your walkway project earlier or later in the season, in temperatures as low as 35 degrees F, with less chance of setting and hardening problems.

However, if your walkway has many steps or landings with exposed edges, Owens recommends fiber-reinforced crack-resistant concrete mix. It contains thousands of little plastic fibers to make it more resistant to shrinkage cracks, edge chipping, impact damage and scaling during freeze/thaw cycles. Crack-resistant concrete takes three days to set up, so your walkway will be out of commission that long, but it can make concrete steps more durable under harsh conditions.

"The right concrete for a project is a matter of trade-offs," Owens says. "Consider setup speed, surface durability and the amount of weight the surface will bear." No matter which product you choose, Owens recommends using as little water as possible. "The lower the water-to-cement ratio, the stronger the concrete and the better the shrinkage resistance."

**HIGH EARLY STRENGTH MIX**

**CRACK-RESISTANT MIX**

**MEET THE PRO**

**Frank Owens** has more than 28 years of experience in the concrete industry and has been with The Quikrete Companies for the past 25 years. He is currently vice president of marketing.

# Big saw for tough cuts

When your patio project calls for cutting tough stuff, this big cut-off saw is just what you need and what's in every pro landscaper's truck. It's basically a gas-powered chain saw body with a 14-in.-diameter diamond blade mounted to it. You wouldn't guess by looking at it, but it's perfect for cutting paver bricks and it's way faster than most other methods. The trick is to make a simple wooden form to hold the brick secure on the ground. Then you just rev up the saw and slice the brick as if it were a pound of butter. The hose fitting on the saw douses the blade with water while you're cutting to keep the blade cool and reduce dust. You can also use the saw to cut stone, retaining wall block or any other concrete or stone product. Cut-off saws like this model are available to rent at suppliers and rental stores.

**Tip:** Lay all your full-size pavers at once and leave off the perimeter ones that need cutting. Rent the saw and hog them all off at once. Then return that saw to save cash.

# Tips for installing veneer stone

If the words "cultured stone" conjure up images of a fake that you can spot a mile away, then you need to take a look at modern manufactured veneer stone. Today's versions look so good that you'll be hard-pressed to tell them from actual stone. And since manufactured stone is cheaper and lighter than the real thing, it's a great DIY choice for any stone veneer project.

There are several national brands of manufactured stone—including Eldorado, Coronado and Cultured Stone—and they all provide detailed installation instructions on their Web sites. But we were sure that a professional would have tons of great tips and advice, so we enlisted Marcus Schilling, a third-generation mason, to show us how he installs stone veneer. And sure enough, we were right.

You can use manufactured stone indoors or out, but exterior applications require special attention to details of waterproofing and flashing. Before installing exterior stone veneer, talk to your local building inspector to see what's required in your area. We'll show you tips for installing manufactured stone indoors; however, most of the tips also apply to exterior applications.

## Stone veneer in a nutshell

Before we launch into the tips, it's helpful for you to have a general idea of the installation process. Almost all stone veneer installations start with a layer or two of building paper, covered by properly installed dimpled and galvanized wire lath. The next step is to cover the lath with a 1/2-in. layer of Type S mortar, which is "scratched" while it's still wet to allow the stone to cling better. After this "scratch coat" dries overnight, the stone is applied with the same type of mortar. If you're using stone intended to look like it's dry-stacked—that is, no mortar between the stones—you're done. Otherwise you'll finish the job by grouting the joints between the stones with mortar.

**MEET THE PRO**

**Marcus Schilling** was introduced to the world of masonry when he was about 7 years old. He helped his dad with all sorts of stonemason tasks, including carrying small stones and cleaning up at the end of the day. And he loved it from the start. His grandpa was a stonemason. His grandpa taught his dad, and his dad taught Marcus and his brothers. And now Marcus is teaching his sons—and us!—the craft of setting stones and laying bricks.

## More tips for working with lath

- Wear gloves and safety glasses.
- Cut wire lath with large tin snips, power metal shears or a diamond blade mounted in an angle grinder.
- Prebend lath at inside corners. Bend it over a board before putting it in place.
- Make sure the lath is installed so it feels rough when your hand is going up, and smooth going down.

## Easy way to cut wire lath

Wire lath can be unruly, and the cut edges are sharp. So anything you can do to keep the stuff under control while you're cutting it is a big bonus. Here's a tip from Marcus on how to make long cuts. Lay the wire lath on some long boards. Measure from the edge of the lath to the edge of the board on each end so the desired cutting line is lined up with the edge of the board. Then secure the lath temporarily with a few staples. Now use the edge of the board as a guide to make the cut. Marcus uses cordless metal shears, but tin snips or aviation snips will also work.

## Speedy troweling

Marcus swears this is the fastest way to get the mud on the wall. Prop up your mud board about 16 in. high and within easy reach. Load it with mortar. Then use your London trowel as shown to transfer the mortar from the mud board to your trowel. Pull the trowel up the wall to embed the mortar in the lath.

LONDON TROWEL

**Tip:** When installing "dry-stack" stones, use a colored mortar or dye the mortar to match the stones.

## What kind of mortar should I use?

You'll find recipes for mixing your own mortar in the stone manufacturer's instructions, but Marcus uses premixed Type S mortar that's labeled for use with veneer stone. Special additives are already included—all you add is water. Look for it at masonry suppliers or ask about it when you buy your stone.

## You don't need a special tool to scratch the mortar

Grooving or scratching the wet mortar provides a better bond for sticking on the stones. You can buy a special rakelike tool for this, but Marcus prefers to use a 3/16-in. square-notched tile mastic trowel. They're cheap and easy to find at home centers and hardware stores. Simply drag it across the wet mortar to make horizontal stripes.

## Stick on the stone like a pro

Marcus makes a swipe across the entire back of the stone with the trowel first to create a good bond for the mortar bed. Then he wipes mortar from the trowel all around the perimeter. This creates a little hollow spot in the middle that will act as a suction cup to hold the stone in place until the mortar hardens. The key is to put on enough mortar to create about a 1/2-in.-thick layer when the stone is pressed against the scratch coat. If any mortar oozes out around the edges, knock it off with the trowel so it doesn't get in the way of grouting.

## Disguise the cut ends of stones

Occasionally you'll have to cut stones to fit. Marcus uses a 10-in. chop saw equipped with a dry-cut diamond blade. But if you're doing only one job, you can get by with a diamond blade mounted in an angle grinder. Regardless of the tool you use, you'll want to disguise or hide the cut ends. After cutting a stone, Marcus cuts angles on the corners to make them look more natural. You can also use a tile nipper or horse-hoof trimmer to chip away at the sharp edge left by cutting. Marcus chooses thin stones to cut if possible. Then he hides the cut edge against a thicker stone. And if he's using mortar that's dyed to match the stone, as you would in a dry-stack installation, Marcus "butters" the end of the stone so it blends in better.

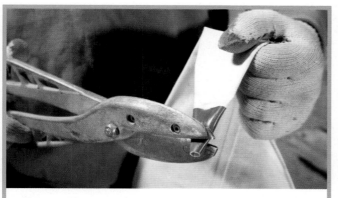

## Cut off the tip of the grout bag

Grout bags come with either metal or plastic tips. Marcus prefers the plastic tips for grouting stone. He cuts the tip to create an opening that's about 5/8 in. in diameter to allow proper mortar flow. Marcus says a common mistake is to mix grouting mortar too stiff. Make sure the mortar is loose enough to ooze from the tip without having to squeeze the bag.

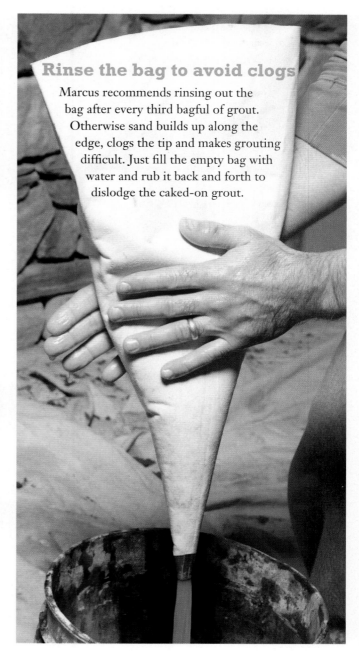

## Rinse the bag to avoid clogs

Marcus recommends rinsing out the bag after every third bagful of grout. Otherwise sand builds up along the edge, clogs the tip and makes grouting difficult. Just fill the empty bag with water and rub it back and forth to dislodge the caked-on grout.

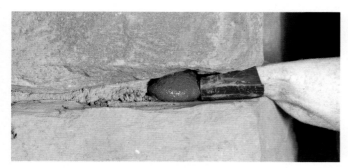

## Fill the joints completely

Marcus says he often encounters hollow grout joints on work done by beginners. Be careful to fill the joints full from back to front as you're grouting. Joints that are hollow underneath will fall out later. Keep the tip pressed deep into the joints so they get filled from the back to the front of the stone.

## Wait! Don't wipe off that wet mortar

When you spill a glob of mortar on the stone, which is almost certain to happen, leave it alone. Let the mortar set up about 30 minutes. Then flick the partially hardened mortar off with the tip of the trowel. Dab the remaining residue with a damp rag to remove it.

## You don't need a special tuckpointing trowel

Marcus finishes the joints using a 3/8-in.-wide tuckpointing trowel that he's cut off to about 5 in. long. He says most masons prefer the shorter length because it gives them much better control. But he says a carpenter's pencil is a great alternative. It's the perfect size and shape for striking your grout joints. Let the grout set up until it's firm to the touch but not hard. Usually this is about 20 to 30 minutes. Then rake the pencil over the grout to smooth and shape it. Finish up by brushing off any loose mortar with a soft masonry brush.

# What's the best cure for spalling concrete?

**THE PROBLEM:**
Water penetrates, freezes and breaks up the concrete surface.

**THE SOLUTION:**
Apply a sealer to lock out water.

**THE RESULT:**
Water can't penetrate; it just beads up on the surface.

The cause of "spalling" or "scaling" concrete is simple. Concrete is porous and soaks up a lot of water. When that water freezes, it expands and breaks up the concrete surface. According to concrete expert Chris Sullivan, prevention is pretty simple too: Apply a sealer to reduce water penetration.

There are many types of sealers. For most sidewalks and driveways, the best choice is an acrylic sealer. Acrylics work by forming a clear coating on concrete. The coating is easy to apply with a roller or sprayer and will last two to five years, depending on weather and traffic. Some products give concrete a glossy "wet" look, while others leave a duller matte finish.

Cost is often a clue to quality. Also check the label; higher-quality acrylics are "non-yellowing" and require new concrete to be fully cured (14 to 28 days, for example). Acrylics cover 100 to 200 sq. ft., depending on the porosity of the concrete.

Home centers carry acrylic sealer (in the masonry aisle), though some sealers don't say "acrylic" on the label. A few common brands are Quikrete High Gloss Sealer, Quikrete Acrylic Cure & Seal, Rust-Oleum Concrete Sealer and Sikagard Sealer.

Acrylic coatings can make concrete slippery. So if you have smooth steps or walkways, there's an alternative you should know about: Penetrating sealers such as "silane" and "siloxane" create a barrier within the concrete rather than on the surface. Available only at specialty concrete suppliers, they usually cost more and degrade faster than acrylic.

**MEET THE PRO**

**Chris Sullivan** is a chemist and vice president of marketing at Chem-Systems, which makes sealers and other concrete-related products.

# Choosing the right modular concrete block

## What kind of wall do you get for your buck?

Walk around most residential neighborhoods and you'll find concrete block retaining and garden walls dotting the landscape. No longer just holding back earth, stabilizing slopes and preventing erosion, modern concrete block walls define pathways, create borders for outdoor "rooms" and serve as focal points in featureless yards.

Building a block wall is a significant investment of time (if you do it yourself) and money (whether you do it yourself or pay someone to do it). Shopping for modular block can be confusing because of the many colors, textures, shapes, styles and stacking systems available. This article will help you sort through your options and discuss what you need to know before you shop so you can buy the right block for your garden or retaining wall.

### In a nutshell

- The more expensive the block, the more it will look like natural stone.
- Each block system will accommodate curves, steps, corners, caps and setbacks differently. Your wall's requirements will help narrow your options.
- When you shop, take along a sketch of the wall's height, length, radius of inside and outside curves, and specific features. Then you'll have everything you need to choose the material and narrow down prices on one trip.
- Even if you plan to hire a pro, shop around to see actual walls rather than depending on contractors' pictures to imagine how yours will look.
- Home centers carry some systems, but you'll find the widest variety of options at landscape suppliers.

TATE CARLSON

**TOP OF THE LINE:** The most expensive block offers the greatest flexibility in design potential, styles, colors and wall size. Big "wow" factor.

VERSA-LOK

**MID-RANGE:** Mid-priced block is good for highly visible walls where function is still the primary concern. It offers a high-end look and feel and is available in many colors and styles.

KEYSTONE

**LEAST EXPENSIVE:** These easy-to-install blocks are often used for garden walls. They're available in a limited number of styles and colors.

# 4 things to think about before you shop for modular blocks

**1** **What's the wall's purpose?**

A freestanding garden wall 3 ft. or less in height that serves a more decorative function gives you more flexibility with the size, style and type of block you choose.

Most manufacturers offer a wide variety of styles in two or three basic sizes. The garden wall size is the most common. These relatively small blocks (about 12 in. long x 4 in. high) are lightweight (less than 25 lbs.) and work best for accent walls around the yard and garden up to about 30 in. high. All four sides are finished and they have special blocks for columns, corners and ends.

Retaining walls, because they're load-bearing and slope into a hill slightly, require larger blocks and beefier connections. These blocks are 16 to 18 in. long x 6 to 8 in. high and weigh 50 to 75 lbs. Big walls usually entail excavating and moving tons of soil and gravel as well as the heavy block itself. These walls can be daunting to do yourself, so think it through before you unknowingly dedicate a whole summer to the task. Most systems are engineered to handle heights up to 4 ft. Retaining walls above that height must be designed or approved by a licensed engineer.

**FREESTANDING WALL BLOCKS** are widely available at home centers, nurseries and landscape suppliers.

**HEAVY-DUTY WALLS** require full-size blocks, which are available at landscape suppliers.

**2** **What kind of look do you want?**

Do you want the block to blend with your property's existing features or to inject something new into the landscape? Although specific shapes, colors and textures vary by region, almost every manufacturer produces four main styles:

**Three-way split**

The corners are split off the face of this block, leaving a highly textured, rounded surface. These are usually the best choice for tighter curves.

**Straight face**

When stacked, it has the classic look of chiseled stone. The uniform texture is a good backdrop for a garden or a good visual base to a house. Its muted appearance will look in style for years. Block size varies. In general, use small block for smaller walls.

**Tumbled or weathered**

The edges are rounded to soften its appearance and make it look more weathered and natural. Different-length blocks can be mixed to further vary the look.

**Mosaics or ashlars**

This combination of tumbled and weathered block in different sizes and colors gives a wall a custom-fitted look. Best used for straight walls; curves require more building experience and block cutting. This type also requires more expert advice for curves, corners and stairs.

## 3 What are your wall's requirements?

The details of your project will help you decide on a block system. Different block systems are suited to different project requirements. For example, all block systems have limits as to how tight a curve they can form without being cut. Systems also vary in how they handle corners, setbacks, cap blocks, columns and steps.

BILL ZUEHLKE (4)

**Solid and semi-solid blocks** are heavy (up to 75 lbs.) but are the most versatile. You can simply split them to form 90-degree corners or any other angle, rather than ordering special blocks.

**Hollow-core blocks** are about half the weight of their solid counterparts and much easier on the back. After you set each course, you fill the cores with gravel, making the wall every bit as strong as a solid block wall. You have to order special blocks for corners and caps.

**Lip systems** (interlock or tongue-and-groove) are popular with DIYers since they go together fast and easy. However, they aren't quite as versatile because you can't vary the setback (the amount each course of wall steps back into the slope). The typical setback is 1-1/4 in. per row.

**A pin or a clip system,** made from tough plastic or fiberglass, anchors each row of blocks to the ones below. These systems are fussier but will let you slide the block forward (no setback) if you need a more vertical wall (such as where a wall meets the corner of a house).

## 4 What's your budget?

The cost of block is only a piece of the total project budget. If you're using a contractor, you'll obviously pay labor costs. A good rule of thumb for a contractor-built wall is to double the materials price—in other words, half labor, half materials. Make sure to agree on the front end whether your contractor will provide final grading and resodding (or will leave your yard a total disaster). Will the driveway be

repaired? Wheel ruts fixed? Topsoil included? These details often account for why one bid is significantly higher or lower than another.

If you plan to build your own wall, beware. There's a lot of heavy work, including tons of fill and footing material to get delivered and moved. Also consider the tools you'll need to rent and other additional costs:

VERSA-LOK

- **Delivery charges for materials.** Don't wreck your back or your vehicle. Block is heavy, even the garden wall variety. Pay the extra charge to place your materials exactly where you want them.
- **Skid steer rental.** Keep in mind that using heavy machinery will damage your yard, so you need to add the costs of grading and resodding as well.
- **A block splitter.** You can also have the landscape yard split the blocks for you.
- **Plate compactor rental.** It's crucial to compact your footing material or you'll have a sagging, crooked wall in the future.
- **Other materials** such as "compactable gravel" for the base, drainage layer material and drain tile.

plants missed by the herbicide. Common brands include Ferti-Lome's Weed-Out, Sta-Green's Crab-Ex Plus and Scotts Turf Builder.

## 2 Check the key ingredient

There are many different trade names for "weed and feed" products on the market. Chemical names can be confusing. Look carefully at the ingredients panel for dithiopyr, prodiamine or pendimethalin. These active ingredients, which are sold under various brand names such as Dimension, Barricade and Scotts Halts, will kill crabgrass in most areas of the country and in many different kinds of turf. However, it's always wise to ask your local extension service which chemicals are best for your area and turf species.

## 3 Don't skip a spring

Killing crabgrass this year doesn't mean you're off the hook next year. Crabgrass seeds can lie dormant in the soil for several years and will germinate once they make their way to the soil surface. Don't be lulled into a false sense of perfect turf. Make a habit every spring of applying a preemergent herbicide to prevent these seeds from getting established. And if your lawn is overtaken by crabgrass right now, applying a preemergent herbicide every spring will eventually wipe it out and prevent those seeds from germinating in the future.

## 4 Time your application by watching your shrubs

Crabgrass germinates when soil temps reach 55 to 60 degrees F, which could be as early as February or as late as May depending on where you live. Applying your preemergent herbicide at the right time is critical because it works by killing germinated crabgrass seeds before they sprout. If you apply it too early, it will lose its potency before the crabgrass sprouts. If you apply it too late, it won't do any good. In the North, a good rule of thumb is to apply preemergent herbicide when lilacs or forsythia is blooming; in the South, when dogwoods are blooming. You can also buy an inexpensive soil thermometer at garden centers to monitor soil temperature.

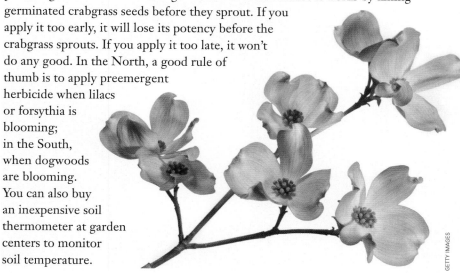

GETTY IMAGES

## 5 Spot-kill crabgrass that comes up

To kill crabgrass that appears later in the summer, spot-spray infested areas with a post-emergent herbicide designed specifically to kill crabgrass and other annual grass weeds—quinclorac is the most common active ingredient. Typical broadleaf herbicides, like the ones that kill dandelions and clover, will not take out crabgrass. The best time to start spot-spraying for crabgrass is when the plants are mature, usually in early to mid-July.

## Consider chemical-free control methods

Preemergent herbicides are the most effective and economical way to control crabgrass. But if you'd rather not use herbicides, you can try hand-weeding individual crabgrass plants in late spring before they get too big. They pull easily in soft ground after a rain.

Corn gluten meal (CGM), a corn byproduct, is another method used to control both crabgrass and broadleaf weeds such as dandelions and clover. It releases a protein that slows the development of weed seedling roots. CGM requires a heavy application rate (20 lbs. per 1,000 sq. ft.), which makes it cumbersome to use and expensive. It's sold at garden centers.

corn gluten

BILL ZUEHLKE

## 6 Keep your lawn healthy

A weak, poorly cared-for lawn is an open invitation to crabgrass and other weeds. The best way to stop crabgrass is to shade it out with a dense, healthy lawn. The key to maintaining a healthy lawn is proper watering, mowing, fertilizing, core aerating, top-dressing with compost and reseeding thin spots.

## 7 Two applications are better than one

Most preemergent herbicides are designed to provide weed control for about eight to 10 weeks. But during unusually hot summers, they don't last that long because warmer soil temperatures degrade them. This makes your lawn vulnerable to crabgrass again by midsummer. To prevent this, use a lawn fertilizer that contains a preemergent herbicide during your second lawn feeding as well as the first. This will extend your crabgrass control into early fall and prevent crabgrass from sneaking back into your lawn during late summer.

## 8 Reseed or kill—not both

Herbicides that kill crabgrass will also kill desirable grasses such as bluegrass, ryegrass and fescue. If you treat your lawn with a preemergent, you cannot seed. And if you seed, you cannot use a preemergent herbicide. The solution is to control crabgrass in the spring and do your seeding in late summer or early fall, making sure to keep these two chores at least eight weeks apart. There are a few preemergent herbicides, such as Tupersan, that are compatible with newly established seed, but they're expensive and can be hard to find.

## 9 Apply a double dose near hot spots

Lawn near driveways, sidewalks and curbs or on south-facing banks absorbs a lot of heat during the summer months, which makes it more susceptible to crabgrass. Limit crabgrass growth in these areas by doing a targeted double treatment. After you've treated your entire lawn, go back and make another pass, about 6 to 8 ft. wide, along these areas (and make sure to sweep it off hard surfaces afterward). This will help keep crabgrass from taking hold along these heat absorbers.

## 10 Know when to throw in the towel

Sometimes a lawn becomes so overrun by crabgrass and other weeds that it makes more sense to start over rather than try to save it. If weeds occupy more than 50 percent of an area, it's best to start over by destroying the entire lawn and reseeding or sodding. Late summer or early fall is the best time of year to take on this project.

# Winterizing a sprinkler system

**Q** Every year I pay the irrigation company to blow out my sprinkler system. I'd like to try it myself, but I don't want to risk leaving water in the system over the winter. Can I do this with my own compressor?

**A** Yes. Just be aware that even the largest home compressor isn't powerful enough to blow out the entire system at once. But you can probably blow it out zone by zone.

If you're into number crunching and you have the original irrigation layout showing the gallons per minute (gpm) of each sprinkler head, just divide the total gpm of each zone by 7.5. That'll give you the cubic feet per minute (cfm) you need to blow it out. Otherwise, just rent a 10-cfm compressor and hose from your local tool rental center.

Set the compressor air pressure regulator to a maximum of 80 psi for rigid PVC pipe systems or 50 psi for flexible black polyethylene pipe. Then turn off the water supply and set the system timer to open just one zone. Next, open the manual drain valve at the end of that zone (if equipped). Then connect the air line to the blow-out port as shown in the photo. Connect the other end of the air hose to the compressor and blow out the line. The heads should pop up and spit out water. Disconnect the hose as soon as they run dry. Don't overdo the blow-out—without water cooling the plastic gears, they can melt in less than a minute. So move on to the next zone and allow the heads to cool. Then go back and blow out each zone a second time.

**PRESSURE VACUUM BACKFLOW (PVB) DEVICE**

**BLOW-OUT PORT**

**TURN OFF**

**TO SPRINKLER ZONES**

## Follow the hookup procedure

Close off both valves on the backflow preventer. Then remove the plug on the blow-out port and screw in a quick-connect hose adapter. Snap on the air hose and connect the other end to the compressor.

## What's the best gas to use in lawn equipment?

"If you can find and afford nonoxygenated gas, it's the way to go," says our favorite motorhead, Rick Muscoplat.

According to Muscoplat, nonoxygenated gas doesn't absorb moisture as quickly as oxygenated gas (which contains ethanol), so you won't have as many carburetor corrosion problems. "Unfortunately," says Muscoplat, "nonoxy gas isn't available everywhere. Often you can only find it at marinas, where you'll pay two or more bucks more per gallon than for regular gas."

Whichever gas you use, Muscoplat suggests adding a fuel stabilizer to keep fuel fresh. Lawn equipment that you plan to store for an extended period should be prepped according to the manufacturer's instructions. Check online in your zip code to find stations that sell nonoxygenated gas.

**MEET THE PRO**

**Rick Muscoplat**

# Topiary tips from Craig Minasian, Disney's plant (and animal) wrangler

**Keeping the animals happy:** "There's a lot of maintenance on the animals that have antlers, horns and stripes, like the zebras. A variety of plants are used on detail areas—palm fiber for antlers and Spanish moss for the zebra stripes."

Whether you're 6 or 60, you can't help but be tickled by an arborvitae elephant or a rhododendron rabbit. In the 1960s, Walt Disney turned the centuries-old art of topiary into an enormously popular part of Disneyland's big "show." There are now more than 100 whimsical characters and animals sculpted out of live plants at the Disney Resorts. The pros who create these character topiaries need to have extensive landscaping knowledge as well as artistic souls. Craig Minasian has both. With 30 years in the landscape industry, he's spent the last four of them as a master senior topiary engineer at the Disneyland Resorts. He learned his craft through Disneyland's formal Character Topiary Maintenance Training and Apprentice program.

## A typical day starts in the dark
"We do most of our work when guests are not around. So we set up lights at 2 a.m. and work under the lights until dawn. My workday is finished by 10 a.m."

"My primary tools are sheep shears (available at farm supply stores), which can be used one-handed and are good for close cuts and detail work like on the faces, and common two-handed garden shears for the bigger areas."

## Secrets to successful topiary
"You need patience and the ability to focus on the whole project and not just the details in front of you. With character topiary, you're trying to fill the base frame. So we're always looking at the holes in the figures and trying to redirect new growth to fill the holes. The challenge is to manage the health and look of each plant to keep it within the frame."

## Craig's tips for the novice "topiary engineer"

- Start small. Buy a prebent wire frame at a garden center or make your own.
- Start with a vine topiary rather than a shrub topiary. Vines are easier to work with and let you practice pruning and managing the different kinds of plants.
- Choose plants that grow quickly and are tolerant of many growing conditions. Good vine topiary plants include English and Boston ivy.
- In cold climates, plant the topiary in a pot that can be moved into the garage during the winter.

# Mr. Lawn can whip your sorry grass into shape!

Achieving a lush lawn doesn't have to be a constant struggle. And you don't have to pay big bucks for a lawn service to douse your yard with chemicals either. Growing healthy, green grass is mainly just a matter of knowing what to give your lawn, and when to give it.

In this story, we'll show you what to do in the spring, summer and fall to get a lawn so nice you could cut it up and sell it as sod. These steps will work for any yard, regardless of climate or soil type. The products shown in this article are available at lawn and garden centers and some home centers.

We worked with lawn care expert **George Dege,** better known as Mr. Lawn. He has been teaching lawn care classes since the 1970s and has helped thousands of homeowners improve their lawns. As the third-generation owner of a lawn and garden center, he has been in the lawn care business "forever."

## Not-so-green acres

Following Mr. Lawn's advice, we worked on the lawn shown here. In March, it had dead patches of grass caused by voles. By August, the grass over the entire lawn was so thick we felt like we were walking on shag carpet. And the lawn looked great too (see above). It was noticeably greener than the neighboring yards.

Once the grass starts turning green, it's time to start your lawn care. That's usually mid to late March for Northerners, early March for Southerners. Don't fret if your lawn is slow to green up. That's good. The thicker the lawn, the less sunlight that reaches the individual blades and the longer it takes for the grass to turn green.

Get rid of the stones and sand that the snowplow or snow blower threw into your yard over the winter. Raking isn't effective—you'll only get about 15 percent of the stones and pebbles. Instead, use a shop vacuum (Photo 1).

The snow piles that sat on your lawn all winter compacted the soil. You can loosen the soil and improve water penetration by applying gypsum (a 40-lb. bag covers 200 sq. ft.). Test your broadcast spreader's dispersal pattern on your driveway. Fill the hopper, set the spread rate so the holes are wide open for gypsum and walk at your normal speed. Then measure how far the gypsum is dispersed on each side of the spreader

(Photo 2). This tells you the distance to move over with each row when you're spreading—you want the spread patterns to overlap by 6 to 8 in. Broadcast spreaders always "throw" farther on the right side than they do the left. You don't need to spread gypsum over the entire lawn, just 10 ft. back from the street and the driveway.

For your spring and summer mowings, cut just the top third of the grass. So if your grass is 3 in. high, take 1 in. off the top. Mowing more than one-third stresses the grass. You can mow the grass shorter in the fall.

Between your second and third mowings, apply a lawn fertilizer with slow-release (time-release) nitrogen (a 20-lb. bag covers 5,000 sq. ft.). Always fill your spreader over a tarp or driveway (Photo 3). Follow the spread rate listed on the fertilizer bag and spread it on the entire lawn.

Fifteen days after applying the fertilizer, spread soil activator on the lawn (Photo 4; a 40-lb. bag covers 4,000 sq. ft.).

**1** **VACUUM THE PEBBLES**
Gravel and sand hinder grass growth, so vacuum them up. Start along the street and vacuum into the yard until you no longer hear stones getting sucked up. Then do the same thing along the driveway.

**2** **CHECK THE SPREADER'S "THROW"**
To apply the right amount of fertilizer, measure from the wheel to the edge of the dispersal pattern. Then space your passes across the lawn so the coverage overlaps by 6 to 8 in. Do this test every time you spread a new product.

**3** **DON'T SPILL ON THE GRASS**
Park your spreader over a tarp or your driveway when filling the hopper. Spills and leaks can saturate one spot of your lawn and kill your grass.

## Your lawn and a chicken's butt—a marriage made in heaven!

Chicken manure is rich in nitrogen, which is a key nutrient for a healthy lawn. No need to get your own flock—it's a whole lot easier to just buy it by the bag.

Proper watering is crucial to a healthy lawn. The best time to water is early morning, when the sun starts to rise. You lose some water to evaporation in the middle of the day. And watering at night leaves the grass wet too long, which can cause fungus and other diseases in the summer.

Give your lawn 3/8 in. of water three times a week. Calculate the amount of time it takes your sprinkler to dispense that much water (Photo 5). Set a timer (sold at home centers and lawn and garden centers) on your hose spigot so you won't have to watch the clock (Photo 6). Increase from 3/8 in. to 1/2 in. when the daytime temperatures are above 80 degrees F.

If you have bare spots in your lawn caused by your dog, sprinkle gypsum on the spot and saturate it with water (Photo 7). Plant new grass seed in the bare spots and keep it watered.

Crabgrass will grow when the soil warms up to 55 degrees F. Apply a crabgrass preventer to keep that nasty weed from coming back. Timing is everything. If you apply the preventer too early, it will be ineffective. And once the seeds germinate, it's too late. In northern states, late April is the best time. Mid-March is recommended for southern states. Check with a local garden center to find the best time for your area.

Apply the preventer wherever you had crabgrass the previous year, which is typically along the street, driveway and sidewalk (Photo 8).

In mid-May, give your lawn its second application of lawn fertilizer.

**4** **IMPROVE YOUR SOIL**
Soil activator helps retain water in sandy soils and loosens clay soils. It also helps aerate the soil, decompose grass clippings and reduce erosion.

CAKE PAN

**5** **MEASURE THE RIGHT AMOUNT OF WATER**
Set a cake pan halfway between your sprinkler and the edge of the spray pattern. Watch your clock to see how long it takes the sprinkler to fill the pan with 3/8 in. of water. Water for that amount of time three times a week, unless it rains.

TIMER

**6** **WATER WITH A TIMER**
If you don't have an automatic sprinkler, a timer frees you from watching the clock every time you water. The timer controls the sprinkler, so you'll be sure the lawn gets the proper amount of water.

GYPSUM

**7** **NEUTRALIZE DOG SPOTS**
Gypsum and water are the antidote for dog spots in your yard. Gypsum neutralizes the dog urine, and the water soaks the area for new grass seed. If you treat the brown spots early, your grass won't die.

CRABGRASS PREVENTER

**8** **STOP CRABGRASS BEFORE IT STARTS**
Apply crabgrass preventer to any areas where crabgrass previously grew. A hand spreader is perfect for small areas, like along the pavement where crabgrass tends to grow.

By midsummer, you should notice a thicker, greener lawn. You'll probably also notice weeds. Spot-kill patches of weeds with an herbicide in a handheld pressure sprayer (Photo 9).

If weeds are popping up all over the lawn, spray them with a dial sprayer (at home centers and lawn and garden centers). Pour concentrated herbicide into the sprayer and hook it up to your garden hose. Turn the dial on the top of the sprayer to the setting recommended on the herbicide container (such as 2 tablespoons per gallon of water). Then spray the weeds (Photo 10).

In mid-August, you could give your lawn a third application of fertilizer, but chicken manure works even better because it contains more nitrogen, which gives the grass a healthy, green look (there's hardly any odor). Mr. Lawn is a fan of Chickity Doo Doo because it also contains 9 percent calcium, which improves root growth. (A 40-lb. bag covers 4,000 sq. ft. Find retailers online.) Within two or three days of applying the manure, you'll see the lawn really green up.

**9** **SPOT-SPRAY INDIVIDUAL WEEDS**
Don't treat the entire lawn if you have just a few weeds. A pump sprayer is more economical than buying spray bottles. Be sure there's no rain in the forecast for 24 hours.

DIAL SPRAYER

**10** **USE YOUR HOSE FOR LARGE AREAS**
Use a dial sprayer hooked up to your hose to kill large areas of weeds. Spray the herbicide on a calm day so the weed killer won't drift onto your plants and flowers.

### DIY success story

"My dad followed Mr. Lawn's advice, and he always had a great-looking lawn. I did the same thing when I bought my first house. I was happy with the results too.

"Two years ago, I bought a new house, and I started Mr. Lawn's program a second time (and yes, I even vacuumed my lawn). I had some bare spots and the grass was sparse in places. By the time I applied Chickity Doo Doo in August, I had the nicest lawn on the block. There was one downside. My lawn was so lush and grew so fast that I sometimes had to mow two or three times a week."

*—Ron Knafla*

### Fall care

Don't neglect your lawn as the growing season comes to an end. It's important to keep treating your soil before the grass goes dormant for the winter. In early to mid September, apply soil activator over your yard, just as you did in the spring.

Two weeks after that, give your lawn its final application of fertilizer for the year. Use a winterizer fertilizer (a 40-lb. bag covers 10,000 sq. ft.). This specialized fertilizer has more potassium to help the grass roots grow deeper, which lets the roots absorb and store nutrients until the ground freezes. When the ground warms up in the spring, the grass uses those nutrients to jump-start its growth.

Keep mowing your lawn until the grass stops growing. Even in Minnesota, that sometimes doesn't happen until the first part of December. On your final mowing of the year, cut the grass to 1 to 1-1/2 in. high (Photo 11).

Now you're done caring for your lawn until spring!

**11** **FACE WINTER WITH SHORT GRASS**
Mow the grass short at the end of the year. This reduces the chance that your lawn will get snow mold and vole damage.

# What's the best garden hose?

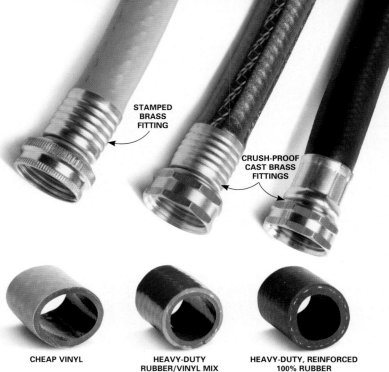

STAMPED BRASS FITTING

CRUSH-PROOF CAST BRASS FITTINGS

The best garden hose doesn't kink or leak, lasts forever, is exactly the right length and weight for your needs and isn't too expensive.

In other words, the best doesn't exist. But happily, high-quality hoses do exist, and they all share a few characteristics. They might be 100 percent rubber or made of a rubber/vinyl composite material, but the label will clearly state that the hose is both heavy-duty and flexible. They have heavy-duty crush-proof cast brass fittings that, unlike stamped brass fittings, won't get deformed when you drive over them, and they come with a lengthy warranty period (usually a lifetime). They're also not cheap. Expect to pay premium prices for a good 50-ft. garden hose.

CHEAP VINYL

HEAVY-DUTY RUBBER/VINYL MIX

HEAVY-DUTY, REINFORCED 100% RUBBER

# What's the best grass to grow under trees?

Growing grass under shade trees isn't easy, but one key to success is choosing the right shade grass species and planting method for your region.

In cool-season areas, you'll get a better result using seed rather than sod. Sod is grown in wide-open fields under conditions that favor sun-loving grasses. Choose red and tall fescues for shady areas in Northern zones. Garden centers will have grass seed mixes formulated for shade. Late summer and mid-spring are the best times to establish cool-season grasses in shady areas.

In warm-season areas, St. Augustine grass is probably your best choice for moderate shade. Unfortunately, this species is not currently available as seed, so the only way to plant it is with plugs, sod or sprigs (a significantly more expensive proposition). St. Augustine grass has limited cold and drought tolerance.

GRASS SEED

GRO·FORMULA #1622

DENSE SHADE

GRASS PLUGS

**Shade seed and fescue mixtures work best in cool-season areas.**

**St. Augustine grass plugs are your best bet in warm-season areas.**

**To help ensure success with shade grasses:**

■ Don't skimp on the prep work. You'll need to rototill before planting and keep the area watered and weed free to give the grass time to fill in.

■ Selectively prune tree limbs to allow more light to reach the turf and improve turf quality.

# 10 must-have hummingbird flowers

## 1 Bee balm

(*Monarda didyma*)
Perennial; zones 4 to 9
**Color:** Red
**Blooms:** Summer
**Size:** 3 to 5 ft. tall; spreads 18 to 36 in.
**Care:** Moist, moderately fertile soil; light shade to full sun. Deadhead flowers to keep them blooming and to limit reseeding.

## 2 Butterfly bush

(*Buddleja* species)
Shrub; zones 4 to 9
**Color:** Purple, pink and white
**Blooms:** Summer to fall
**Size:** 6 to 15 ft. tall; 4 to 10 ft. wide
**Care:** Grow in sun to light shade.
**Caution:** Considered invasive in some regions.

## 3 Butterfly weed

(*Asclepias tuberosa*)
Perennial; zones 4 to 9
**Color:** Orange
**Blooms:** Summer to fall
**Size:** 1-1/2 to 3 ft. tall; spreads 12 in. wide
**Care:** Moist well-drained to dry soil; full sun. These plants will wander to where they're best suited in your garden.

Phlox

## 4 Cardinal flower

(*Lobelia cardinalis*)
Perennial; zones 3 to 9
**Color:** Red
**Blooms:** Summer
**Size:** 3 to 4 ft. tall; 2 ft. wide
**Care:** Fertile and moist soil, partial shade to full sun. Works beautifully with other native plantings.

## 5 Columbine

(*Aquilegia* species)
Perennial; zones 3 to 9
**Color:** Red, pink, blue, purple
**Blooms:** Spring to early summer
**Size:** 1 to 3 ft. tall; 6 to 24 in. wide
**Care:** Low-maintenance plants that prefer moist, but not wet, soil. Reseeds itself.

## 6 Fuchsia

(*Fuchsia* species)
Perennial; zones 10 and 11; annual to north
**Color:** Red, pinks, purple, white
**Blooms:** Until frost
**Size:** Trailing to 3 ft. or available in shrub form.
**Care:** Requires moist soil: Check pots twice a day in hot weather. Pinch back flowers.

## 7 Phlox

(*Phlox* species)
Perennial; zones 3 to 8
**Color:** Pink, red, blue and purple
**Blooms:** Spring to fall
**Size:** Up to 3 ft. tall; 12 to 24 in. wide
**Care:** Needs well-draining soil in full sun. Deadhead to extend bloom time.

Salvia

## 8 Salvia

(*Salvia splendens*)
Annual
**Color:** Red
**Blooms:** Until frost
**Size:** 1 to 3 ft. tall; 9 to 14 in. wide
**Care:** Keep soil at roots cool and moist; grow in full sun. Deadhead flowers to keep blooming.

## 9 Snapdragon

(*Antirrhinum*)
Annual
**Color:** Varies with variety
**Blooms:** Until frost
**Size:** 6 in. to 4 ft. tall; 6 in. to 2 ft. wide
**Care:** Grows in full sun to part shade in moist soil. Regular deadheading needed.

## 10 Trumpet vine

(*Campsis radicans*)
Perennial; zones 4 to 9
**Color:** Orange-red
**Blooms:** Summer
**Size:** Climbs to 40 ft
**Care:** Grows in full sun in moist to dry soil. Tolerates poor soil and needs little or no fertilizer.

## 2 Forgetting the tamper-resistant receptacles

Tamper-resistant receptacles are designed to stop a kid from inserting an object such as a paper clip. They're required for all locations, indoors and out. Tamper-resistant receptacles are a great invention, so use them—it's code.

**TAMPER RESISTANT**

### Common violation

Replacing an existing receptacle with a conventional one. When an existing receptacle is replaced, the NEC requires the installation of a tamper-resistant receptacle.

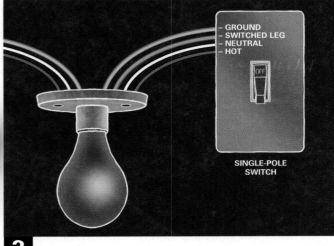

- GROUND
- SWITCHED LEG
- NEUTRAL
- HOT

OFF

SINGLE-POLE SWITCH

## 3 Wiring switches without a neutral

All switch locations now need a neutral wire. This code was mainly implemented to accommodate potential future uses. Electronic switches require a small amount of constant electricity and therefore need a neutral wire run to them. There are exceptions to this code, but if the walls are currently open anyway, don't make the next guy fish in a wire. Do it right and make sure there's a neutral wire in the box.

### Common violation

One common occurrence of a missing neutral wire is a dead-end single-pole switch loop. One way to solve this problem is to run a three-wire cable with ground to the last switch on the run.

## 4 Using a ground rod electrode when a better system is available

For a long time, metal underground water piping was considered the best grounding electrode available, but virtually all underground water piping today is plastic. And it turns out that rebar in concrete footings or the foundation for a house is actually a more effective grounding system than the ground rods we've been using for decades. So if there's rebar in the new footings, that rebar needs to be used as the primary grounding electrode. This new provision in the NEC requires a lot of coordination between the trades and project managers. Electricians usually show up long after the concrete guys have moved on, but good communication is much easier work than busting up concrete.

### The bottom line

If a new home has footings with at least 20 ft. of 1/2-in. rebar, the rebar embedded in those footings needs to be used as the primary grounding electrode.

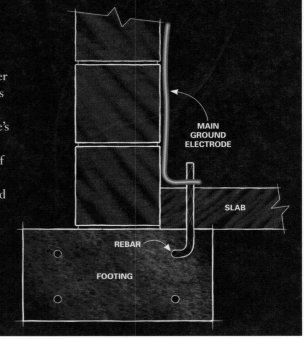

MAIN GROUND ELECTRODE

SLAB

REBAR

FOOTING

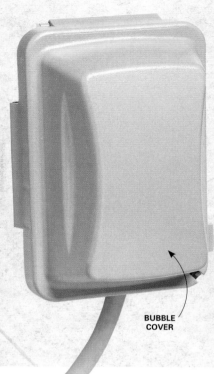

**BUBBLE COVER**

## 5 Installing a flat weather-resistant cover on an outdoor receptacle

Flat covers provide protection only when a receptacle isn't in use, but it's not uncommon for extension cords to be plugged in for extended periods of time; for holiday lights, for example. In-use or "bubble covers" provide protection at all times. The NEC defines a "wet location" as an area that is subject to saturation with water or other liquids, and unprotected locations exposed to the weather. The NEC has another definition for "damp locations" that is more subjective, but if you think the receptacle is going to get wet, use an in-use cover. And don't forget the weather-resistant receptacle. The NEC requires that all 15- and 20-amp receptacles be rated as weather-resistant and tamper-resistant when installed in *both* wet and damp locations.

**DOES NOT MEET CODE**

### Common violation

Often it's assumed that an exterior outlet that's sheltered by a roof overhang can be covered with one of the older, flap-style outlet covers. But that decision is up to the inspector, so it's better to play it safe and install a bubble cover.

## 6 Crowding a service panel

A service panel requires a working clearance that's 30 in. wide, 3 ft. deep and 6 ft. 8 in. high. Here's a good rule of thumb: If you can't park a refrigerator in front of the panel, you don't have enough working space. These clearances are designed to protect the person working on the panel. It's difficult to work safely when your arms are pinned to your sides. Also, the panel needs to be readily accessible, meaning the area should not be used as storage space or require a ladder for access.

**REFRIGERATOR FOOTPRINT**

### Common violations

- Panels in closets, crawl spaces and bathrooms.
- Panels encroached upon by laundry tubs, sump basket, ducting and pipes.

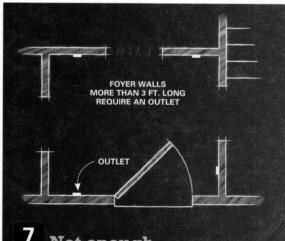

**FOYER WALLS MORE THAN 3 FT. LONG REQUIRE AN OUTLET**

**OUTLET**

## 7 Not enough receptacles in the foyer

The purpose of this code is to reduce the use of extension cords. From any point along a wall line, a receptacle outlet needs to be within reach of a 6-ft. appliance cord, and that 6 ft. cannot be measured across a passageway. The bottom line is that extension cords start fires and create tripping hazards—the fewer of them, the better.

### Common violation

Failure to install receptacles in walls that are 3 ft. long or longer.

## 8 Insufficient bonding

Grounding is not bonding. Plumbing, phone lines, coaxial cable and gas piping systems need to be not only *grounded* but also *bonded* to one another. Bonding equalizes the voltage potential between conductive systems. This greatly reduces the risk of a person becoming the path for current flow between two conductive systems in case one of the systems becomes energized. Also, in a lightning strike, equalized voltage potential minimizes the risk of a very high current jumping (arcing) between two systems and causing a fire.

### Common violations

- Replacing an old fuse box and assuming the system is bonded.
- Unbonded satellite and cable installations.

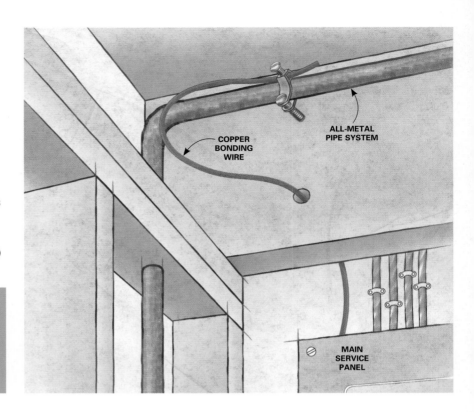

**COPPER BONDING WIRE**

**ALL-METAL PIPE SYSTEM**

**MAIN SERVICE PANEL**

## What's the best electrical tape?

**MEET THE PRO**

**Al Hildenbrand** is a licensed Minnesota Class "A" Master Electrician with a bachelor of science degree in electrical engineering. He's the owner of Al's Electric Works in Minneapolis, MN.

"A lot of electricians, including me, swear by Scotch 33+," says master electrician Al Hildenbrand. "It's an amazing tape. The glue is stable and non-gumming and non-running, so it doesn't leave a residue on your hands or the material if removed. But more importantly, the plastic has a 'stretch' and 'return memory.' When the tape is pulled off the roll, it stretches slightly, and over the next five to 10 minutes, attempts to return to its original length.

"This 'memory' helps to put a slight compression on a smoothly wrapped splice to hold it in place. And the 'stretch' allows an irregular surface to be wrapped over the high spots, where the stretch is greatest; the 'memory' generally allows the tape on either side to snug down onto the smaller diameters. The result is a smoother, tighter and more uniform insulating of what is being covered."

**SCOTCH SUPER 33+ VINYL ELECTRICAL TAPE**

# Pro wiring tips

Even if you have years of wiring experience under your belt, there are always a few tricks you may not know. And a good way to discover them is to watch another veteran at work. That's what we did. It didn't take long to discover some real gems.

This section features tips, tricks and techniques from two master electricians with decades of experience between them. From straightening cable to labeling wires, here are tips to help you wire better and faster.

## Peel UF like a banana

Underground feeder (UF) cable has a tough plastic sheathing that allows you to bury it directly in the ground without running it through a conduit (of course, it has to be buried deep enough to satisfy the electrical code). But that tough sheathing is also difficult to remove—unless you know this trick.

Start by separating the black and white wires from the bare copper by grabbing each with pliers and twisting (Photo 1). They're easy to tear apart once you get them started. Pull them apart until you have about a foot of separated wires. Next, remove the sheathing from the insulated wires by grabbing the end of the wire with one pliers and the sheathing with another pliers and working them apart. After you get the sheathing separated from the insulated wire at the top, peel it off (Photo 2). Repeat the process to remove the sheathing from the black wire. Finally, cut off the loose sheathing with scissors or a knife.

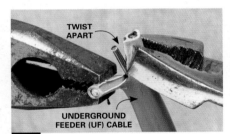

**1** **SEPARATE THE END.** Twist the end of the UF with two pairs of pliers to separate the wires.

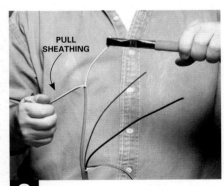

**2** **STRIP OFF THE SHEATHING.** Peel the sheathing from the wires and cut it off.

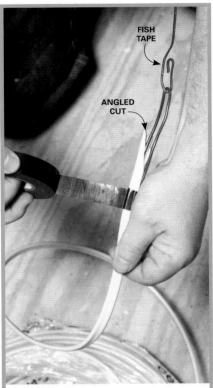

**CONNECT IT SECURELY.** Bend one wire back to form a big loop and wrap the whole works with electrical tape.

## No-snag fish tape connections

After going to all the trouble of working your fish tape to its destination, the last thing you want is to lose the cable or get your tape stuck on something inside the wall as you pull it back. Here's how to avoid both problems (photo above). Start by stripping an 8-in. length of cable. Using a side cutters, cut off all but one wire. Cut at a steep angle to avoid a "shoulder" that could catch on something. Then bend the single wire around the loop on the end of the fish tape and wrap the whole works with electrical tape to form a smooth bundle. Now you can pull the wire without worrying that it might fall off, and the smooth lump won't get snagged by or stuck on obstructions.

## Troubleshooting GFCIs

We asked our electrical pros what problems they run into with GFCIs and how to solve them. For starters, we found that most complaints occur when several outlets are protected by one GFCI. There are several possible causes, ranging from a light or appliance with a ground fault that's plugged into a downstream outlet, to a defective GFCI or even a circuit with too much cable.

To determine whether the problem is with the GFCI itself or downstream, turn off the power to the GFCI and disconnect the wires from the "load" terminals. Push the reset button (if it doesn't click, you'll have to reset it after the power is back on) and plug a GFCI tester into the GFCI outlet before you turn the power back on. If the GFCI trips after you turn the power on, replace it. If it holds, then the problem is with one of the downstream outlets. To avoid the time-consuming process of troubleshooting the "load" outlets, the easiest and best solution is to replace each of them with a new tamper-resistant GFCI.

# Identify roughed-in wires

Save yourself a lot of headaches by identifying the wires as you install them. It's a lot harder to figure out which wires go where when they're covered with drywall. The electricians we talked to use a "code" for marking wires, and so can you. Photo 1 shows one example. Another method is to use a label (Photo 2). But by the time you get back to connect switches and outlets, you might find that drywallers, tapers and painters have covered the label or knocked it off. That's why it's best to use nonlabel coding whenever possible. Develop a system and write it down. You'll never have to guess which are the "line" and "load," and which wires are the travelers for your three-way switch.

## Two ways to I.D. wires

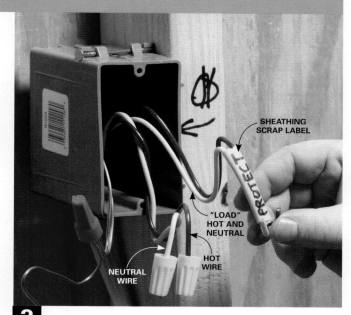

**TWIST TRAVELERS**

**TIGHTLY TWIST COMMON WIRE**

**SHEATHING SCRAP LABEL**

**"LOAD" HOT AND NEUTRAL**

**NEUTRAL WIRE**

**HOT WIRE**

**1** CODE YOUR WIRES. Here's one example. Wrap three-way switch "travelers" loosely and wrap the common wire tightly around them for easy identification later.

**2** LABEL WIRES. You can also use scraps of plastic sheathing to label the wires. Here we labeled the wires that will be GFCI protected.

## Test before touching

When you've done a lot of wiring, it's easy to get complacent about whether the power is off. But don't. Use a noncontact voltage detector to check every wire in the box or area you're working. Always check the tester on a wire or cord you know is live to make sure it's working before you rely on it. Noncontact voltage detectors are available at home centers, hardware stores and online. The tool shown here has a green light that indicates it's turned on and working—a nice feature that's well worth the extra money.

**AVOID SURPRISES.** Test all the wires in a box with a noncontact voltage detector before you touch anything.

## Multiple switches, one hot wire

A box with three switches is crowded enough without adding extra wire connectors and pigtails. Here's a wiring method that eliminates extra connections and creates a neater installation. Instead of running a separate pigtail from the hot wire to each switch, just leave the hot wire extra long. To connect the switches, simply score the wire with your wire stripper and push the insulation to expose about 3/4 in. of bare wire (Photo 1). Wrap this bare section at least three-quarters of the way around the screw terminal of the first switch. Repeat the process for the remaining intermediate switches (Photo 2). Connect the last switch in the usual manner, looping the wire around the screw in a clockwise direction.

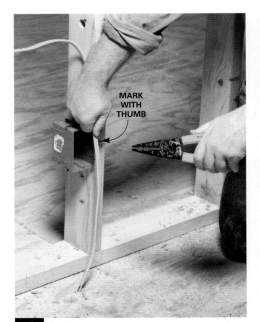

**1 SAVE BOX SPACE. Run a continuous hot wire from switch to switch. Score the insulation and slide it to expose bare wire.**

**2 GO FROM SWITCH TO SWITCH. Wrap the exposed section of wire around the screw and run it to the next switch.**

## Strip sheathing first

It's tempting to push your roughed-in cable through the knockouts in the box and worry about how to strip the sheathing later. But that's the hard way. It's much easier to remove the sheathing before you push the wires into the box. The only trick is to make sure you have the cable in about the right spot before marking it (Photo 1) and removing the sheathing (Photo 2). As long as you don't have the cable stretched tight, there will be enough "play" to make final adjustments after you've inserted the conductors into the box. Remember, the electrical code requires that at least 1/4 in. of sheathing be visible inside the box.

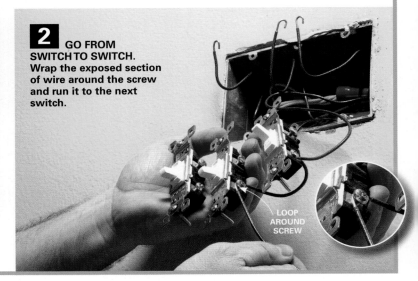

**1 MARK THE SPOT. Hold the cable near the box and mark it with your thumb where it extends slightly past the box.**

**2 STRIP THE SHEATHING. Score the sheathing at the "thumb mark" and slide it off. Then feed the wires into the box.**

## Uncoil without kinks

Pulling plastic-sheathed cable through holes in the framing is a lot easier if you straighten it out first. If you simply pull the cable from the center of the coil, it'll kink as you pull it through the studs.

The trick is to lift a handful of coils from the center of the roll (Photo 1) and toss them across the floor as if you're throwing a coiled rope. Next, walk along the length of cable, straightening it as you go (Photo 2). The electricians we talked to prefer this method because they can keep the cable contained in the plastic wrapper for easier handling and neater storage.

**1** AVOID KINKS. Don't just pull cable from the roll. Instead, lift a few loops from the center of the roll. Four loops will reach about 12 ft.

**2** STRAIGHTEN BEFORE PULLING. Toss the coil across the floor. Then straighten it by hand before pulling it through the framing.

## Pack boxes neatly

If you've done much wiring, I'm sure you've had times when you could barely push the switch or outlet into the box because there were so many wires. The solution is to arrange the wires neatly and then fold them carefully into the box. Here's how to keep wires neat and compact: First, gather all the bare ground wires along with a long pigtail and connect them. Fold them into the back of the box, leaving the pigtail extended. Next, do the same for the neutral wires. If you're connecting switches as we show here, you don't need a neutral pigtail. Leave the hot wire extra long and fold it back and forth across the bottom of the box. (See "Multiple Switches, One Hot Wire" on p. 98 for how to connect switches to this wire.) Put a wire connector cap on the hot wire to identify it. The neatly packed box makes it easy to identify the wires and leaves you plenty of room for the switches.

**FOLD THE WIRES.** Neatly packed wires save space and eliminate confusion.

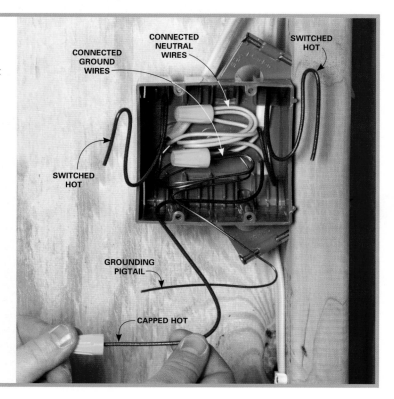

CONNECTED GROUND WIRES

CONNECTED NEUTRAL WIRES

SWITCHED HOT

SWITCHED HOT

GROUNDING PIGTAIL

CAPPED HOT

## Probe for the screw hole

Many fixtures have a canopy that's held in place by two screws. Aligning the first screw is easy enough because you can tilt the canopy a little and aim for the screw hole above it. To align the second screw, stick a skinny screwdriver or a nail into the canopy hole and rotate the canopy until you find the screw hole.

## Third hand

Connecting a fixture takes three hands: one to hold the fixture and two to make the connections. If you don't have a third hand, hang the fixture from a scrap of wire or a coat hanger while you make the connections.

## Buy better connectors

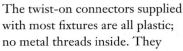

The twist-on connectors supplied with most fixtures are all plastic; no metal threads inside. They just don't grip the wires for an easy, secure connection. So spend an extra few bucks on a pack of assorted small connectors with metal threads when you buy the fixture.

## Check your wiring before you buy

If your home was built before 1985, beware: Many new light fixtures can't be connected to pre-1985 wiring because the insulation on the wiring can't withstand the heat generated by the fixture. These fixtures carry a warning on the label: "Use wire rated for at least 90 degrees C."

If you know your wiring was installed before 1985, you'll have to choose a fixture that doesn't carry this warning. Hanging fixtures, for example, usually don't require newer wiring because they don't heat the wiring as much as fixtures that mount directly against the ceiling. The alternative is to replace the wiring, which may be a small job, or huge, depending on the situation.

If you don't know the age of your wiring, look at the fine print. If you have plastic sheathed cable (Romex is one common brand) and can see the outer sheathing, look for "NM-B" or "UF-B." Or look for "THHN" or "THWN-2" on the insulation of individual wires. If you see any of these, the wiring can handle the heat.

## Make a strong connection

Light fixtures almost always require a connection between solid wire and stranded. That's frustrating because the connector twists and pushes the stranded wire but doesn't grab it. Here's the solution: First, cut off the old exposed solid wire and then strip off 1/2 in. of the insulation. On the stranded wire, strip off 5/8 in. Hold the wires together so the stranded wire extends about 1/8 in. beyond the solid wire and twist on the connector. The end of the stranded wire will bunch up inside the tip of the connector, locked in place for a secure connection.

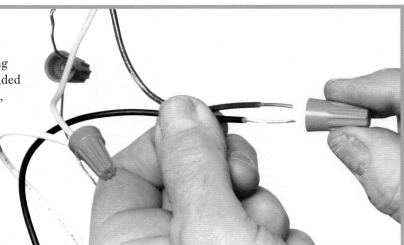

## Why work in the dark?

If the light fixture and outlets in the room are on different circuits, plug in a couple of lamps before you shut off the power to the fixture. Otherwise, strap on a camping headlamp. You'll find them everywhere.

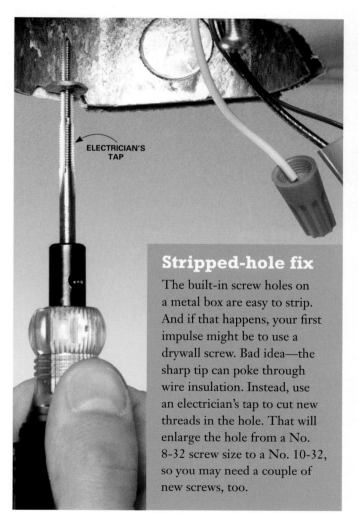

ELECTRICIAN'S TAP

## Stripped-hole fix

The built-in screw holes on a metal box are easy to strip. And if that happens, your first impulse might be to use a drywall screw. Bad idea—the sharp tip can poke through wire insulation. Instead, use an electrician's tap to cut new threads in the hole. That will enlarge the hole from a No. 8-32 screw size to a No. 10-32, so you may need a couple of new screws, too.

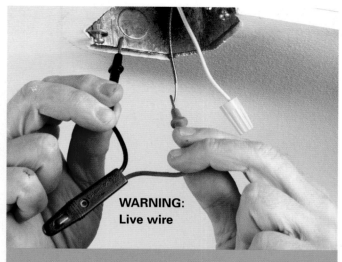

**WARNING: Live wire**

## Check for ground

Your new light fixture will have a ground wire (green coated or bare copper). But if you have an older metal box, there may not be a ground wire inside the box to connect to. Adding a ground wire to the box isn't difficult; just connect a 6-in. section of bare copper wire to the box by driving a No. 10-32 ground screw (available at home centers) into a threaded hole in the box. But before you do that, you have to make sure the box itself is grounded.

Here's how: Turn the power on and make sure the light switch is turned on. Find the hot wire (typically black or red) using your noncontact voltage tester. Next, you'll need a circuit tester (sold at home centers). Touch one of the tester's probes to the bare end of the hot wire and the other to the box. If the light glows, the box is grounded. If not, a ground wire will need to be run to the box to meet electrical code. That's a job for a licensed electrician, unless you're a very knowledgeable DIYer.

## Chandelier chain too long? There's a tool for that!

Raising a chandelier is as easy as removing a few chain links. But opening and closing links without scratching or misshaping them can be a pain. That's why some whiz kid invented chain pliers. This tool bends links open and closed gently and neatly. Search online for "chain pliers." Sure, it's a splurge, but don't you want a tool none of your buddies have ever seen?

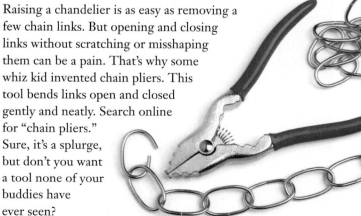

OUT WITH THE OLD: Empty the tank with a hand pump before running the carburetor dry. Reload with fresh gas next time you run the generator.

## Old fuel is your worst enemy

Stale fuel is the No. 1 cause of generator starting problems. Manufacturers advise adding fuel stabilizer to the gas to minimize fuel breakdown, varnish and gum buildup. But it's no guarantee against problems. Repair shops recommend emptying the fuel tank and the carburetor once you're past storm season. If your carburetor has a drain, wait for the engine to cool before draining. If not, empty the tank and then run the generator until it's out of gas. Always use fresh, stabilized gas in your generator.

## Backfeeding kills

The Internet is full of articles explaining how to "backfeed" power into your home's wiring system with a "dual male-ended" extension cord. Some of our Field Editors have even admitted trying it (we'll reprimand them). But backfeeding is illegal—and for good reason. It can (and does) kill family members, neighbors and power company linemen every year. In other words, it's a terrible idea. If you really want to avoid running extension cords around your house, pony up for a transfer switch ($300). Then pay an electrician about $1,000 to install it. That's the only safe alternative to multiple extension cords. Period.

## DON'T!
## It's just plain dangerous

Forget about using a double-ended cord to run power backward into a receptacle. Instead, run separate extension cords or install a transfer switch.

## Store gasoline safely

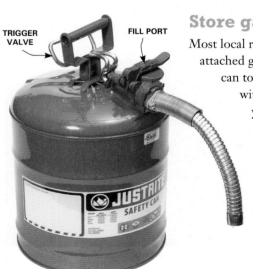

TRIGGER VALVE

FILL PORT

Most local residential fire codes limit how much gasoline you can store in your home or attached garage (usually 10 gallons or less). So you may be tempted to buy one large gas can to cut down on refill runs. Don't. There's no way you can pour 60 lbs. of gas without spilling. Plus, most generator tanks don't hold that much, so you increase your chances of overfilling. Instead, buy two high-quality 5-gallon cans. While you're at it, consider spending more for a high-quality steel gas can with a trigger control valve.

A BETTER GAS CAN MEANS LESS SPILLAGE: The trigger valve on this gas can gives you total control over the fill. There's a separate refill opening so you never have to remove the spout.

## Lock it down

The only thing worse than the rumbling sound of an engine outside your bedroom window is the sound of silence after someone steals your expensive generator. Combine security and electrical safety by digging a hole and sinking a grounding rod and an eye bolt in concrete. Encase the whole thing in 4-in. ABS or PVC drainpipe, with a screw-on cleanout fitting. Spray-paint the lid green so it blends in with your lawn. If you don't want to sink a permanent concrete pier, at least screw in ground anchors to secure the chain.

**STOP CROOKS AND PREVENT SHOCKS. Protect yourself from accidental electrocution by connecting the generator to a grounding rod. Then secure the unit to the eye bolt with a hardened steel chain and heavy-duty padlock.**

GROUND ROD

SCREW LID

## Use a heavy-duty cord

Generators are loud, so most people park them as far away from the house as possible. (Be considerate of your neighbors, though.) That's OK as long as you use heavy-duty 12-gauge cords and limit the run to 100 ft. Lighter cords or longer runs mean more voltage drop. And decreased voltage can cause premature appliance motor burnout.

## Replacing a dimmer? Check the rating

If you're installing a dimmer switch, keep in mind that each switch is rated to handle a maximum wattage. If you're trying to dim six 100-watt lightbulbs, use a switch rated for at least 600 watts. Newer models are fairly generous with their allowances (usually about 600 watts), but that won't cut it if you're trying to dim seven 100-watt bulbs.

**CHECK THE RATING. Make sure the wattage rating on your new dimmer is at least as high as the old one.**

## Adjustable-depth electrical box

An electrical box that can be adjusted until it's flush with the wall is a perfect solution when you're thinking about adding tile or paneling but aren't sure how thick the finished wall will be. There are a few different versions of adjustable boxes. Turning a screw in the box shown here moves the box in and out and allows

you to fine-tune the box position after you've completed the wall covering. Adjustable-depth boxes cost a little more than regular boxes but are worth every penny in areas where you think you'll add tile, paneling or cabinetry and don't want to guess at the depth.

## Occupancy and vacancy sensors

Residential occupancy and vacancy sensors have come of age. Most residential sensors use passive infrared (PIR) technology to detect heat and motion and turn lights on and off accordingly. They can cut lighting costs by 50 percent in rooms where lights are frequently left on when no one is in them. Wall-mount sensors install just like a light switch and are available as switches or dimmers. Most require a neutral wire, but there are a few models that don't. The smartest sensors are designed to screen out background interference and detect small movements and natural light. They also work with LED, CFL, incandescent, halogen and other bulb and load types.

### Occupancy vs. vacancy sensor—what's the difference?

An occupancy sensor automatically turns lights ON and OFF. Great for areas where lights are accidentally left on a lot, like in a kid's room, or where your hands are full, like in a laundry area.

A vacancy sensor has a manual ON and automatic OFF (you can preset different times). It's good for bedrooms, so the light doesn't automatically turn on if a spouse enters while you're sleeping, or in the hallway, so your pet doesn't trigger the light.

**Lutron's Maestro occupancy/ vacancy sensor switch** functions in both modes depending on how it's programmed. It's available in two models—one for small rooms and one for larger rooms. It includes a push-button manual control switch and is available as a dimming sensor as well. It does not require a neutral wire.

**Leviton's Universal Dimming Sensor** is an occupancy sensor and dimmer in one unit. It has a 180-degree field of view for up to 900 sq. ft. of coverage and includes manual presets for delayed-off time settings. Compatible with dimmable LED, CFL and incandescent bulbs. It does not require a neutral.

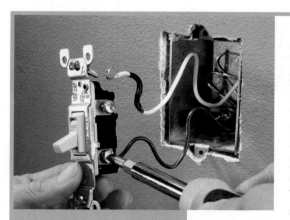

**No neutral:** If your switch is wired like this one— connected to a white and a black wire—both wires are hot and neither can serve as a neutral.

### Check the wiring before you buy

Many of the new, sophisticated smart switches require a neutral wire to run the circuitry inside the switch—particularly those compatible with LED and CFL bulbs. Before you buy a new switch, check the packaging. Most will specifically tell you if a neutral is required, as shown at right. To see if you have a neutral wire in your switch box:

- Turn off the power and use a noncontact voltage detector to check that the circuit is off before you remove the cover plate.
- Remove the cover plate and unscrew and remove the switch. The photo above shows one common situation without a neutral wire.

## Bath fan timers

Timers for bath fans are important because excess humidity can cause everything from window condensation and mildew to moisture and rot inside walls. Timers connected to exhaust fans must be rated to run electric motors, which makes them more expensive than those running incandescent lamps.

Some new wall switch timers have dual controls for turning off both lights and fans after a preset time. For the ultimate in smart bath fan timers, buy a humidity-sensing fan designed to automatically turn on and off as moisture levels at the ceiling rise and fall.

**Lutron's Maestro Countdown Timer** can be set to operate the fan or light for five to 60 minutes before turning off automatically. It also has a tap-twice manual override. Orange LEDs indicate the time remaining before the device turns off. This single timer does not require a neutral. It's also available as a dual timer for both light and fan control.

**Broan's UltraSense bath fans** automatically turn on when they detect humidity at the ceiling and turn off when humidity levels fall. These fans are available in single- and multi-speed versions. The latter automatically increase their speed to remove shower steam as quickly as possible. Models with motion sensors increase the fan speed automatically for humidity and odor control when someone enters the room.

## Outside lighting timers

Automated outdoor lighting is convenient, but the smartest timers are astronomic versions that turn lights off and on from a memory of 365 days of sunrise and sunset times based on your home's location. Those with randomized settings can vary on and off times, which adds a heightened level of security by fooling burglars into thinking someone is home when you're away. The newest (and most expensive) astronomic timer switches are compatible with CFL and LED bulbs in addition to incandescent and halogen bulbs. Noncompatible timers can cause CFLs to flicker and shorten their life span.

**Intermatic's EI600 Series In-Wall timers** do not require a neutral wire. This timer series is highly recommended by lighting pros, and users report they are easy to install and program.

**Leviton's Vizia indoor/ outdoor programmable timer** comes with three different-color faceplates and a five-year warranty. It requires a neutral wire.

You can save up to $55 a year by replacing an incandescent bulb with a dimmable LED and using it regularly at low levels. Beyond energy savings, dimmers add comfort and convenience. However, dimming technology has had a hard time keeping pace with advances in CFL and LED bulbs. Problems include:

- **Reduced dimming range.** Unlike incandescent bulbs, most CFL and LED bulbs will not dim to very low levels. Some dimmable LED bulbs can get close, but it depends on a specific bulb's circuitry.

- **Lights dropping out.** CFL and LED bulbs will sometimes turn off before the slider reaches the bottom.

- **Lights not turning on.** After you dim a CFL or LED bulb, it sometimes won't turn on until you move the dimmer slider up. This "pop-on" effect can really be frustrating in a three-way situation where a light can be controlled from several switches, not just using the dimmer.

- **Lights turn off unexpectedly.** Dimmable CFL and LED bulbs can be affected by line voltage fluctuations and they can turn off (not just dim or flicker, like incandescents) when a hair dryer or vacuum cleaner is used.

The good news is that dimmer switch technology is improving. The newest switches work well and can effectively dim mixed light sources on the same circuit. The bad news is these switches are pricey and they require pricey dimmable LED and CFL bulbs (they also work fine with incandescent and halogen bulbs). A list of compatible bulbs can be found on manufacturer Web sites. Some require a neutral and some do not, so check the packaging carefully.

**Leviton's SureSlide Universal Dimmer** has an on/off preset function that remembers your preferred setting and is compatible with Decora wiring devices and wallplates. It does require a neutral.

**Lutron's C-L Dimmer Collection** includes adjustable dials that accommodate a broad range of dimmable bulbs. Available at amazon.com. Check Lutron for a list of compatible bulbs.

**Lutron's Credenza C-L Lamp dimmer** plugs into any outlet to dim table and floor lamps with incandescent and halogen as well as dimmable CFL and LED bulbs. The regular Credenza lamp dimmer lets you use a standard halogen or incandescent lightbulb instead of a more expensive three-way bulb and also plugs into standard outlets.

# Keep your A/C cool and save a bundle

**1 COMB OUT THE MATS.**
Match the correct end of the fin comb to the fin spacing on your coils. Then insert the comb and pull up to straighten the fins. Wear leather gloves to prevent nasty cuts.

**2 CLEAN OUT THE CRUD.**
Suck up all the spider webs, leaves, dust and dirt before you spray the coils.

**3 APPLY A FOAM CLEANER.**
Shoot the spray over the entire surface of both coils and let the foam do the work for you. If the buildup is heavy, brush in the direction of the fins with a nylon-bristle brush.

Most people assume warm air from their A/C unit means it's low on refrigerant. That's not always the cause. Many times, window and through-the-wall A/C units can't blow cold air because the evaporator and condenser coils or cooling fins are clogged. Professional cleaning can get expensive. But you can do the entire job yourself in about an hour. If cleaning doesn't do the trick, you can always call in a pro (or buy a newer, more efficient unit). Here's how to clean your A/C unit.

First remove the plastic filter holder/trim panel. It usually snaps off. Then remove it from the window or slide it out of the wall (get help—it's heavy).

If you're working on a window unit, remove the mounting frame and the case. The case screws are usually located along the bottom edge. Note the location of any odd-length screws since they have to go back in the same spots upon reassembly.

Then straighten the bent cooling fins with a fin comb (Photo 1). The Frigidaire fin comb kit shown here is cheap and fits most brands of air conditioners.

Buy two cans of A/C coil cleaner (sold online). Vacuum all visible buildup from both coils (Photo 2). Then spray both coils with the cleaner (Photo 3). While the foam works, clean the fan blades with household cleaner and a rag. If the fan motor has plastic- or rubber-capped oiling ports, pop them and squeeze in a few drops of electric motor oil.

**FIN COMB KIT**

Wash (or replace) the air filter and reinstall the unit. It just might blow a lot cooler. If not, you have other problems!

**4 SERVICE THE FAN MOTOR.**
Pop off the plastic or rubber caps on the motor's oiling ports. Then squeeze a few drops into each port and recap.

# Whole-house fan

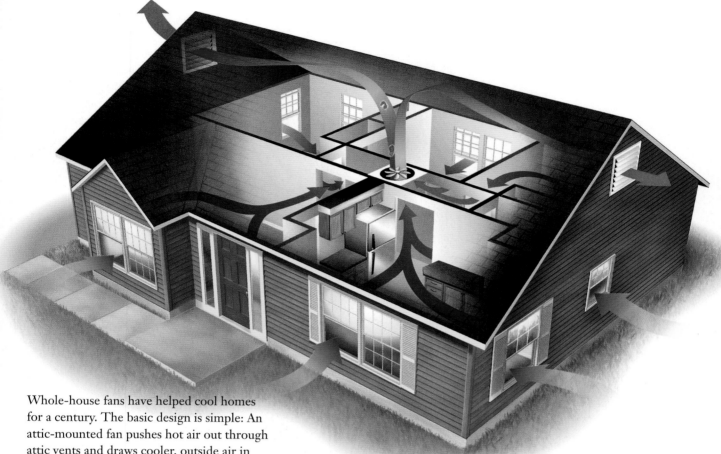

Whole-house fans have helped cool homes for a century. The basic design is simple: An attic-mounted fan pushes hot air out through attic vents and draws cooler, outside air in through open doors and windows. This rapid air exchange—large fans can purge a house of hot air in two to three minutes—not only removes built-up heat but also creates a pleasant breeze.

Fans had been supplanted by air conditioners for the past several decades but are now resurging in popularity. Why? First, they sip electricity while air conditioners guzzle power. Second, the latest generation of fans sport self-sealing insulated shutters that close when the fan's not operating. (Unless you jury-rig your own cold-weather cap, older units behave just like an open window in the winter.) This auto-insulating feature prevents vast amounts of heat from escaping through the fan when it's not in use.

## Choosing a system

A local HVAC installer can help you find the fan that best fits your home and climate. Bear in mind that size isn't everything. Larger fans are great for moving air quickly, but when you weigh the increased size against installation requirements, insulation, appearance, noise and cost, you may opt for a smaller fan. (Depending on your needs and floor plan, several smaller fans may provide better airflow.)

Attic ventilation is almost as important as the fan. A fan won't work if the hot air doesn't have an easy way out; without adequate ventilation the fan may force hot air down on you! Fans require 1 sq. ft. of net free vent area per 750 cfm. If you don't want to install additional venting, it may make sense to stick with a smaller fan.

## Finding the right fan for you

These days, there are several different types of fans to choose from (see photos, p. 115). In addition to the large traditional models, manufacturers have come up with types that are easier to install and better insulated.

Before you buy, contact your utility company to see if you're eligible for an energy rebate. You may also be able to reclaim a portion of the cost as an energy tax credit on your income taxes.

## Caution

When you use a whole-house fan, it's important to open doors and windows. Otherwise the fan may cause gas-burning appliances, such as your furnace or water heater, to backdraft exhaust fumes and carbon monoxide into your home.

## Standard fan

### 4,500 to 6,900 cfm

Because they're the most affordable and widely available, large-diameter fans are still a good solution for homeowners living in warmer regions. These fans cost less up front, but installation may be more difficult. Moving a joist in order to frame out a box for the fan, or installing additional attic venting might wind up costing more than

the fan itself. Another disadvantage is that during the winter, the vented opening works like an open window, giving warm, moist air an easy path out and into your attic. To prevent heat loss, you'll need to build an insulated box to cover your fan during the off-season.

## Insulated-door fan

### 1,000 to 1,700 cfm

If you live in an area with frequent cold snaps, you'll want a fan that holds in the heat when it's not in use. Door fans come with insulated (R-22 or R-38) panels that open every time you turn the fans on. This feature not only helps during winter months but also keeps heat out during the summer when you're

running your A/C. These models don't move as much air as standard fans, but they tend to run quieter, so they can be run all night. Like standard fans, these units are usually installed in a hallway, but some smaller models are specially designed to fit in between or around existing trusses or joists to make installation easier.

## Inline fan

### 1,500 cfm

Fan/insulated duct units don't move as much air as standard fans, but by investing in one fan per bedroom, you can provide a breeze effect in the room(s) you most want to cool. The small intake port is not only less obtrusive than the large louvered panels needed with other fans but also easier to install. (A flexible duct connects the intake port to the fan.) Like insulated door fans, inline fans have damper doors within them that prevent warm air from leaking out in winter.

## How fans save on cooling expenses

Depending on the severity of your summers, a fan can work as an efficient prechiller before you switch on your A/C, or even as your sole source of cooling. Using only a tenth as much power as your A/C, a fan bringing in cooler night and/or morning air can lower inside temperatures by 5 degrees (or more) in just a few minutes. Homeowners living in dry climates with wide day/night temperature swings may be able to do without their A/C system by simply switching the fan on during cool hours and then turning off the fan and shutting the house during the hottest times of the day.

Granted, whole-house fans aren't perfect. They can't cool inside temps lower than outside temps, nor can they dehumidify. If you live in a humid region, you'll still need to lean on your A/C in the dog days of summer. And while most folks may prefer fresh outside air, if you suffer from allergies, realize that fans draw in outdoor pollen and dust.

# 5 things you need to know about geothermal heat

A geothermal heat pump can save you so much money in energy costs (while helping the environment) that you will be tempted to install one immediately.

## However...

A geothermal system costs so much to install that you will be tempted to forget the whole thing.

## Rebates, incentives and more information

You'll find a variety of federal, state and local financing, rebates and incentives available. Check with your local utility. For more information, search online for "geothermal heat pumps."

## Is geothermal right for you?

About 100,000 geothermal heat pumps are installed in the United States each year, and according to Bob Donley, customer support manager at GeoSystems LLC in Minnesota, interest in geothermal is really on the rise. "In 2008 alone, the industry saw a 40 percent increase in homeowner interest." Donley says you're a good candidate for a geothermal system if you:

- Can stomach the up-front costs and plan to stay in your house for at least four to seven years (new construction) or 10 to 12 years (retrofit) to recoup initial costs through energy/cost savings.
- Live on a large lot with a pond or a well. This would allow you to use a less expensive loop system (see Figure D, p. 118).
- Are building a new house and can roll the up-front costs right into the mortgage. You'll be saving on heating and cooling costs on day one.
- Have an existing house with very high energy bills. This most likely means you currently use propane, oil or electricity for heating and cooling.

## 1 It works like your fridge

Your fridge removes heat from its interior and transfers it to your kitchen. A geothermal heat pump uses the same principle, but it transfers heat from the ground to your house (or vice versa). It does this through long loops of underground pipes filled with liquid (water or an antifreeze solution). The loops are hooked up to a geothermal heat pump in your home, which acts as both a furnace and an air conditioner.

During the heating season, the liquid pulls heat from the ground and delivers it to the geothermal unit and then to refrigerant coils, where the heat is distributed through a forced-air or hydronic system. During the cooling season, the process runs in reverse. The pump removes heat from your house and transfers it to the earth. Many units can provide domestic hot water as well.

A geothermal heat pump is vastly more efficient than conventional heating systems because it doesn't burn fuel to create warmth; it simply moves existing heat from one place to another. And because temperatures underground remain a relatively constant 50 degrees F year-round, the system requires a lot less energy to cool your home than conventional AC systems or air-source heat pumps, which use outside air as a transfer medium.

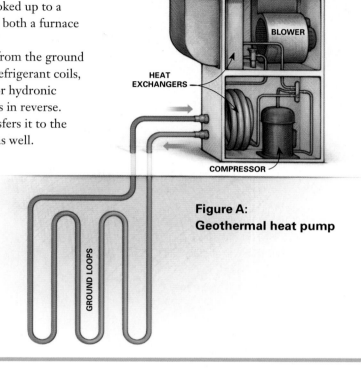

BLOWER

HEAT EXCHANGERS

COMPRESSOR

GROUND LOOPS

**Figure A:
Geothermal heat pump**

## 2 The up-front costs are scary

Let's not sugarcoat it—installing a geothermal system is expensive. It costs $10,000 to $30,000 depending on your soil conditions, plot size, system configuration, site accessibility and the amount of digging and drilling required. For a typical 2,000-sq.-ft. home, a geothermal retrofit ranges from $10,000 to $20,000. The system may require ductwork modifications along with extensive excavation. In a new home, installation costs would be on the lower end. Even so, a geothermal system will cost about 40 percent more than a traditional HVAC system.

Recouping these costs through energy savings could take as little as four years or as long as 15 years depending on utility rates and the cost of installation. It takes some homework and professional estimates to figure out whether a geothermal system makes financial sense in your situation.

## 3 It has real benefits

- Has much lower operating costs than other systems. A geothermal heat pump will immediately save you 30 to 60 percent on your heating and 20 to 50 percent on your cooling costs over conventional heating and cooling systems.
- Uses clean, renewable energy (the sun). With a geothermal heat pump, there's no onsite combustion and therefore no emissions of carbon dioxide, carbon monoxide or other greenhouse gases. Nor are there any combustion-related safety or air quality issues inside the house. (However, the pump unit uses electricity, which may be generated using fossil fuels.)
- Can be installed in both new construction and retrofit situations. However, it's a lot more expensive in retrofits requiring ductwork modifications.
- Is much quieter than other cooling systems. There's no noisy outdoor compressor or fan. The indoor unit is generally as loud as a refrigerator.
- Is low-maintenance and long-lived. The indoor components typically last about 25 years (compared with 15 years or less for a furnace or conventional A/C unit) and more than 50 years for the ground loop. The system has fewer moving parts and is protected from outdoor elements, so it requires minimal maintenance.

# 4 Type of loop affects the cost

The three closed-loop systems shown on the right are the most common. There is also a less common open-loop system that circulates surface water or water from a well through the system and returns it to the ground through a discharge pipe.

The best system, loop length and design for a particular home depend on a variety of factors such as climate, soil conditions, available land, required heating and cooling load, and local installation costs at the site.

# 5 There are downsides (besides the cost)

- Not a DIY project. Sizing, design and installation require pro expertise for the most efficient system.
- Still relatively new, so there are fewer installers and less competition (which is why prices remain high).
- Installation is highly disruptive to the landscape and may not be possible on some lots. Heavy drilling or digging equipment will definitely crush your prize petunias.

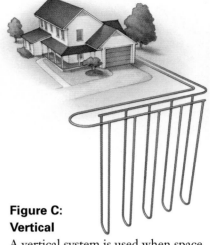

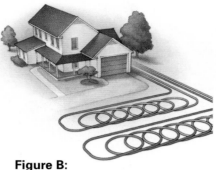

**Figure B:
Horizontal**

Layered coils or straight runs (see p. 116) of polyethylene pipe are placed in 6-ft.-deep trenches. This is the cheapest underground option, but it requires a lot of open space. A 2,000-sq.-ft. house requires 400 ft. of 2-ft.-wide trenches.

**Figure C:
Vertical**

A vertical system is used when space is limited. Four-inch-diameter holes are drilled about 15 ft. apart and 100 to 400 ft. deep. Two pipes are inserted and connect at the bottom.

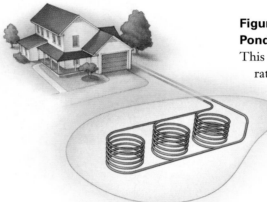

**Figure D:
Pond/lake**

This system draws heat from water rather than from the soil. If there's a body of water nearby, this is the lowest-cost option. A blanket of water covers coils anchored on racks about 10 ft. deep.

# Get smart metering

Smart metering programs vary among utility companies, but the basic idea is the same: The utility installs a special "smart" meter that tracks how much electricity you're using. The utility uses that data to make sure its power grid doesn't get overloaded and cause blackouts. If the grid nears capacity, the utility can shut off major appliances in homes for short periods of time. (Not all companies offer smart metering—check with your local utility.

What's in it for you? Money! Some programs pay you a monthly fee for signing up. Others let you view your home's usage online in real time so you can better manage your electrical consumption. Others let you choose "real-time" or "time-of-use" pricing that allows you to pay less for electricity that's used during off-peak hours (for example, on weekdays from early afternoon until 8 p.m.). These plans reward you for using electricity when it's cheapest. Smart metering makes the most sense if you're away from home all day—you won't notice or care if things get turned off.

**TIME-OF-USE METERS replace the existing meter and attach to the meter box. They enable you to pay less for electricity used at certain times of the day.**

# LEDs: Ready for prime time

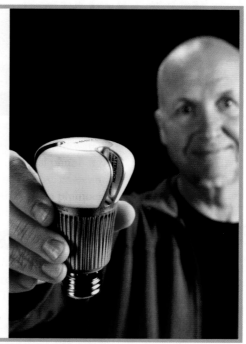

I've been trying out a few LED bulbs at home, and I'm convinced they are the future. I tried CFLs and found them frustrating: slow starting, shorter-than-advertised life span and a pain to dispose of because of the mercury. LEDs are a different story: bright, warm light; instant-on; and they really seem to last (I haven't been able to burn one out). Most home centers now have a good selection of 40-, 60- and 75-watt replacement bulbs, in configurations for lamps, recessed fixtures, even chandeliers. They're dimmable, too, though sometimes the existing dimmer will need to be replaced with one designed for LEDs.

The drawback is the up-front cost. However, LED bulbs should last as long as 20 to 30 incandescents, plus they use significantly less electricity. My recommendation: If you use a light regularly and leave it on for more than just a few minutes, and you're going to be in your house for more than a few years, go LED. You'll save money, and you'll like the light.

*—Ken Collier, editor in chief*

# CFL bulbs in outdoor fixture won't turn off

**Q** I installed outdoor-rated CFL bulbs in my outdoor motion sensor fixture. They always turn on, but sometimes they don't turn off unless I flip the indoor switch. The fixture worked fine with incandescent bulbs. What gives?

**A** Older motion sensor fixtures were designed for incandescent bulbs. The electronic ballasts in some CFLs interfere with the solid-state circuitry in the motion sensor.

First visit the sensor manufacturer's Web site and look for compatible CFL bulbs. If you can't find any, either buy a CFL-compatible fixture or go back to incandescent bulbs.

# Hybrid water heaters

**Q** The ads for hybrid electric water heaters claim energy savings of almost 50 percent. How can a heat pump with a mechanical compressor be more efficient than electric heating coils that are supposedly 100 percent efficient?

**A** Simple. It's more energy efficient to move existing heat produced by natural gas or propane from the surrounding area into the water inside the tank than to create heat. If you have an electric water heater, it would be wise to check out the savings from a hybrid.

Hybrid water heaters use the same electrical supply as your existing heater and require only minor changes to existing plumbing. And prices on hybrid water heaters have dropped lately, making them an even better investment. Call your local utility or go online to check for rebates and tax incentives in your area.

# Joining threaded plumbing fittings

Wrapping Teflon tape around pipe threads to create a seal is standard procedure for DIYers. But it's not foolproof. Burrs inside the female fitting can catch the tape and roll it around. The leak will only show up after you've finished the job and turned on the water. At that point, you'll have a mess on your hands, cutting and refitting pipes.

Here's a tip from master plumber Les Zell. Go ahead and wrap Teflon tape around the male threads just like always. Then add pipe thread sealant as shown. The sealant will fill any gaps caused by tape failures. It's cheap insurance against a leak. Les says he's never had a leak since he started adding this second step.

**ADD A DAB OF PIPE DOPE.**
**Grab a brush full of pipe thread sealant and wipe it right on top of the Teflon tape. Then assemble the fittings.**

# Caulking the toilet to the floor

GLUING EDGE

**CAULK THE FLOOR.**
**Cut the caulk tube tip square and drag the caulk gun toward you as you lay in a thick bead of caulk along the inside edge of the tape.**

Toilets should be caulked to the floor to prevent side-to-side movement that can break the wax seal (and to prevent splashes or overflows from puddling under the toilet and rotting the floor). DIYers often set the toilet and then apply a tiny bead of caulk along the outside edge. That doesn't always provide a good enough bond to the floor, and it leaves a prominent caulk line. There's an easier way to secure the toilet and provide a cleaner caulk line. Just follow this tip from master plumber Les Zell.

First set the toilet in place (without the wax ring) and square it up to the wall. Then make an outline of the toilet on the floor with masking tape. Remove the toilet and turn it on its side. Measure the depth and width of the gluing edge of the bowl. Next, move your caulk gun to the inset depth you just measured and apply caulk directly to the floor, maintaining the inset depth as you follow the tape (photo at left). Install the wax ring and lower the toilet onto the flange. Stand on the toilet to compress the wax ring and ensure good contact with the caulk. Then use paper towels to clean up any caulk that oozed out.

# Waste and venting Q&A

## When should I use a Y?

In a drain system, use a Y-fitting to connect horizontal pipes. Along with a 45-degree "street" fitting, you can use a Y-fitting to run vertical drainpipes into horizontal pipes as shown. A Y-fitting can also be used in vent systems.

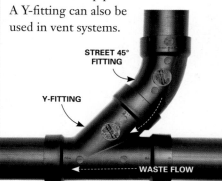

STREET 45° FITTING

Y-FITTING

WASTE FLOW

## When should I use a T-fitting?

Use a T-fitting in drain lines to connect a horizontal pipe to vertical pipes. It can also be used to tie vent lines into horizontal drains or to join vent lines.

WASTE FLOW

T-FITTING

**Plumbing codes vary by locality.** The rules we give in this article generally follow the strictest codes. Your local rules may be more lenient about issues like vent sizing, the choice of fittings, etc.

## What's a street fitting?

Standard fittings have hubs that fit over pipes. A street fitting has a "streeted" end that fits into a hub, so you can connect it directly to another fitting without using a section of pipe. That saves labor and space.

HUB

STREETED END

## Why does the home center carry three types of L-fittings?

WASTE FLOW

STANDARD L-FITTING

A standard L-fitting is used for horizontal-to-vertical flow in drain systems.

A "sweep" or "long-turn" L-fitting is OK for almost any situation and is required in two situations: horizontal-to-horizontal turns and vertical-to-horizontal turns (as shown). But it can be used in any situation where space allows.

WASTE FLOW

LONG-TURN L-FITTING

VENT L-FITTING

A vent L-fitting can be used anywhere in the vent system, but *only* in the vent system—never where waste flows. The other two types of L-fittings are OK for venting, too.

## What's the vent for?

A plumbing vent is kind of like the air intake on a gas can; it lets in air. Without venting, a slug of sewage racing through a waste line creates air pressure and a vacuum in the pipe. That means noisy, gurgling drains. Even worse, a vacuum can suck all the water out of traps, allowing sewer gas to flow freely into your home. Yuck.

## Vent-to-trap distance —there's a limit

Every drain needs a trap (see note below), and every trap needs a vent. The maximum distance between the trap and vent depends on the diameter of the pipe. Memorize this table for midterm exams:

| Pipe size | Max. horizontal distance to vent |
|-----------|-----------------------------------|
| 1-1/4"    | 30"                               |
| 1-1/2"    | 42"                               |
| 2"        | 5'                                |
| 3"        | 6'                                |
| 4"        | 10'                               |

**Note**: A toilet has a built-in trap, so it doesn't need one in the drain line. It still needs a vent, though.

## Can vents run horizontally?

Yes, but horizontal vent lines must be at least 6 in. above the "spill line," which is the level where water would overflow the rim of a sink, tub or toilet.

## What size vent pipes do I need?

A typical bathroom (sink, toilet, shower or tub) requires a 2-in. vent. You could run smaller pipes to the sink or shower, but it's usually easier to use one size for the whole system.

# PEX Q&A

If you haven't discovered PEX yet, you're missing the biggest revolution in plumbing since the flush toilet. PEX is flexible plastic tubing that you can use for everything from plumbing repairs to installing water lines in an entire house. You'll find PEX tubing, fittings and tools at home centers, hardware stores and online. In this article, we'll answer the most common questions about PEX and give you some tips for working with it.

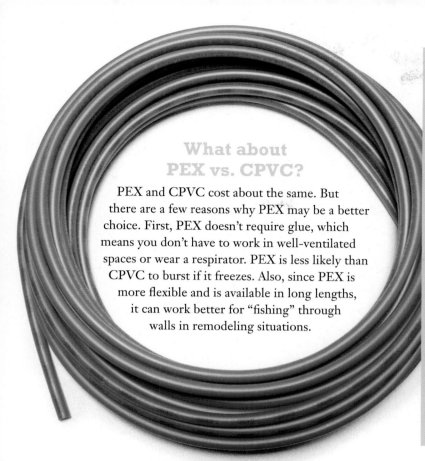

## What about PEX vs. CPVC?

PEX and CPVC cost about the same. But there are a few reasons why PEX may be a better choice. First, PEX doesn't require glue, which means you don't have to work in well-ventilated spaces or wear a respirator. PEX is less likely than CPVC to burst if it freezes. Also, since PEX is more flexible and is available in long lengths, it can work better for "fishing" through walls in remodeling situations.

## Which is better— PEX or copper?

PEX (cross-linked polyethylene) has several advantages over copper:

- **PEX is cheaper than copper.** Some of the savings will be offset by the need for a special tool to install the fittings, but if you're doing a medium to large plumbing job, you'll usually save by using PEX instead of copper.
- **PEX is faster to install than copper.** If you use a manifold and "home-run" system (shown in the top photo on p. 128), it's like running a garden hose to each fixture—super-fast and easy. But even if you install PEX in a conventional main line and branch system, the connections are quicker to make than soldering copper.
- **PEX won't corrode like copper.** If you live in an area with acidic water, copper can corrode over time. PEX is unaffected by acidic water and is therefore a better choice in these areas.

## Do I need special tools?

No. You can use stab-in or compression fittings to make the connections. But they're too expensive to be practical on large projects. For most jobs, you'll want to invest in a special tool to make connections. There are several PEX connection methods, but only two that are affordable enough to be practical for DIYers: crimp rings and cinch clamps, as shown below.

Crimp rings are a band of metal, usually copper, that you slip over the fitting and compress with a crimp ring tool. The main drawback to the crimp ring method is that you'll need either separate crimping tools for 1/2-in. and 3/4-in. fittings, or a universal tool with a swappable insert (not shown). This adds a little up-front cost to this method.

CINCH CLAMP

CINCH CLAMP TOOL

Cinch clamps work more like the traditional band clamps you're probably familiar with. You slip the cinch clamp tool (shown) over the protruding tab and squeeze to tighten the cinch clamp. The same tool works for all sizes of cinch clamps. Cinch clamp tools are also less expensive than crimping tools. We like the one-handed version shown in the photo because you can hold the ring in place with one hand while tightening it with the other.

The only other special tool you need is a scissors-like cutter for the tubing (bottom photo).

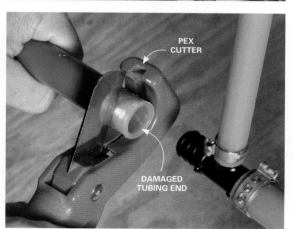

PEX CUTTER

DAMAGED TUBING END

"PRO" CRIMP RING

CINCH CLAMP

COPPER CRIMP RING

## How do I splice PEX into my existing pipe?

There are several methods. The easiest is to cut out a section of pipe and slip in a stab-in tee (top photo). SharkBite is one common brand of stab-in fitting. This method doesn't require soldering, which can be a big time-saver. But check with your plumbing inspector if you're planning to bury this connection in a wall or ceiling. Some areas don't allow stab-in fittings to be concealed. Another method is to solder in a tee and a PEX adapter. Then slip the PEX tubing over the adapter and attach it with your chosen connection method (bottom photo). You can also use a stab-in tee to connect PEX to CPVC. Read the label to find the compatible fitting.

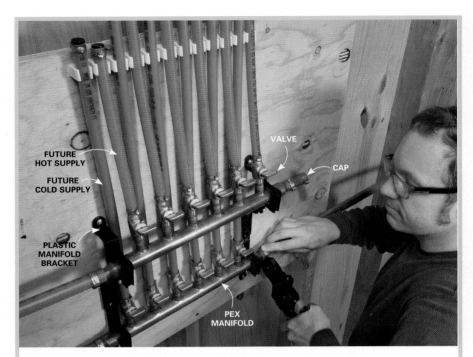

FUTURE HOT SUPPLY
FUTURE COLD SUPPLY
PLASTIC MANIFOLD BRACKET
VALVE
CAP
PEX MANIFOLD

COPPER WATER SUPPLY
STAB-IN "TEE"
PEX

COPPER TO PEX ADAPTER
PEX
COPPER "TEE"
CINCH CLAMP

## Does it meet code?

There is no unified national plumbing code. Before starting your plumbing job, check with your local inspector for specific local requirements.

## Do I have to use manifolds with PEX?

No. You can install PEX just as you would other pipe, with main lines and branches to each fixture. But you lose a lot of the benefits of PEX with this system since it requires so many fittings. With the home-run system, you install a manifold in the utility room or some area that's close to the main water line and water heater, and run a separate PEX tube to each fixture as shown above. This system uses more tubing but is fast and only requires two connections: one at the manifold and another at the fixture end. You can also use a hybrid system where you run 3/4-in. hot and cold lines to a set of fixtures—for example, a bathroom—and install a smaller manifold behind an access panel. Then make short runs of 1/2-in. PEX tubing to each fixture.

## Do I have to use red for hot and blue for cold?

No. The colors are just to help you keep track of the hot and cold lines. You can use white PEX for everything if you prefer.

## Is PEX reliable?

PEX has been used for decades in other countries, where there are thousands of homes with 30-year-old, leak-free PEX. Most of the problems with PEX systems (in the United States and elsewhere) have been caused by sloppy installation or faulty fittings rather than the tubing itself.

## Can I connect PEX to my water heater?

No. First extend a pipe 18 in. from your water heater and connect the PEX to the pipe.

## Will PEX break or split if it freezes?

Probably not. Manufacturers are reluctant to say so, but reports from the field suggest PEX can withstand freezing. You should still protect the tubing from freezing, but since it can expand and contract, it's less likely to break than rigid piping.

## How do I connect PEX to my plumbing fixtures?

There are several methods. If the connection will be visible, like under a wall-hung sink, and you would prefer the look of a copper tube coming out of the wall, use a copper stub-out (top photo). You can connect a compression-type shutoff valve to the 1/2-in. copper stub-out and then connect your fixture. In areas that are concealed, like under a kitchen sink or vanity cabinet, you can eliminate a joint by running PEX directly to the shutoff valve. Use a drop-ear bend support to hold the tubing in a tight bend (bottom photo). There are several types of shutoff valves that connect directly to PEX.

If you're using a manifold system with valves, you may not need to install a shutoff valve at the fixture. Ask your plumbing inspector. We recommend adding one, though. It doesn't raise the cost much and is more convenient than running downstairs to shut off the water when a repair is needed.

COPPER STUB-OUT

DROP-EAR BEND SUPPORT

HOT WATER SUPPLY

COLD WATER SUPPLY

## Which tubing should I use for interior water lines?

For water lines, there are three grades: PEX-A, PEX-B and PEX-C. They're manufactured differently, PEX-A being slightly more flexible. If you're ordering online, go ahead and spend a few cents extra for PEX-A. But don't go running around town looking for it; the difference isn't that big. The plumbers we talked to would be willing to use any of the three types in their own homes. PEX is also popular for in-floor radiant heating systems, for which you need PEX tubing with an oxygen barrier.

EXPANSION/CONTRACTION LOOP

## What about expansion?

PEX expands and contracts more than copper, so don't stretch it tight. Let it droop a little between fasteners. On long runs, it's a good idea to install a loop as shown to allow for contraction. Another advantage of the loop is that if you mess up and need a little extra tubing, you can steal it from the loop. Also, since PEX moves as it expands and contracts, make sure to drill oversize holes through studs or joists so it can slide easily, and don't use metal straps to attach it. Use plastic straps instead.

MISPLACED CINCH CLAMP

CUTOFF WHEEL

CINCH CLAMP

ROTARY TOOL

## What if I goof? Can I take it apart?

Sure—there's a special tool for cutting off crimp rings, and you can use side cutters to remove cinch clamps. But a rotary tool (Dremel is one brand) fitted with a cutoff blade works great for cutting either type of connector (see photo). After you remove the crimp ring or cinch clamp and pull the PEX from the fitting, cut off the end of the tubing to get a fresh section for the new connection. If you damage the fitting with the rotary tool, replace the fitting rather than risk a leak.

# Best toilet plunger

The best toilet plunger is one that's designed for a toilet. A lot of people don't know there's a difference, and they're using a standard "cup" plunger, which is actually designed for flat surfaces on a sink, tub or shower. Use a cup plunger on a toilet clog and you won't get a solid seal, Instead, it'll slip around and cause "splash back." (Yuck.)

"The plunger we carry on our trucks has a fold-out flange," says St. Paul plumbing contractor Charlie Avoles. "The extra piece of rubber will go further into the waste opening in a toilet for a good seal while plunging. When we don't want to use the flange, it folds up into the wide part, so you can use it like a standard plunger."

**FOLD-OUT FLANGE**

## Charlie's tips for unplugging a toilet:

- Plunge slowly and remember that when it comes to dislodging a clog, the pull-back motion is often just as important as the push-down motion.
- You need standing water in the toilet to create enough force in the plunging action.
- Try plunging 12 to 15 times before you give up. Sometimes plunging just won't free up the clog, and you have to resort to removing the toilet to get at the toilet trap.

**MEET THE PRO**

**Charlie Avoles** is co-owner of St. Paul PipeWorks Plumbing and Remodeling.

# Best faucet valve

If you want a kitchen, bath or shower faucet that will never, ever drip, Gray Uhl, trends director at American Standard, has some simple advice: Buy one that says "ceramic valve" on the packaging. Ceramic valves are tough enough to grind up sand and other particles in water, smooth enough to seal with light pressure and—unlike rubber parts—durable enough to last for decades. The ceramic material used in valves is incredibly hard (about five times harder than carbon steel), so it costs a bit more to make them. But you won't notice that on the price tag. Ceramic faucets cost about the same as the other faucets you'll find at home centers. Uhl predicts that within a few years, you won't find any nonceramic valves on home center shelves.

**Ceramic parts are tiny but tough. Friction and particles in the water slowly destroy other valves but have almost no effect on ceramic.**

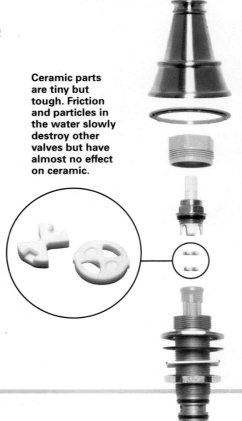

**MEET THE PRO**

When **Gray Uhl** was a little kid, he spent Saturdays at American Standard's research lab while his father worked on early versions of the ceramic valve. Today, Gray works on faucet design for the same company.

# Tips for using plastic pipe

We asked Les Zell, our resident master plumber, to tell us some of his tips on working with plastic plumbing. Not surprisingly, with 25 years in the biz, he had plenty to share. Here are a few of his best.

## ABS vs. PVC

Les says "I pretty much only use ABS black pipe and rarely use the white PVC stuff. It's all about the glue. Gluing ABS is a one-step process, which makes it faster to work with than PVC. Purple PVC primer is messy, emits noxious fumes and it's just ugly."

ABS cement lasts longer in the can and dries clear, making it more forgiving if you get a drip or two on the floor. ABS cement also dries faster, which reduces the risk of connections pushing apart before they set up. Les believes the labor saved by using ABS more than makes up for the extra money spent on pipe and fittings. ABS is also lighter and more flexible. He says that makes it easier to flex for bending it into tight spaces.

"It's not only me. None of my plumber buddies use PVC either." The only downside—retailers don't always carry ABS.

## Les on plumbing wisdom

Les believes that new plumbers will learn 75 percent of what they need to know during the first year on the job, but that it takes 20 years to learn the next 24 percent, and the rest is unknowable.

## Les loves tubing cutters

For pipes up to 2 in., Les prefers a tubing cutter (a giant version of the type used for copper tubing). "It makes a perfectly straight cut with no burrs or shavings to clean up. But best of all, it doesn't take up much room in the tool bucket." You can get them at home centers.

DULL BLADE

## Use dull blades for bigger or tighter cuts

When Les cuts larger pipe or has trouble getting the tubing cutter into tight spaces, he uses a recip saw fitted with an older, dull wood blade. "A new wood blade with aggressive teeth tends to grab on to the pipe and rattle the whole works, and a metal blade melts the plastic rather than cuts it."

## Don't glue yourself into a corner

In many assemblies, there are pipes that move and pipes that don't. If you start gluing fittings together willy-nilly, you may end up in a situation where you're unable to attach the last fitting because one or both of the pipes don't move enough to slide the fitting on.

"The last fitting to be glued should be the one on a pipe that has a little wiggle room." That's usually where a vertical run meets a horizontal one so you can snug on an elbow or a tee from two directions.

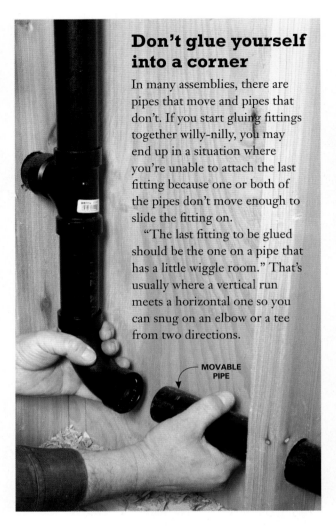

MOVABLE PIPE

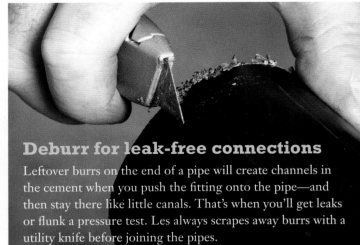

## Deburr for leak-free connections

Leftover burrs on the end of a pipe will create channels in the cement when you push the fitting onto the pipe—and then stay there like little canals. That's when you'll get leaks or flunk a pressure test. Les always scrapes away burrs with a utility knife before joining the pipes.

## Seal the ends!

FOAM CORE

Most ABS pipes have either a cellular or a foam core that air will actually pass right through. "If you don't believe it, wrap your lips around the pipe wall and blow through it." If you don't seal pipe ends with cement, air will escape into the porous center core and find its way out of the plumbing system, and you'll fail a pressure test every time. "Can you even imagine that disaster? You'd have to replumb everything!"

## You can reuse a landlocked fitting

SOCKET SAVER

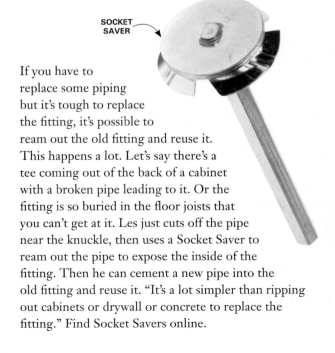

If you have to replace some piping but it's tough to replace the fitting, it's possible to ream out the old fitting and reuse it. This happens a lot. Let's say there's a tee coming out of the back of a cabinet with a broken pipe leading to it. Or the fitting is so buried in the floor joists that you can't get at it. Les just cuts off the pipe near the knuckle, then uses a Socket Saver to ream out the pipe to expose the inside of the fitting. Then he can cement a new pipe into the old fitting and reuse it. "It's a lot simpler than ripping out cabinets or drywall or concrete to replace the fitting." Find Socket Savers online.

## Avoid callbacks—use straps

Changes in temperature can cause changes in the length of plastic pipes. When you hang pipe from plastic J-hooks, you'll hear a tick when the pipe slips past the J-hook. Les says he gets tons of service calls from panicky customers believing these ticks to be water drips from a leaky pipe. "But they can never find the leak!" He generally uses plastic straps and never gets false alarm calls on his plumbing.

PLASTIC STRAP

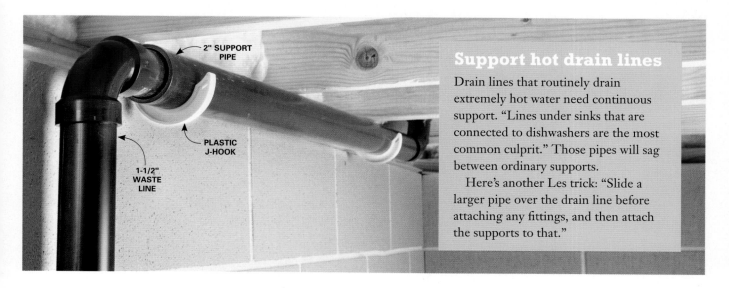

## Support hot drain lines

Drain lines that routinely drain extremely hot water need continuous support. "Lines under sinks that are connected to dishwashers are the most common culprit." Those pipes will sag between ordinary supports.

Here's another Les trick: "Slide a larger pipe over the drain line before attaching any fittings, and then attach the supports to that."

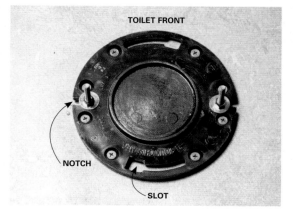

## Skip those closet flange slots

Les has serviced dozens of toilets with broken closet flanges. Toilets are top-heavy, which stresses the closet bolts that hold a toilet to the closet flange. The plastic on the sides of the adjustable slots that receive the bolts is thin and prone to cracking. Les always turns the flange 90 degrees and anchors the toilet using the notches instead. He makes sure the notches are parallel to the wall behind the toilet. "One more thing: Don't use flanges with metal collars—metal rusts."

## Learn Les's elbow rule

For pipes under 3 in., there are three basic types of 90-degree elbows: vent, short sweep and long sweep. Vent elbows are easily identified by their drastic bend and can only be used on a vent run that carries air, not water.

Les has a good system to remember when to use the other two types of elbows. "If water is speeding up as it turns the corner (usually going from horizontal to vertical), use a short sweep. If water is slowing down (usually from vertical to horizontal), use a long sweep."

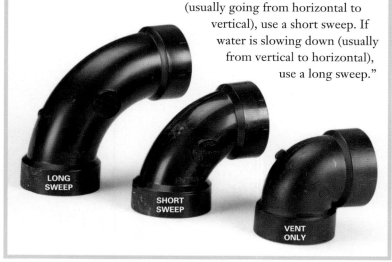

# Chapter Nine

# TILING

# Modern tricks for modern tile

Tile just keeps getting bigger and bigger—in popularity and in size. The materials have changed too: Ceramic is still around, but porcelain and glass are now almost as common. Our tile guru, Dean, has had to change how he works. Here are some of his tips.

**MEET THE PRO**

**Dean Sorem** has been setting tile for more than three decades and prides himself on keeping up with the latest products, tools and techniques. He and his crew recently spent an entire day setting just 12 huge, 24 x 48-in. tiles.

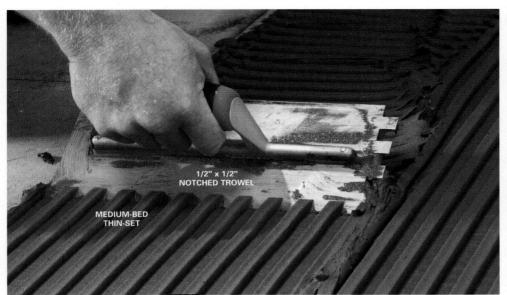

**MEDIUM-BED THIN-SET**

**1/2" x 1/2" NOTCHED TROWEL**

**CARDBOARD SHIMS**

**3/4" x 3/4" NOTCHED TROWEL**

## **1** Pick a large-notched trowel for big tile

Tiles as large as 2 ft. square have become more popular, and these monsters require a deep layer of thin-set to allow for adjustments. To get the right amount of thin-set, use a 1/2 x 1/2-in. notched trowel for tiles up to 16 in. square, and a 3/4 x 3/4-in. notched trowel for larger tiles. Don't forget: Using large-notched trowels means you'll need a lot more thin-set. As a general rule, a 50-lb. bag of thin-set will cover about 40 to 50 sq. ft. using a 1/2 x 1/2-in. notched trowel, and about 30 to 40 sq. ft. using a 3/4 x 3/4-in. notched trowel. When you use large-notched trowels like this, look for thin-set labeled "medium bed," "large tile" or "large format."

## **2** Flatten the framing

Old-school tile setters made up for wavy walls by installing wire lath and floating a layer of mortar over it. But modern tile backer boards simply follow along the crooked wall, and if you don't fix the wall, you'll have a wavy tile job.

The best solution is to straighten the walls before you install the backer board. Lay a straightedge against the walls to find high and low spots. In most cases, you can fix problems by adding shims to the face of the studs until the faces all line up. But if you have just one protruding stud, then it may be quicker to plane it down with a power planer or replace it if you can.

Dean prefers thin paper shims as shown (available in the drywall section of some home centers) because they provide precise control over shim thickness and can be offset to create a tapered shim. You can make your own thin shims from heavy felt paper or thin cardboard. Staple the shims in place.

## **3** Cut without cracking the tile

You'll need a diamond wet saw to cut large porcelain tiles. Dean recommends renting a contractor-quality saw rather than buying a cheapie. But even with a saw like this, tiles larger than about 8 in. square have a tendency to crack before you finish the cut, often ruining the tile. You can help prevent this by pressing the two pieces together as you near completion of the cut. Holding the tile like this stabilizes it and dampens vibration, resulting in a cleaner cut.

**DIAMOND WET SAW**

**PORCELAIN TILE**

## 4 Back-butter large tile

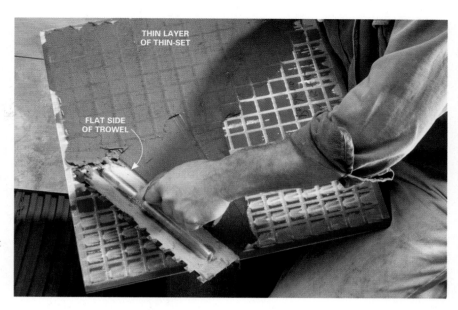

The increased surface area of tiles larger than about 8 x 8 in. makes it critical that you butter the back to ensure a strong bond. It takes only a few extra seconds per tile to spread a thin layer of thin-set on the back of the tile with the flat side of the trowel. Then when you set the tile, this thin layer bonds easily with the layer you've troweled onto the floor or wall and creates a strong connection.

Dean also butters the back of larger transparent glass tiles to provide a consistent color. Otherwise you'll see air bubbles and other imperfections in the thin-set through the transparent glass.

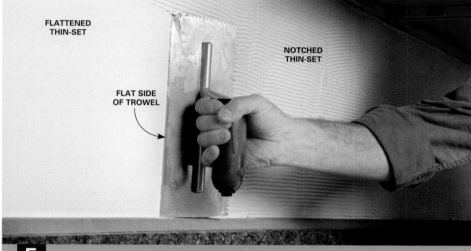

## 5 Flatten thin-set before installing mosaic tile

Mosaic tile is typically thin, and it has a lot of grout joints. If you simply apply thin-set with a notched trowel and embed the sheets of mosaic in it, the ridges of thin-set will squeeze out of all those grout joints and you'll have a real mess to clean up.

The way to avoid this is to flatten the ridges with the flat side of the trowel before you set the mosaic tiles in it. Use the notched side of a 1/4 x 1/4-in. V-notched trowel first to apply the right amount of thin-set. Then flip the trowel over to the flat side and, holding the trowel fairly flat to the surface and using medium pressure, flatten the ridges. Now you can safely embed the sheets of mosaic tile without worrying about thin-set filling the grout joints.

## 7 Clean grout joints with a toothbrush

No matter how careful you are, you're bound to end up with some thin-set in the joints between tiles. And if you allow it to harden, it'll interfere with your grout job. A toothbrush works great to clean excess thin-set from grout joints, especially for the skinny joints between mosaic tiles. Let the thin-set get firm, but not hard, before you start the cleanup process. If you try to clean up thin-set too soon, you risk disturbing the tiles.

## 6 Upgrade your grout sponge

It's hard to get the last bit of grout haze off using a grout sponge. After the grout dries, you usually have to come back and polish off the remaining cloudy layer with a rag. But if you finish your grout cleanup with a microfiber sponge, you'll end up with a job so clean you may not have to do anything more.

Start your cleanup with the plain side of the sponge after the grout firms up. Then when the joints are nicely shaped and most of the grout is off the face of the tile, switch to the microfiber side of the sponge. You'll find microfiber sponges at home centers and tile shops.

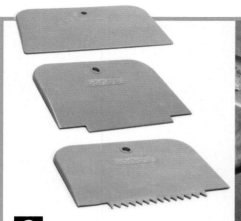

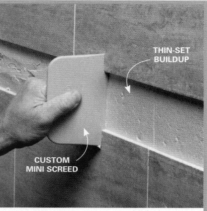

THIN-SET BUILDUP

CUSTOM MINI SCREED

## 8 Make a custom trowel

Dean has discovered that inexpensive auto-body filler spatulas, available at home centers and auto parts stores, are perfect for making custom trowels for special circumstances. One way Dean uses a custom-made trowel is for insetting thinner tiles into a field of thicker tiles. After finishing the field tile installation, he cuts notches on each edge of the spatula with a utility knife to create a mini screed. He cuts the notches about 1/16 in. deeper than the thickness of the decorative tile to allow for thin-set. Then he uses this trowel to add a layer of thin-set that acts as a shim when it hardens (top photo). After this layer hardens, he cuts 3/16-in.-deep teeth in the spatula to make a notched trowel and uses it to apply thin-set (middle photo). Now when he sets the decorative tile, it's perfectly flush with the field tile (bottom photo).

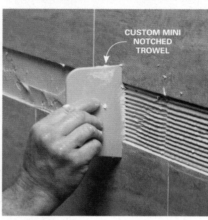

CUSTOM MINI NOTCHED TROWEL

MOSAIC DECORATIVE BAND

## 9 Finish your job with premium grout

There's been a revolution in grout technology over the past several years, and all of the big-name grout producers have modern grout that's easier to apply, denser, more stain resistant and more colorfast than standard grout. These new grouts also cure faster and are resistant to mold and mildew.

You no longer have to mix in latex additives, worry about uneven or blotchy grout joints or decide between sanded and unsanded grout. Power Grout, Custom Building Product's Prism and Fusion Pro grouts, and Laticrete's PermaColor are a few examples of premium grout. You may have to visit a specialty tile store to find them, though. The formulas vary, but all of these will outperform standard grout. And some, like Power Grout and Fusion Pro, don't even require sealing, saving you time and money.

Premium grouts are more expensive, of course, and might add a little to the total cost of your project. But considering all the other costs (and all your hard work), premium grout is a bargain.

## 10 Level mosaic tile with a block

Mosaic tiles are so small and numerous that getting their faces flush using just your fingers is nearly impossible. But tamping them with a flat block of wood creates a perfectly aligned surface in no time. Make a tamping block out of any flat scrap of wood. An 8-in. length of hardwood 1x6 or a 6 x 8-in. rectangle of plywood is perfect. After you set several square feet of mosaic tile, pat the tile into the thin-set with the tamping block. Hold the block in place and bump it with your fist to flatten the mosaic. Repeat the tamping process on each new section of tile you install.

HARDWOOD BLOCK

# Planning and prep tips

Most pros in any trade are creatures of habit. When something works, they stick with it. Whether you're a tile novice or a remodeler who occasionally tackles a tile job, you're sure to find at least a few tips here that'll come in handy on your next tiling project.

## Measure tile with spacers

Mock up and measure a row of tile to determine the layout. If you'll be using spacers to create grout lines, add them between the tiles before you measure. Use the measurement to determine whether you should shift the layout to get a wider tile in the corner and to determine the layout for the end walls of a tub or shower.

SPACER

CHALK LINE

SELF-LEVELING LASER LEVEL

## Plan layouts with a laser level

Laser levels save time and increase accuracy. Use a self-leveling laser to help plan the tile layout. Project a level line around the room and measure from it to determine the size of the cut tiles along the edges. Then, after figuring out an ideal layout, use the laser as a guide to chalk layout lines. The laser saves time by eliminating the fussy job of extending level lines around the room with a 4-ft. level. Most also project level and plumb.

Self-leveling lasers reduce setup time and can be swiveled without readjustment. Mount the laser on an inexpensive camera tripod for maximum versatility. More-expensive lasers project perpendicular lines on the floor that you can use to plan floor layouts.

## Draw a start line above the tub

Draw level and plumb layout lines on the wall to guide your installation. Measure a row of tile to determine the location of the plumb line on the back wall. Subtract about 3/4 in. from the height of the tile and use this measurement to locate the height of the level line above the tub or shower.

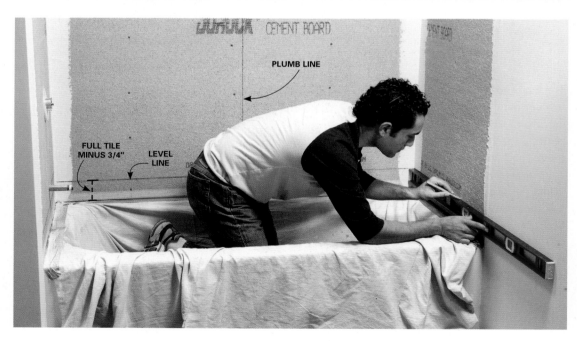

CEMENT BOARD

PLUMB LINE

FULL TILE MINUS 3/4"

LEVEL LINE

## Start from a straight board

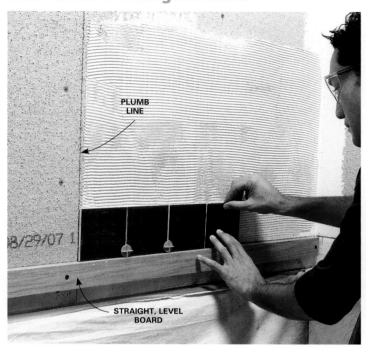

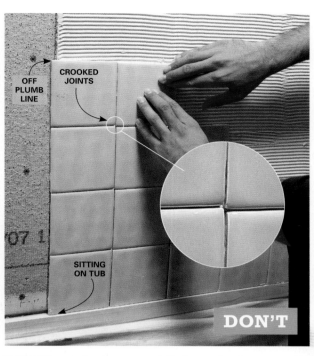

Screw a straight board to the level line and stack tile on the board. When you've completed tiling above the board and the tiles are held firmly, remove the board and cut the first row of tile to fit. Leave a 1/8-in. space between the tub and the tile to allow installation of a flexible bead of caulk. This tip also allows you to wrap tile around tub corners as shown in the photo below.

DON'T start the first row of tile by resting it against the tub or shower. It'll cause trouble because most tubs and showers aren't perfectly straight or level. Your tile will wander from the plumb line, and misaligned grout lines will be your only solution.

## Wrap sidewall tiles around the tub

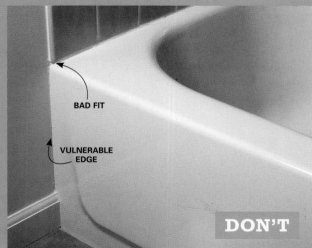

Plan the tile layout so a column of tile extends past the end of the tub. Use the method shown in the bottom photo on p. 141 to determine how wide the corner tile needs to be in order to extend the tile beyond the tub. Plan to extend the tile 2 or 3 in. beyond the tub and to leave at least a half-tile along the wall if possible.

DON'T stop tile even with the end of the tub. This leaves the walls along the front of the tub vulnerable to water damage and doesn't look as finished as tile extending to the floor.

# Either start from the corner or split the center

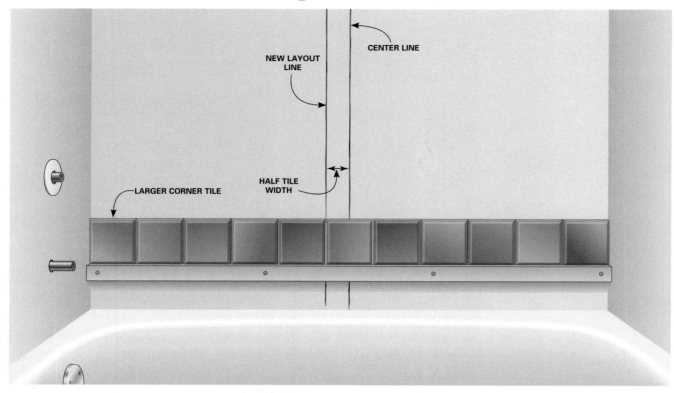

Locate the starting plumb line to leave the widest possible same-sized tiles at each corner. Lay out the tile on the floor and use the back wall measurement to determine how wide the corner tiles will be. If starting with the edge of a full tile in the center of the back wall leaves a skinny strip in the corner, shift the plumb line by half the width of the tile. This will increase the size of the corner tiles.

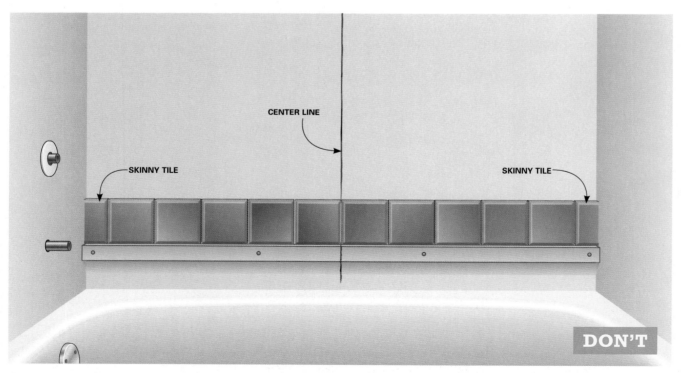

DON'T leave a skinny strip of tile in the corners. Plan for the widest possible corner tile for the most attractive tile job.

## Polish stone edges

To save money and get a better-looking job, you can make your own trim pieces for marble, granite and other stone tile jobs. Take the top of a shower curb, for example. You would have to buy enough bullnose trim to cover both edges, and you'd end up with a grout joint down the center where the two rows of bullnose meet. Instead, you can cover the curb with one piece of stone, polished on both edges.

Use the honeycomb-style dry

diamond polishing pads with hook-and-loop fasteners. They allow you to quickly run through a series of grits from 60 to 800 or higher without wasting a lot of time changing pads. One caveat, though. This type of disc requires a variable-speed grinder because the maximum allowable rpm is about 4,000. If you own a single-speed grinder that runs at 10,000 rpm, you'll need a set of PVA Marble Edge Polisher discs that are safe to run at high speed (they polish all kinds of stone). Search online for "marble polishing discs."

Polishing stone is a dusty operation, so work outside. Start by using the coarsest grit to remove the saw marks from all the edges. Then progress through the grits until you reach the

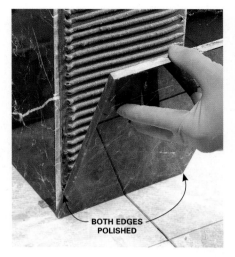

**BOTH EDGES POLISHED**

level of sheen you desire. Use light pressure to avoid overheating the disc and wearing it out prematurely. You'll have to progress through the finest grit to create a glossy surface.

## Level the floor

Tiling a wavy floor is a nightmare. You push and pry to get each tile flush with its neighbors and you still end up with "lippage" (edges that protrude above adjoining tiles, usually at corners). So before you tile, check the floor with a 4-ft. straightedge. If you find low spots more than 1/4 in. deep, screed thin-set over them to create a flat surface.

For really bad floors, self-leveling compound (also called "self-leveling underlayment") is a lifesaver. You just mix the powder with water and pour to create a flat, smooth surface. Some products require metal or plastic lath; some don't.

Self-leveling compound is almost goof-proof, but there are two big pitfalls. First, it will slowly seep into the tiniest crack or hole, leaving a crater in the surface. So before you put down the lath, grab a caulk gun and fill every little gap—even small nail holes. Second, you have to work fast. Most compounds begin to harden in about 30 minutes. To get the whole floor poured in that time frame, you need at least one helper to mix the compound while you pour. And even with help, you'll have to move quickly.

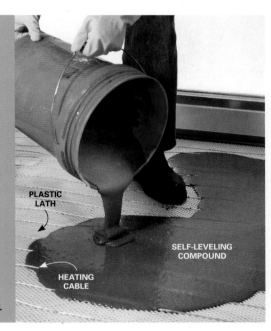

**PLASTIC LATH**

**SELF-LEVELING COMPOUND**

**HEATING CABLE**

**REDGARD**

**PAINT PAD APPLICATOR**

## Waterproof wet areas

It's a surprise to most people that a tiled wall or floor isn't waterproof. Some types of tile are porous, and most grout isn't waterproof either. Water can seep through tile and grout and leak into cracks at corners and other intersections. The only sure way to keep water from reaching the backer board is to waterproof all areas that may be exposed to water. That's easy with the new waterproofing coatings. Shown here is the RedGard brand, but there are others. A good rule of thumb is "If in doubt, coat it with waterproofing."

Follow the application instructions on the container. Apply the waterproofer with an inexpensive paint pad because it works like a trowel, allowing you to quickly spread a thick, even layer over the surface.

# Beyond the basics

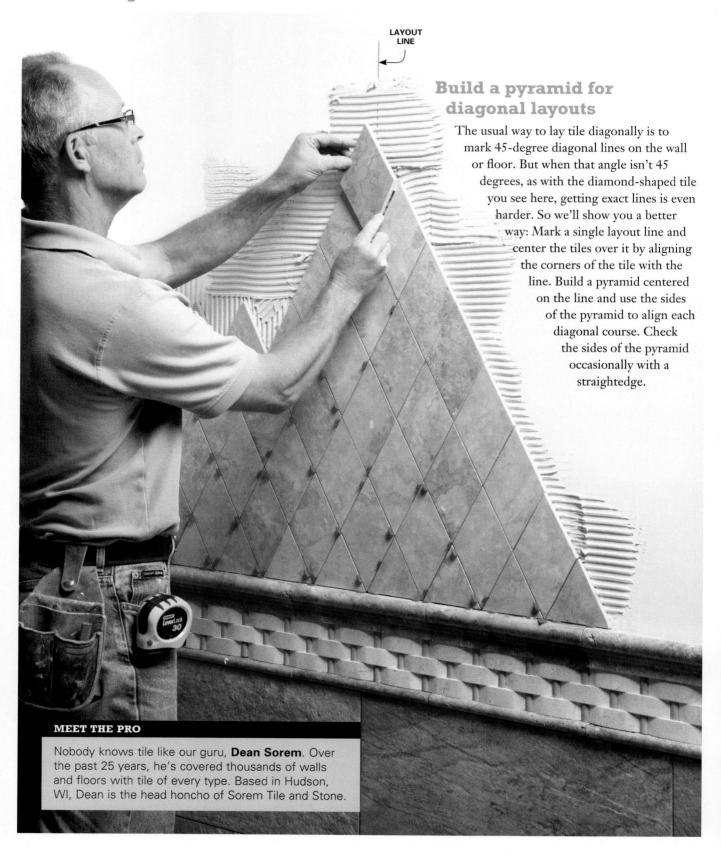

LAYOUT LINE

## Build a pyramid for diagonal layouts

The usual way to lay tile diagonally is to mark 45-degree diagonal lines on the wall or floor. But when that angle isn't 45 degrees, as with the diamond-shaped tile you see here, getting exact lines is even harder. So we'll show you a better way: Mark a single layout line and center the tiles over it by aligning the corners of the tile with the line. Build a pyramid centered on the line and use the sides of the pyramid to align each diagonal course. Check the sides of the pyramid occasionally with a straightedge.

**MEET THE PRO**

Nobody knows tile like our guru, **Dean Sorem**. Over the past 25 years, he's covered thousands of walls and floors with tile of every type. Based in Hudson, WI, Dean is the head honcho of Sorem Tile and Stone.

## Special mortar for big tiles

Thin-set mortar is the best bedding adhesive for most tile. But if you're setting tiles larger than 12 x 12 in., look for terms like "medium bed," "large tile" or "large format" on the bag label. Bigger tile requires a thicker bed, and unlike standard thin-set, medium-bed mortar doesn't lose its bonding strength when you lay it on thick. It's also firmer and shrinks less, so tiles stay in position better while the mortar hardens. Medium-bed mortar is available at tile stores and some home centers.

LOOK FOR THIS!

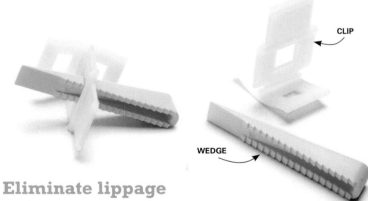

NICHE TRIM

## Size a niche to suit the tile

If you're planning a wall niche, lay out the tile and take some measurements to determine the size of the niche. If you custom-size the niche to fit between full tiles, you'll get a better-looking installation and avoid some cutting. With a diagonal tile layout like the one shown here, you'll get full tiles and half tiles. If trim will frame the niche, be sure to factor it into the layout.

CLIP

WEDGE

## Eliminate lippage

"Lippage" is the technical term for uneven tile edges (though "@%&#!" is more common). Lippage is hard to avoid with large tile and easy to see with narrow grout lines or tile that has square—rather than rounded—edges. In any of those circumstances, leveling clips and wedges help you lay tile flat. Just slip the clip under the tile and push in the wedge. After the thin-set hardens, break off the exposed clip. LASH brand clips are available at some home centers or online.

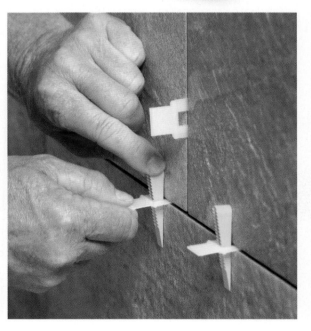

## Clean cuts in porcelain

Porcelain tile is incredibly hard—and incredibly brittle. So it often chips along cuts or cracks before the cut is complete. Here's a three-step routine that eliminates those problems. The first step only works with saws that allow you to adjust the depth of cut. If yours doesn't, you can still make the second and third cuts to avoid cracks.

**1 SCORE.** Make a shallow cut across the tile—about 1/8 in. deep. This minimizes chipping.

**2 SLIT.** Cut a finishing end slit about 2 in. long. This prevents cracking as you approach the end of the main cut.

**3 SLICE.** Make the main cut as usual. Don't rush it; slow, steady pressure creates the cleanest cut.

| AVERAGE COVERAGE / COBERTURA PROMEDIO | | |
|---|---|---|
| TILE SIZE<br>TAMAÑO DE AZUELOS Y BALDOSAS | TROWEL SIZE<br>TAMAÑO DE LLANA | PER 25 LB BAG<br>POR BOLSA DE 11 34 KG |
| Up to 8"<br>Hasta 20 cm | 1/4" x 1/4" x 1/4" Square-Notch<br>6 x 6 x 6 mm Dentada Cuadrada | 45 - 50 sq. ft.<br>4.2 - 4.6 m² |
| 8" to 12"<br>20 a 30 cm | 1/4" x 3/8" x 1/4" Square-Notch<br>6 x 9 x 6 mm Dentada Cuadrada | 32 - 35 sq. ft.<br>2.9 - 3.3 m² |
| 12" or larger<br>30 cm o más | 1/2" x 1/2" x 1/2" Square-Notch<br>13 x 13 x 13 mm Dentada Cuadrada | 23 - 25 sq. ft.<br>2.1 - 2.3 m² |

## Don't trust this chart

Your thin-set probably has a chart like this on the label. Don't rely on it. The recommendations are a good starting point, but they don't guarantee a thin-set bed thick enough to provide full contact with the tile. And without full contact, you don't get full support or adhesion.

As the chart shows, larger tiles require larger trowel notches (to provide a thicker bed). But other factors matter too: the flatness of the wall or floor, or the texture of the tile's back. So the only reliable way to know that the bed is thick enough is to set the first few tiles, then immediately pry them up. If the tile hasn't made full contact, you'll see it. The easiest solution is to use the next notch size. With tiles larger than 12 in., it's a good idea to also "back-butter" them with thin-set. Also keep an eye on "squeeze-out" during the job. If you don't see thin-set squeezing out between tiles, pull up a tile to check coverage.

## Gentle smudge remover

When you're shopping for tile supplies, take a detour to the sandpaper aisle and pick up a pack of fine abrasive pads. Along with a little water, they're great for removing stubborn thin-set smudges on the face of tile. And they won't scratch the glossy glaze.

## Get a handle on tile

A suction cup lets you lift a sunken tile or adjust a crooked one. Some home centers and hardware stores carry them; most don't. To shop online, search for "suction cup handle." Keep in mind that they only work on smooth-faced tile.

## Absolutely essential trowel

Tile setters use a margin trowel for everything: prying up sunken tiles, nudging crooked ones, cleaning out grout lines, mixing up small batches of thin-set or grout, scooping mix out of the bucket and scraping up messes. Makes a great back scratcher, too. If you're setting tile, you've got to have one (sold at home centers).

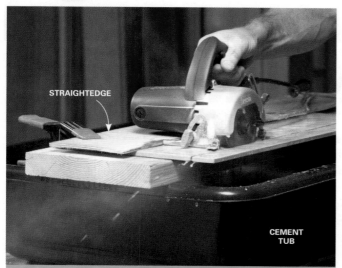

STRAIGHTEDGE

CEMENT TUB

## Big cuts without a big saw

Huge tiles are popular these days, and the best way to cut them is with a big, expensive tile saw. Here's the next best way: a handheld wet saw guided by a straight-edge (we used a plywood scrap). The Ryobi TC400 saw shown, along with the three-step cutting method shown on p. 148, gave us perfectly straight cuts in porcelain tile (but with some chipping). A cement-mixing tub caught most of the mess.

BACKER STRIP

## Tough scrubber for tools

Thin-set today is a lot stickier and tougher than it used to be. That's a good thing for your tile job, but not so good for your tools. For easier cleanup, toss a coarse sanding sponge into your water bucket. The grit cuts through partially dried thin-set or grout. And unlike rags or sponges, it doesn't snag on the teeth of notched trowels.

## Built-out trim

If you're using tile trim, it's often necessary to "build out" the trim so it protrudes from the surrounding field tile. A strip of tile backer can help you get the build-out just right. Any kind of backer board will do; just slather one side with thin-set or mastic and stick it in place. In this case, the trim wasn't quite thick enough to overhang the tile below, so we set the trim over a strip of 1/4-in. backer. To make adjustments of less than 1/4 in., you don't need a strip of backer; simply apply a heavier bed of thin-set.

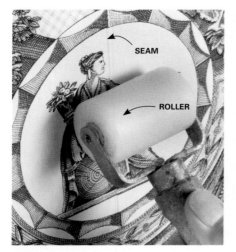

SEAM

ROLLER

## Roll every seam

To keep the edges from curling, you need to set them with a roller. But the same rule that applies to the smoother applies to the roller: Don't press too hard or you'll squeeze out too much adhesive.

## Overlap and cut both pieces at once

Sometimes, rather than butting one panel up to another, you'll need to create your own seam. The best way to do this is to lap one panel over the other and cut down the middle of the overlap. Then peel the two pieces apart and pull out the small strip that was cut off the underlying piece.

If you don't have a steady hand, you can use a drywall knife as a cutting guide. Try not to penetrate the drywall paper. Angle the knife blade down low so more than just the tip of the blade is doing the cutting. Bob uses a knife with blades that snap off. Blades are a lot cheaper than wallpaper, so he snaps off a section after every cut.

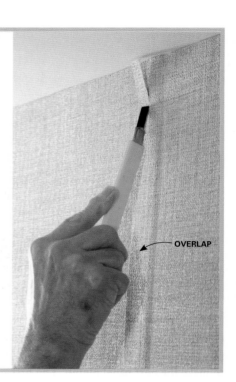

OVERLAP

## Wipe down as you go

It's a lot easier to clean up the paste before it has fully cured, so Bob sponges off every panel with warm water as he goes. He uses natural sponges, one in each hand. He swipes with the first and makes a final pass with the other. He uses a few drops of dish soap when he's working with particularly sticky paste. To avoid creating suds, Bob squeezes the sponges out while they're still submerged in water, then he gives them another small squeeze above the water bucket.

NATURAL SPONGE

## Tools of the trade

Hanging wallpaper doesn't require a huge investment. You probably already own many of the tools. Bob's most expensive tools are his beech cutting table and his magnesium straightedge. You can substitute an old door slab and a level.

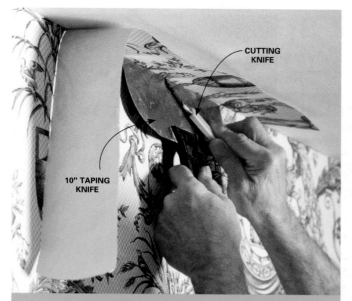

**CUTTING KNIFE**

**10" TAPING KNIFE**

## Use a taping knife as a cutting guide

Leave an extra 2 in. at the top and bottom, and use a drywall knife as a guide to trim it. Bob prefers a 10-in. knife so he doesn't have to move it as often as he would a smaller one. Hold the knife down close to the wall to avoid cutting into the ceiling.

## Make relief cuts before trimming

When you're up against trim or other obstacles, you'll need to make a relief cut before trimming the paper. You could make the cut with a knife, but scissors are better to avoid scratching the trim.

**CORNER**

## What's the best paintbrush for cutting in with latex paint?

Professional painter—and ballroom dancer extraordinaire—Bill Nunn says the clear choice is a high-quality synthetic "sash" paintbrush. (That's the type with the angled bristles.)

"They can be found in nylon, a nylon and polyester blend, and Chinex. Nylon is a soft and fine filament and feathers paint well. In combination with polyester, it has a firmer feel and can help you spread a heavier paint. The firmness is usually marked on the paper wrapper, to which I always return a brush at day's end to preserve the shape. Chinex is a trade name for a synthetic bristle designed to help you with cleanup. It sheds paint well, especially the newer acrylics, but also applies oil paint well."

**MEET THE PRO**

For more than 30 years, **Bill Nunn**, owner of William Nunn Painting, has specialized in interior and exterior painting, wallcoverings and wood finishing.

# A smooth, fast polyurethane finish

You may think a brush is the best tool for applying polyurethane finish, but think again! Use this method for a perfect finish every time.

## Sand out the pencil marks

Begin by drawing light, squiggly pencil lines on the surface at each grit stage. When the pencil lines disappear, you're ready to move on to the next grit. You're wasting your time sanding coarse, open-grained woods like ash or oak super-smooth. Start at 80 grit and end with 100 or 120 grit. Sanding through all the grits to 220 grit won't improve the finish one bit. But with closed-grained woods like maple or birch, don't skip any grit steps, and go all the way to 220 grit.

## A clean work area is key

The more dust-free the project and the surrounding surfaces, the less work you'll have and the more flawless your finish will be. Before you start, vacuum the project, the workbench and the floor. Under the piece to be finished, spread out 6-mil poly to protect the floor from drips and spills and to make cleanup easy. Reuse these sheets several times, then toss them. Don't finish on the same day you sand; the dust stays in the air for hours. Start finishing with clean clothes and hair.

## Wipe down with mineral spirits

Wipe down the project with a tack cloth or a lint-free cloth saturated with solvent. You can use an old, clean cotton

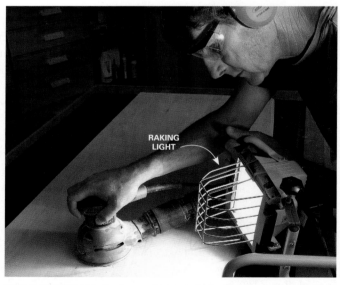

**USE A LIGHT** held at a low, raking angle to check for scratches, dirt and any other imperfections while you sand and apply finish coats.

T-shirt for this and the wipe-on step shown later. This step removes nearly all traces of dust. It only takes a few minutes for the solvent to evaporate so you can get started on finishing. Don't use water; it'll raise the grain and you'll have to sand again.

**LOSE THE DUST.** Wipe down every square inch of the workpiece with a lint-free cotton cloth dampened with mineral spirits or denatured alcohol.

6" MICROFIBER ROLLER

VARNISH IN BAKING SHEET

**ROLL ON POLY FAST—THEN QUIT.** Dampen the roller with mineral spirits and roll the poly on all of the large flat areas and cabinet interiors. Coat the surface and quit. Don't continue to work the finish.

FRESHLY COATED BOTTOM

STANDOFF

**FINISH BOTH SIDES AT ONCE.** Coat the bottom first and then flip over the top, resting it on standoffs while you roll the finish on the top. The Painter's Pyramid (standoff) shown is available at home centers.

## Use a roller on large flat surfaces

You can get the poly on fast and evenly with little rollers—no brushstrokes, puddles or thin spots. Some rollers may cause bubbles, but 6-in. microfiber rollers dampened with mineral spirits work great. There's always a bit of leftover lint, but only on the first coat. A Teflon baking tray makes a great rolling pan.

Don't worry when you see the finish right after you lay it down. It'll look like it's full of flaws. Just roll it out and use the raking light to make sure the surface is completely covered. Don't keep working the finish. Let it be, and it will flatten out. Keep a can of spray poly handy in case of bubbles. A light mist knocks them out.

After each coat, redip the roller in mineral spirits, put it into a zippered plastic bag for the next coat and leave the wet tray to dry. In a couple of hours, the dried poly just peels right out of the pan. It's usually best to put two coats on cabinet interiors and sides, and three coats on tabletops for extra protection.

## Finish both sides at once

With a solid wood top like this one, finish both the top and the bottom surfaces, even if the bottom won't show. Skip this step and the top can twist, cup or warp. To save drying time, coat the bottom and then immediately flip it over to finish the top. Right after the top is rolled out, roll the edges and then go around them with a dry foam brush to eliminate any drips or thick spots. You can skip the final coat on the underside. Being short a single coat on the underside isn't a big deal.

## Zero cleanup with wipe-on poly

After the roll-on coats are dry, use wipe-on oil poly (use the same sheen you chose for the roll-on poly) for the face frames, legs, doors or any other narrow, small or intricate areas. Do this after the large areas are dry so you don't smudge adjacent areas. This is a great method because only two things get dirty: a glove and a cotton rag, both of which you can toss after each coat. (Spread them out to dry first.) You can put on two to four coats in one day depending on the temperature and humidity. There are no drips, sags or runs—ever.

**DRYWALL CIRCLE GAUGE**

**KEYHOLE SAW**

## Mark your holes with a drywall circle gauge

Scribe holes with a drywall circle gauge, and then make the cuts with a drywall saw. With just these two tools, you can cut a wide variety of hole sizes.

## Repair panels with flat latex caulk

Wade insists that only rookies damage ceiling panels. But when a panel does get damaged at his job site, he uses a little white caulk (or "apprentice putty" as he calls it) to patch it up. Make sure you use a flat latex caulk—shiny silicone will stand out worse than the hole. If the damaged area is bigger than a pencil eraser, you may want to set that panel aside to be used as a partial in another location.

## What's the best paint for a stucco patch?

According to Steve Revnew at Sherwin-Williams, dealing with patched stucco requires a two-step process. "Since the patch is new stucco, before you paint, prime the patch with a masonry primer designed with specific resistance to high pH and efflorescence." Revnew says these primers typically have elastomeric properties that provide for expansion and contraction throughout the life of the stucco. "If you don't do this, you risk paint failure."

Revnew suggests painting with a high-quality 100 percent acrylic latex. "These products allow moisture to escape and give great color and gloss retention." To find the right primer and paint for your stucco project, read the can label or ask at the paint store. High-quality options include Sherwin-Williams' Loxon line and SuperPaint, Behr's Elastomeric Masonry, Stucco & Brick Paint and UGL's DRYLOK masonry waterproofer.

**MEET THE PRO**

**Steven Revnew** is vice president for product innovation at Sherwin-Williams. A chemist by training, Revnew practiced his profession in the Sherwin-Williams research and development labs before venturing into the world of marketing and sales.

# Prevent peeling paint on exterior wood

This is the million-dollar question when you're painting your house, right? And the answer may be the best-kept secret in the painting world—use a water-repellent preservative (WRP). WRP is perfect for moisture-prone spots like garage door trim and windowsills. But most painters—pros and DIYers alike—have never heard of it. Here's how it works:

Peeling often begins with a tiny crack in the paint. A little water sneaks in and the wood swells, stretching the paint and causing more cracks. As the surface warms and the water evaporates, it pushes against the paint from behind. Each time this cycle occurs, the crack grows and the paint bond weakens. Peeling soon begins.

WRP prevents this cycle. Applied to bare wood before primer and paint, it keeps wood from absorbing water after the paint cracks. Mark Knaebe, U.S. Forest Service wood surface chemist, says WRP is very effective, but it needs to be applied with a light hand.

"A small amount of WRP greatly reduces the amount of water entering the wood," says Knaebe. "But it also decreases paint adhesion. So there are two competing things going on. Ultimately, the slight

**WRP may be the best-kept secret in the painting world.**

decrease in adhesion is more than made up for by the absence of water trying to push the paint off when the surface is warmed."

Knaebe also says it's important to keep sunlight from hitting the bare wood during paint prep. "Sunlight destroys lignin, the natural glue that holds wood fibers together. If you apply paint to a surface without lignin, it won't be long before that surface peels away from the rest of the wood."

Knaebe suggests prepping your wood for paint in small sections so the bare wood is exposed to the sun for minutes instead of hours or days. Scrape off the paint, sand the top

Finding a paintable WRP is a little tricky. Labels don't always make it clear whether the product is paintable or not. Here's a list of some widely available paintable WRPs:

- Blue Label Penofin
- Cuprinol Clear Deck & Wood Seal
- Olympic Clear Wood Preservative
- Weatherscreen Clear Wood Preservative
- Woodlife Classic
- Woodlife Coppercoat

layer of wood, apply a paintable WRP to moisture-prone areas and follow the manufacturer's instructions about how long to wait before priming and painting. Everywhere else, prime immediately after sanding.

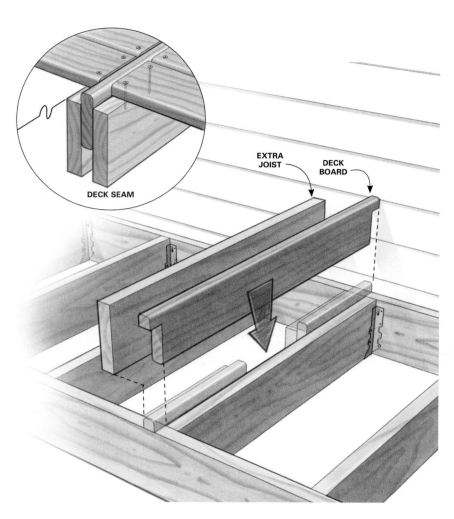

**DECK SEAM**

**EXTRA JOIST**

**DECK BOARD**

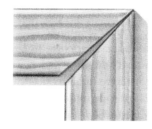

## Get over lag screws

There are few reasons to use lag screws anymore. Construction screws may look wimpy, but they're actually stronger than lags. And you don't have to spend five minutes cranking each one in with a ratchet.

Give construction screws a try on your next deck. You can drive them with any 18-volt screw gun without predrilling—they don't split wood. The price may shock you (they cost four times as much), but you'll never go back to lags.

## Seam a deck

The traditional way most builders go about decking is to randomly stagger joints. The result is that end-to-end deck boards share the 1-1/2-in. thickness of each joist. That can cause problems, especially with wood decks. With only 3/4 in. of nailing surface, fasteners will cause ends to split, and since the board ends have to be tight, untreated wood will rot.

I use a faster, more material-efficient method I call seaming. It's simply strategically placing a seam (or seams, on bigger decks) and using the same length boards for each section. Each seam is a sandwich made of an elevated vertical decking board with joists on both sides. The advantages are many. It's faster than random seaming; all decking ends have a full 1-1/2 in. of framing, so it cuts down on fastener splits; and you can leave 1/4-in. gaps at the ends so end grain can dry out after it gets wet.

The vertical deck board is for looks only. It makes everything look planned and polished. And there's virtually no waste. If I need to build a 20-ft.-wide deck, I'll make it about 19 ft. 6 in. and use all 10-ft. decking on both halves. That allows for 1-in. overhangs and cutting off some bad ends.

Seaming also works well for solid composite decking, which comes in fewer lengths. If, for example, I'm building a composite deck, 12- and 20-ft. lengths might be the only options. For a 16-ft.-wide deck, I might seam it to have a 4-ft. "sidewalk" down the middle for zero waste. Of course, everything depends on the design and the homeowner. But think about it next time to figure out the best approach.

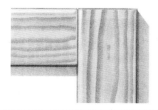

## Avoid miters

Avoid miters in wood decking when you can, especially in wide boards. Here's why: Wood installed outdoors immediately starts shrinking—or in some conditions, expanding—mostly in width. Miters will always open up unevenly, and your perfect miter will look like a hack job in no time. Whenever possible, use simple butt joints. They don't look as professional as miters at first, but they look better in the long run.

## Cobble together a layout frame

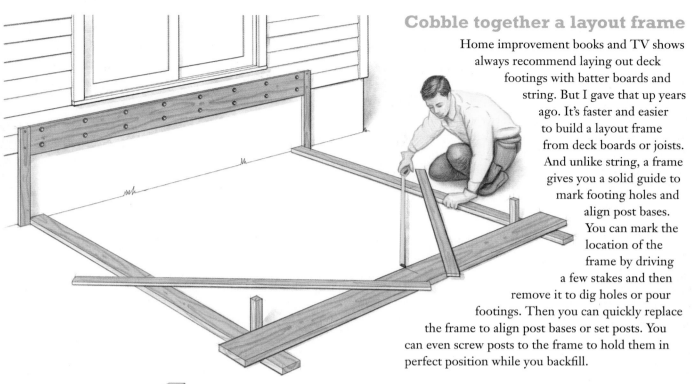

Home improvement books and TV shows always recommend laying out deck footings with batter boards and string. But I gave that up years ago. It's faster and easier to build a layout frame from deck boards or joists. And unlike string, a frame gives you a solid guide to mark footing holes and align post bases. You can mark the location of the frame by driving a few stakes and then remove it to dig holes or pour footings. Then you can quickly replace the frame to align post bases or set posts. You can even screw posts to the frame to hold them in perfect position while you backfill.

## Check the end grain on 4x4s

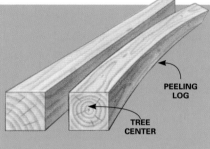

PEELING LOG

TREE CENTER

When buying 4x4s, don't just sight them for straightness; always look at the ends. Try to avoid 4x4s that include the center of the tree, especially anywhere near the center of the 4x4. Those can twist into airplane propellers in no time. This is particularly true of 8-footers because those are often the leftovers from "peeling logs," the outer layers of which have been shaved off to make plywood veneer. When I order 4x4s over the phone and need eights, I always order tens to reduce the chances of getting 4x4 leftovers from peelers.

## Leave a little step below doors

There are so many reasons not to snug decks right under door thresholds. The screen and sliding door tracks on patio doors get full of debris. Storm doors have to bulldoze their way through leaves in the fall. And those leaves will get blown or kicked into the house every time the door opens. Splashing water rots out wood casing and jamb trim. And last but not least, water will inevitably work its way under any threshold and rot out the subfloor and then the framing. It's nearly impossible to flash between ledgers and thresholds if the decking is flush to thresholds. Leave a 3-in. step: The house and its owner will be a lot happier in the long run.

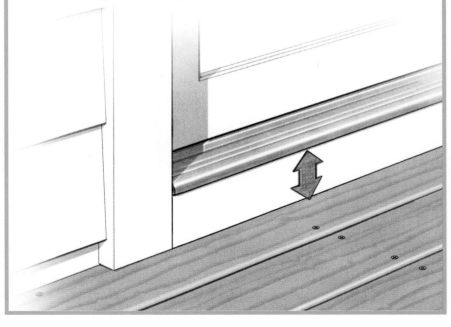

# The da Vinci of decks

For the third year in a row, Eric Mortenson has been named a Twin Cities Best Contractor by Angie's List, the largest home improvement review service in the United States. Winners are in the top 1 percent of U.S. contractors of the 18,000 eligible for the award. Mortenson specializes in high-end decks and three-season porches, and his clients call him meticulous, driven and hard-working. According to one satisfied client, "The building inspector said he seldom sees such craftsmanship and quality anymore."

**Construction philosophy:** "I build everything as if I were building it for myself. When your work becomes art and you're really focusing on quality and beauty, the rest of it takes care of itself."

**On materials:** "It used to be I built 20 percent composite and 80 percent wood. In the last three years, it's changed completely and 80 percent are going with composite. I like to use composites on the horizontal surfaces and cedar for the railing. Cedar is beautiful, it's stronger than a composite rail and having a little bit of wood in there gives the overall deck a less sterile feeling."

**Determining a successful project:** "I always try to do something on every job that the client didn't expect. It really doesn't take that much longer to do something that's got well-thought-out, elegant details in it."

**What experience has taught him:** "You need to have a complete vision and see the finished product before you start. The magic is in the details. You need to know how you're going to finish off that corner, how that border is going to work, and how you're going to tie it to the house before you even buy the materials. When I was younger, I thought I could figure it out as I went, but that doesn't work well."

## Eric's deck-building secrets

- "Sikkens Log & Siding is my favorite stain for any exterior wood vertical surface like garage doors, deck rails, etc. It's a two-coat system and it's expensive, but well worth it. It's stunning and looks like an interior surface, and it'll hold up for five or more years in between coats."

DINGO AUGER

- How to dig footings fast: "Rent a Toro Dingo auger for a half-day. They rent them all over the U.S., they work in all sorts of rough soils, and they make an awful job a lot easier."

- "For putting in joist hanger nails, a palm nailer is a huge time-saver. My first choice is a pneumatic air nailer because it makes the process fast and it's very powerful. But my battery-powered palm nailer can also come in really handy, especially in tight spots and awkward positions where dragging around an air hose is inconvenient."

SIKKENS LOG & SIDING

BATTERY-POWERED PALM NAILER

PNEUMATIC PALM NAILER

# Lessons from a 10-year-old deck

TATE CARLSON

When we built this dream deck 10 years ago in Little Canada, MN, we made the promise that it would last as long as the house. That's a pretty bold statement. After 10 nasty Minnesota winters, we decided to hold our own feet to the fire and go back to see how the deck was holding up.

—*Travis Larson, senior editor*

## Trex composite decking

Yes, it looks great in the photo and indeed, looks nearly as good in person. No sagging, no rot, nothing bad. And despite heavy use, there's no sign of any wear. The decking doesn't look quite as fresh as new; falling leaves, dirt and party plate spills have all conspired against it. But it wouldn't take much more than a good cleaning to spruce it up.

**The lesson:** If you want split-proof, rot-proof, low-maintenance decking, skip the wood and go with composite decking. It's come a long way in the past 10 years, with much better colors and more realistic grain patterns. We endorse it.

## Stain

All of the exposed cedar got two coats of semitransparent stain during construction. Some of the stain has worn off. There aren't any huge swaths of peeling going on. If you squint your eyes, it still looks pretty fresh, but it's about ready for a recoat.

**The lesson:** If you want stain, put on at least two coats and buy the best, even if it is expensive.

## Cedar siding and trim

TATE CARLSON

The cedar and the joinery have held up well, with one exception. The corner boards on the planters have begun to rot where they contact the decking.

**The lesson:** Seal any end grain with stain before installation. Space end grain above horizontal surfaces at least 1/2 in. to keep it from wicking up moisture.

## Framing

We crawled under the deck to do some probing with a screwdriver to check for rot. Not a sign of it. The pressure-treated framing was absolutely solid everywhere. We even dug down around the wooden posts to check those below grade. They were rock-solid, too. But since we used foundation-grade lumber for the posts, that was no surprise.

**The lesson:** Choose or special-order 2x6 and 2x4 foundation-grade treated lumber if you're planning on using below-grade wooden posts like ours. Build "sandwiches" with the lumber—it'll never rot.

# Tree houses

When building on one main trunk, level the main platform by cantilevering the beams and supporting them from below.

SEAN MILROY

## Site considerations

- Choose a healthy, long-lived hardwood for maximum support, with load-bearing branches at least 8 in. in diameter (larger if the species is a softwood).
- The best trees include maple, oak, fir, beech and hemlock.
- You don't have to build it very high, just high enough so nobody gets a bump on the head when walking underneath it.

## Keep weight and stability in mind

- Build the platform as close to the trunk as possible and add diagonal bracing for extra strength to support uneven loads.
- Put the load over the base of the tree, not on one side.
- For heavy tree houses, consider spreading the weight among several trees.
- A tree house will act as a sail in strong winds, which can add a large load to the tree's roots. In high-wind areas, build your tree house in the lower third of the tree.

To accommodate tree movement and growth, allow gaps around any branches or trunks that penetrate the tree house.

## Don't restrict tree growth

- Don't constrict branches with rope, straps or wire. This can strangle the tree.
- Add spacers between the beams and the tree to allow movement.
- Use extra-long large bolts. This leaves most of the shaft exposed so you can mount items on the ends and lets the tree grow over the shaft (see "Use the Right Fasteners," p. 179).
- Allow a 2-in. gap around the tree if it passes through the floor and a 3-in. gap if it passes through the roof (photo above).

## Use the right fasteners

- Don't run bolts through the tree. Lag bolts cause less tree damage than through bolts.
- Don't use too many fasteners. One large bolt is better than many screws or nails. You get the same strength but with fewer puncture wounds to the tree.
- Whenever possible, perch your tree house on top of fasteners rather than pinning beams to the tree. This gives the tree room to move and grow.
- Even for smaller, lighter tree houses where the load is spread over three or four attachment points, consider using 1-in.- or 1-1/4-in.- diameter lag bolts.
- You can order floating brackets and tree house fasteners from specialty suppliers (Search "tree house fasteners" online) or special-order them from home centers. These bolts are pricey and often require special tools. But they allow the tree more room to grow (they can support heavy loads up to 5 in. from the tree) and they hold more weight than normal bolts.

Allow for flexible supports, especially if you use more than one tree, so that trees can move in the wind. Special floating brackets allow the tree to sway.

Large, strong custom bolts can support tree house beams with only one puncture point in the tree. These specialty tree house fasteners (known as TABs or GLs) are worth considering if you want your tree house to last more than a few years, you want to keep tree damage to a minimum and the tree house you're building is large.

Minimize tree damage by perching beams and braces on top of specialty fasteners instead of pinning them to the tree.

## Level the floor

It's much easier to build the rest of the structure if the floor is level and can support the entire weight of the tree house. Consider these methods:

- Lay beams across the branches and shim until level.
- Run the beams between trunks of different trees.
- Cantilever the beams out from a single trunk and support them from above or below.

To keep a large tree house stable, center the load over the trunk and spread the weight among several branches.

# Chapter Twelve

# CARS, TRUCKS, MOTORCYCLES AND RVS

# Clean up your greasy engine

If you're a clean freak, you've probably been degreasing your engine for years. But if you've never done it, here are two good reasons why you should. First, a clean engine is easier to work on. Second, a clean engine brings more at resale. But you can't just spray it with degreaser and hose it down. We'll show you how to prepare the engine to protect critical electrical connections. We'll also give you some tips for doing the job in an environmentally safe way.

**1** **PROTECT EVERYTHING ELECTRICAL.** Wrap ignition wires and coils and all electrical connectors with plastic wrap. Then add a flag of fluorescent surveyor's tape so you don't forget to remove the wrap later.

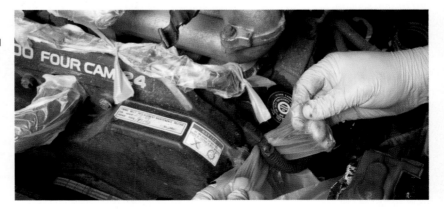

## Picking a degreasing product

Degreasing products come in two types: solvent and water-based. Both types work on greasy engines. And both require special environmental handling once they're applied—even if the label says "environmentally safe" or "biodegradable." Because once the degreasing solution starts dissolving the grease, it's considered hazardous waste.

We prefer solvent-based degreasers because they work faster and seem to cut through heavy grease buildup better than most water-based products. The downside is their strong solvent smell. If you're sensitive to solvents, choose a concentrated water-based product instead.

To get better "cling" on vertical surfaces, choose either a foam or a gel formula degreaser.

While you're at the auto parts store, pick up a drip pan and three 3-packs of absorbent mat.

## Warm it up, wrap it up and spray away

Degreasers work best when the grease is warm and soft. So start the engine and let it run for about five minutes. Then shut it off and let it cool down until you can safely touch the exhaust manifold. Never spray cleaners (especially flammable solvent types) on a hot engine.

If you're using a concentrated water-based product, test it on a greasy spot. If it doesn't cut the grease fast enough, add more concentrated degreaser to the brew.

Next, seal all the electrical connections (Photo 1, p. 181). Then set the absorbent mats under the engine to soak up the runoff (Photo 2). Prep the worst areas (Photo 3). Then apply the degreaser (Photo 4). Aim carefully to prevent the overspray from reaching painted areas. Rinse lightly with water and remove the plastic wrap. When you're done, place the wet mats in sunlight to allow the water to evaporate. Then dispose of the mats following local regulations.

For extra protection, spray an engine protectant onto the dry engine. The spray imparts a slight shine and a protective layer of grease to make cleanup even easier next time.

**2 SOAK UP THE HAZARDOUS WASTE.**
Spread absorbent mats on a drip pan and slide the pan under the engine.

**3 SCRATCH THE SURFACE ON THE WORST AREAS.**
Break up the baked-on crud with a wire brush before you apply the degreaser. Brush gently or switch to a nylon brush around plastic components.

**4 SPRAY, SOAK AND RINSE.**
Spray the degreaser over the entire engine and let it soak for the recommended time. Apply additional coats (if needed) to really greasy areas. Then rinse with a water mist, using as little water as possible.

# Six-point vs. 12-point sockets

"Twelve-point sockets work great for most household repairs and projects," says TFH resident gearhead Rick Muscoplat. "But for vehicle, mower or motorcycle repairs, I always use six-point sockets. They have thicker walls and apply force to the flat shoulder of the hex bolt/nut instead of the corners. So I can apply more torque without rounding off shoulder corners."

The number of points refers to the number of angles cut into the socket. Most modern fasteners have a hexagonal shape (six sides). But 12-point sockets do offer some advantages for the average homeowner. The biggest plus of a 12-point socket is that it gives you twice the number of starting positions. So you only need to rotate the socket a maximum of 30 degrees before it slips onto the fastener (as opposed to 60 degrees for a six-point socket). That's an important feature when you're working in tight spaces or hard-to-see locations—like inside an appliance.

"It's not a bad idea to have 12-point tools around," says Muscoplat. "But if I had to choose only one type, I'd go with the six-pointers."

**MEET THE PRO**

**Rick Muscoplat** writes the Car & Garage department each issue and has been turning wrenches (and sockets) his whole life.

# Racing oil is for racing

Ever heard someone brag about running racing oil in a muscle car? Well, the joke's on them, because racing oil isn't meant for daily or even occasional driving. In fact, running racing oil in a nontrack vehicle can increase the likelihood of sludge buildup in the engine. And, it can damage the $1,200 catalytic converter.

Racing oil contains three times more antiwear and friction-reducing additives (for less wear and more horsepower) than ordinary oil. To make room for that spiked dose, the manufacturers yank the detergent, anticorrosive, antifoam and dispersant additives—precisely the additives you need most to keep your street engine running clean for 3,000 miles. The bottom line: Racing oil is for racing only—get it?

### Racing oil tidbits

- Race teams use lower-viscosity oil with more friction modifiers to qualify. Then they change to a higher-viscosity oil for the race.
- Racing teams go through racing oil at the rate of about 2,130 qts. of oil per car per season.
- In a typical NASCAR race, oil temps can run as high as 320 degrees F.
- Pit crews bring about 60 qts. of oil to every race.
- Teams analyze the oil after every race. They check for viscosity change, the level of metals worn away, oxidation (indicates how the oil held up to heat) and additive depletion.

# Ask the mechanic: Squeal-chirp!

**Q** I have a squealing drive belt. How do I fix it?

**A** A squealing belt is a sign of improper belt tension, a misaligned or worn pulley, a worn belt or a sluggish idler roller bearing. Since most late-model vehicles use a spring-loaded self-tensioning mechanism, check that first. Attach a socket or ratchet to the tensioner and rotate it. It should turn smoothly and return to its original position on its own. If you feel any binding or have to manually move it back into position, it's worn out. Replace it. If the tensioner checks out, use an automotive stethoscope to identify the source of the squeal. Just remove the probe from the end of the stethoscope and hold it next to each belt-driven component while you run the engine. Then listen for the squealing sound. Replace the noisy component.

Never use "belt dressing" to silence a squealing belt. The sticky spray never fixes the root cause of the squeal. Worse yet, the sticky goo collects road dust and sand and grinds up the belt and pulleys. That'll cost you far more when the squeal returns.

# Car additives that work

Walk down the additives aisle at any auto parts store, and you'll see a few hundred products all claiming to increase your gas mileage and convert your daily driver into a race car. Other "miracle in a bottle"–type products claim to seal your leaking engine, fix your transmission or restore an old, tired engine to "like new" condition. Do they work? Some do. But most are a waste of money. I'll walk you through the maze of products and separate fact from, well, snake oil. Let's start with the most effective additive—fuel injector cleaner.

## Oil additives

Skip any oil additives unless you have an old car (early '80s or older). Those engines were built with high-friction flat tappet lifters, so they need a boost of antiwear additive with ZDDP (zinc dialkyl dithio phosphate). Shop for brands like ZDDP Plus or Hy-Per Lube Zinc. Don't use ZDDP additives with a post-'80s engine—extra ZDDP can damage your catalytic converter.

Hoping to restore your worn engine to "like new" condition with a restorative additive? Dream on—it's just not going to happen. The same holds true for oil treatments that contain Teflon or other ingredients that claim to reduce friction and wear. Save your cash for something more beneficial, such as regular oil and filter changes.

**Your older engine needs a wear additive**
Older engines (pre-1980s) need additional wear protection. Pour in a zinc-enriched additive at each oil change.

## Fuel additives

All gasoline contains fuel injector cleaner. But Top Tier gasoline (marked on the pump at the gas station) contains a higher dose of it. So my first piece of advice is to spend a few cents more per gallon and fill your tank with Top Tier gas. If you can't find a station that carries Top Tier gas (check online for "top tier gas") and you make a lot of short runs or drive in stop-and-go traffic, you may get better gas mileage and improve engine performance by adding a fuel system cleaner to your tank. Chevron Techron and CRC Guaranteed to Pass fuel system cleaners both do a very good job. Just add a bottle to your tank once every 3,000 miles and your engine will thank you.

If you drive a diesel, Marvel Diesel Supplement or STP Diesel Fuel Treatment will clean the fuel system and lubricate the injectors. They'll also reduce the risk of fuel waxing during cold weather.

**Fuel system cleaners that work**
Read the bottle instructions for dosing amounts. Add the cleaners directly to the fuel tank.

**MEET THE PRO**

LARRY CARLEY

**Larry Carley** is the technical editor for prestigious professional automotive publications like *Engine Builder*, *Brake and Front End*, *Tomorrow's Technician* and *ImportCar*. With more than 2,500 automotive articles under his belt, Larry is well suited to offer advice on additives.

## Head gasket sealers

If you constantly have to top off your coolant but can't find any sign of an external leak, you probably have a leaking head gasket. Skip the inexpensive head gasket sealers (they require at least two full days of water-flushing procedures). Instead, spend the extra bucks for Bar's Leaks HG-1 Head Gasket & Cooling Sealant or K&W FiberLock Head Gasket & Block Repair

There's an important caveat to using any head gasket sealer. Your engine must be able to run for about 20 minutes without overheating or losing its coolant. If your engine overheats right away or loses coolant too fast, forget about a head gasket sealer—the cylinder head is probably warped. That'll require machine shop service and a new gasket. If the head gasket sealer works, you don't need to add new sealer when you change your coolant.

**Seal a head gasket**
Pour the head gasket sealer directly into the radiator and run the engine for the specified period shown on the label.

## Transmission additives

If your transmission is slow to shift or reluctant to go into gear, and has plenty of fluid, it's most likely ready to give up the ghost. If you're a gambler, you can try a transmission "fix-in-bottle" additive. It may buy you a few more months of driving (at best). But don't think you've fixed the problem. Your transmission is going to fail and probably sooner rather than later.

If your transmission shifts well but leaks fluid, you can add a transmission leak-stop product. They work by swelling the seals to slow the leak. But they're not a permanent fix. Eventually you'll have to replace the leaky seals or gaskets.

For older transmissions with no shifting problems, add a bottle of a fluid conditioner like LubeGard, Prolong or Lucas Transmission Fix. It bolsters the performance of older nonsynthetic transmission fluids. You don't need a conditioner if you're driving a late-model vehicle with the newer long-life synthetic transmission fluids like Mercon V, Dexron VI or Chrysler ATF+4.

**Transmission additive for older vehicles**
To extend the life of an older but fully functional transmission, pour in a bottle of transmission fluid conditioner.

## Cooling system

If you notice coolant puddles on your driveway, check for a cracked radiator, heater hose or a loose hose clamp. Repair that first. Next, check for a leaking core plug (also called a freeze plug). Core plugs are cheap and easy to replace if you can access the area easily.

But if it turns out your leak is coming from your radiator, heater core or an inaccessible core plug, try adding a cooling system sealer product like Bar's Leaks No. PLT11 or Gunk C312. If the product seals the leak, great. If not, you haven't lost much money. Just remember to add another dose of sealer next time you change your coolant. If the sealer doesn't work, you'll have to bite the bullet and replace the leaking component.

If your vehicle is overheating, forget about pouring in an additive (such as a wetting agent) to stop the overheating. None of them work. You'll waste your money and risk permanent engine damage (a minimum $1,000 repair) simply by driving around waiting to see if the additive works. Just fork over the dough to fix the underlying cooling problem.

Another product to avoid is water pump lubricant. Fresh coolant does a fine job of lubricating the water pump.

**Seal the cooling system**
Add leak-stop products directly to the radiator. If your vehicle doesn't have a radiator cap, remove the upper hose, siphon out some coolant and pour it into the radiator with a funnel.

# Avoid brake job rip-offs

You'll buy at least three brake jobs during the life of your vehicle. And if you don't learn how to spot the rip-offs, you'll waste upward of $1,000 on parts and services you don't really need. Brake job rip-offs happen far more often than you think. I'll lift the curtain on these shady practices and show you how to get a good brake job and avoid getting taken.

—*Rick Muscoplat,*
*contributing editor*

### Anatomy of a brake system

Stop on a dime with three simple components. The exploded photo shows the caliper (the squeezing machine), the brake pads (the friction material) and the rotor (the part that gets squeezed).

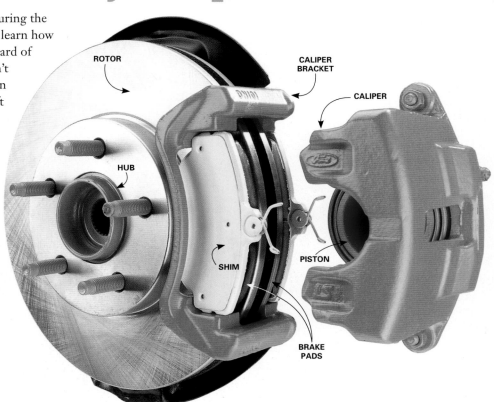

ROTOR

CALIPER BRACKET

CALIPER

HUB

SHIM

PISTON

BRAKE PADS

CALIPER BRACKET

NEW PINS

CORRODED PIN

### New caliper pins save you big $$$

Fix a binding caliper with new slide pins and high-temperature synthetic grease. That'll save you a fortune, and the caliper will slide freely for another 40,000 miles.

## Rip-off #1

## Buying calipers when you don't need them

Brake calipers work in a push-pull process to squeeze the brake pads against the rotors (see "Anatomy of a Brake System," above). First, the caliper piston pushes the inboard pad outward until it touches the rotor. Then the caliper slides backward, pulling the outboard against the other side of the rotor. When you back off the brakes, the piston retracts slightly and the caliper releases pressure on the pads.

But if the caliper binds on the slide pins, the brake pads wear unevenly and quickly. Binding is a very common problem. But that doesn't mean you have to replace the calipers. Instead, the shop simply needs to replace the slide pins (for a fraction of the price of calipers) and lubricate them with high-temperature synthetic grease. So if replacement calipers are recommended, ask if they can be fixed by replacing the slide pins.

In most cases, calipers can be reused. But don't argue if you're told that the brake caliper is leaking fluid or the piston won't retract. Then it must be rebuilt or replaced.

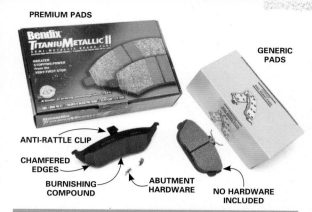

PREMIUM PADS

GENERIC PADS

ANTI-RATTLE CLIP

CHAMFERED EDGES

BURNISHING COMPOUND

ABUTMENT HARDWARE

NO HARDWARE INCLUDED

**You get what you pay for**
Demand brand-name parts. Top-quality manufacturers are proud to put their name right on the package. Generic brake parts are almost always packaged in plain white or yellow boxes. Brand name? Nowhere.

## Rip-off #2
## Paying premium prices for generic pads

Lots of companies build mediocre brake pads and pass them off as a premium product at bargain-basement prices. They're really no bargain because they wear out quickly, chew up your rotors and increase your stopping distance.

How can you tell "real" premium pads from the impostors? First, top-quality brake part manufacturers always put their name on the box (photo at left). And even though they may offer several quality levels (good, better, best), their "good" pads are almost always of higher quality than a premium pad from a "no-name" company. Second, real premium pads usually include all the required hardware (shims, anti-rattle clips and abutment hardware) at no extra cost. So if the shop claims it's installing premium pads, but the price quote includes additional charges for the hardware, well, you can tell where this is going.

## Rip-off #3
## Getting up-sold to ceramic pads

There are lots of myths surrounding ceramic brake pads, and shops are happy to recite them to help you justify an "upgrade." They'll say that ceramic is simply the best brake pad material you can buy. Not true. Another is that they outlast semimetallic pads and provide better braking. Not true either. What is true about ceramics is that they run quieter and give off less brake dust—period.

If you haul heavy loads or do a lot of stop-and-go driving, semi-metallic pads last longer and provide better braking than ceramic pads. So before you fall for the ceramic upgrade routine, think about what type of pad came with the vehicle and what kind of driving you do. If you do mainly light hauling and light braking and are really into the look of your aluminum wheels, then go for the ceramic pads.

## Rip-off #4
## Getting inferior rotors for premium prices

The brake parts market is flooded with inferior rotors that wholesale for as little as $10 a pop. Some shops buy those instead of premium rotors, charge you the higher price and pocket the difference. To the untrained eye, the generic rotors look just like the high-quality versions. But when you place them side by side, the differences are staggering. The friction surfaces on the generic rotors are noticeably thinner and they weigh about 20 percent less (photo at right). With less metal to absorb heat and fewer cooling fins to dissipate it, the generic rotors heat up faster, warp more often (creating pedal pulsation), make more noise and simply wear out faster. They're a lousy choice all the way around—even if you're trying to save money.

Just as with brake pads, ask the shop for a quote that's based on brand-name professional grade (as opposed to "service-grade") rotors.

ECONOMY ROTOR

PREMIUM ROTOR

**Less metal is a bad idea**
Compare the weights of these two rotors for the same vehicle. The economy rotor weighs 20 percent less than the premium brand.

## How to find a reputable brake shop

Call a few shops and ask what brand, type and quality-level pads and rotors they use. Well-known brands are Bendix, Raybestos, Akebono, Hawk, Wagner, NAPA/United, Carquest, Centric, Motorcraft, ACDelco, Monroe, Brembo and EBC.

Ask for a price quote—any reputable shop will provide a fairly firm quote that includes machining the rotors, replacing the slide pins and installing high-quality pads and hardware. If a shop balks at providing a phone quote, call a different one.

# How to buy tires

## Nobody likes buying tires.

The choices are mind-boggling, and the tire ratings and tread designs confusing. I'll be honest with you: I don't have any "insider secrets" on how to save big bucks on tires. Tires, all of 'em, are expensive—period. But I can give you some tips on how to pick the right tires for your vehicle. And I'll warn you away from the most common tire-buying mistakes. When you're done reading, you'll still have to drop a ton of dough on new tires. But you'll be less intimidated by the process and more confident about picking the right tires for your vehicle.

—*Rick Muscoplat, contributing editor*

### Get the original specs

Don't assume the tires on your car are the right size. Instead, buy tires based on the original factory specs. Find the specs on a sticker right on the driver's door or door pillar. Jot down the tire size and the load and speed rating. Don't get talked into buying the wrong tire. If the tire store doesn't stock the recommended tire, ask the staff to order it for you. Installing the wrong size can affect speedometer readings and cause shifting problems.

## Set your top priorities

The most common mistake tire buyers make is to choose tires based solely on price. Here's a better way to approach the tire-buying process. Start by ranking the following tire features in order of importance to you: traction, tread wear, noise, handling/ride comfort and warranty. Shop for tires based on your top three priorities. However, if you're on a really tight budget, you may have to settle for your top priority and ditch the rest.

The U.S. Department of Transportation mandates tire testing to arrive at traction, temperature and tread wear ratings. Other tire features, such as appearance and warranty, come down to personal preference.

Ranking your priorities is a great first step if you're buying a set of four tires. But if you're buying only two tires, it's a whole new ballgame. In that case, you have to buy two new tires that match the "keeper" tires. Buy new tires with a tread design that's as close as possible to that of the two old tires. Match the traction ratings as well. Mismatching new and old tires can cause uneven braking and instability in turns.

Once you pick out the two new tires, make sure the dealer mounts them on the rear of the vehicle (even if it's front-wheel drive). New rubber on the rear greatly reduces the likelihood of rear-end fishtailing during acceleration and hard stops.

### Noise

You want the most aggressive tread design for best performance in snow. But that same aggressive design will make more noise at highway speeds. If you do a lot of highway driving and noise bothers you, shop for a "touring" style tire. They're designed for a quieter ride.

### Handling/ride comfort

Tires with high tread wear ratings and high-performance tires are usually made with harder rubber, so they're far more responsive to minor steering changes—especially at higher speeds. But the tradeoff is you'll have a harsher ride. If you don't mind losing an occasional dental filling, go for those tires. Otherwise, pick a tire that provides a more comfortable ride.

## Temperature

This rating tells you how fast the tire can run under load while still dissipating heat at an acceptable level. It's a pretty worthless rating for most consumers. An "A" tire will cost more and won't get you any better performance under normal street driving conditions. "B" or "C" tires work fine for most drivers.

## Traction

The traction rating tells you how well the tire's rubber compound generates traction on wet pavement. The ratings are AA, A, B, C. "AA" is the best traction. "C" is the worst. Buy an "AA" tire if you drive in the rain or on snow or ice. If money is tight, drop down to an "A." If you rarely encounter those conditions or want to spend less, drop down to a "B." Only buy a "C" tire if you drive full time on bone-dry roads.

## Tread wear

The tread wear rating gives you a rough idea of how long the tread will last when compared with a test-track "base" tire. So a tire rated "400" should last four times longer than the "100" base tire. But each manufacturer uses its own formula to extrapolate tread wear from the test. So use tread wear ratings to compare different tire models from a single manufacturer. Don't compare tread wear ratings across manufacturers. If you just need new rubber on your commuter clunker and don't expect the vehicle to last long, you can save money by buying a "100" tire. But if you have the cash and want the maximum tread life, buy a "500" (or greater) tire.

# Burglarproof your alloy wheels

**LOCKING NUT KEY**

**LOCKING NUT**

Many late-model vehicles come with alloy wheels and low-profile tires (there's a shorter distance between the rim and the tread). Because the rim rides so close to the pavement, shops are seeing a dramatic increase in the number of bent alloy wheels. Since new factory wheels are expensive, vehicle owners usually opt for a used wheel from a recycling yard. And that's creating a shortage of used alloy wheels.

And the result is ... you guessed it: Alloy wheel theft is on the rise. Police reports show that thieves can strip all four wheels from a vehicle in about five minutes.

If you have alloy wheels, install locking lug nuts to deter the crooks. Locking lug nuts aren't foolproof, but it takes a special socket to remove them, and that slows down the thieves.

A set of four locking nuts are available from any auto parts store. Remove one lug nut from each wheel and install a locking nut in its place. Want more security? Add two per wheel.

# Top ATV and motorcycle repairs

**MEET THE PRO**

**Josh Fischer** is the owner of Josh Fischer's Unlimited Motor Sports Repair in New Prague, MN.

## Tire pressure matters!

Many ATV owners have lost their low-pressure tire gauge and use an auto tire gauge instead. Big mistake! It won't give you an accurate reading. ATV owners often overfill their tires, sometimes by as much as 20 to 30 lbs. That reduces traction and increases the "bounce" factor that could throw you from the machine. In 2006, ATV accidents in the United States resulted in an estimated 882 deaths and 146,600 visits to the emergency room. Don't be the next statistic. Inflate your tires to the proper pressure.

**Fill your tires to the ATV manufacturer's recommended pressure** (it's printed on a label stuck to the machine and in your owner's manual), never to the maximum pressure shown on the tire sidewall.

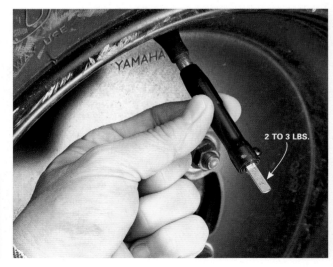

2 TO 3 LBS.

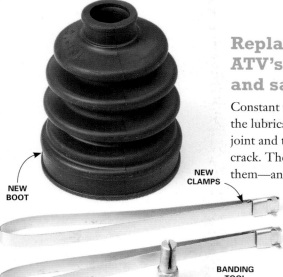

**NEW BOOT**

**NEW CLAMPS**

**BANDING TOOL**

## Replace your ATV's CV boots and save $100

Constant velocity (CV) boots keep the lubricating grease inside the joint and the dirt out—until they crack. Then you have to replace them—and fast! Once they're open to the environment, the grease attracts dirt, which grinds up the metal parts in no time. Instead of replacing an inexpensive boot, you'll be buying the entire joint.

It's easy to check the condition of the CV boots. Just look for fresh grease around the pleats. If you see any, the boot is toast.

Replacing a CV boot is fairly simple maintenance, but you'll have to remove the axle shaft from the machine. To do that, you'll have to jack up the machine and support it with jack stands (see your service manual for jacking and support locations). Then remove the wheel and the axle nut.

Next, remove the axle from the differential. Most axle styles pop out with a crowbar, but some require a special procedure, so refer to your service manual. Service manuals are worth the investment if you plan to do your own work (check the dealer or online for prices and availability).

You can buy individual CV boots, but as long as you have the axle shaft out of the machine, it's best to replace both of them at once. You'll also need a banding tool. Buy one from your local dealer, or buy one online. Once the axle is out, follow the boot replacement procedure shown.

**RETAINING BAND**

**1** Cut the retaining bands with side cutters and slice the old boot lengthwise with a utility knife to remove it. Clean the joint in degreaser until you can see the retaining clip. Compress or expand the C-clip (depending on the style), and pop the joint off the axle.

**2** Soak the disassembled joint in degreaser, scrub the parts with a toothbrush, rinse with clean degreaser and wipe the parts dry. Slide the boot over the axle shaft and crimp the band clamp. Then fill the joint with new grease.

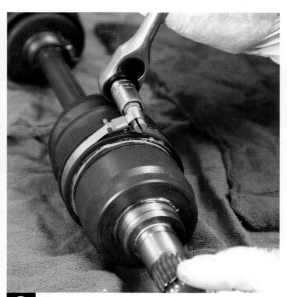

**3** Slip the large end of the boot over the joint. Burp the air out of the boot and crimp the remaining band. Tighten just enough to prevent the boot from rotating.

## Clean and maintain your ATV air filter

Most owners operate their ATVs in dirty conditions. That's fine; they're designed for that. But you have to keep the air filter clean. According to pros, just about every machine that comes in for service has a seriously clogged filter. A dirty filter lowers your gas mileage and causes poor engine performance. Cleaning the filter is messy, but anybody can do it.

Buy an air filter cleaning kit from your dealer. It contains a bottle of cleaning solution and a spray can of filter oil. You'll also need a plastic cleaning tub, rags, a bucket of soapy water and chemical-resistant gloves.

**Remove the foam filter and wipe any debris from the outside. Then dunk the filter in the cleaning solution for the recommended time. Squeeze out the excess solution. Rinse the filter with water and let it dry.**

**Pour fresh oil on the cleaned filter element. Then squeeze the foam to spread the oil into the pores. Reinstall it on the carburetor.**

## Clean and lubricate your motorcycle chain

Cleaning and lubing your motorcycle chain takes only a few minutes and can dramatically increase the life of the chain. Many bike owners do it wrong. Lube needs to be applied to the part of the chain that meshes with the cogs. If you apply it to the outside of the chain, centrifugal force will throw it off before it can penetrate to the chain's innards. A Grunge Brush (sold online) will scrub the crud off the chain (Photo 1).

**1** **Dunk the brush in degreaser and slide it up and down the chain. Rotate the chain and repeat until you've cleaned the entire chain. Rinse with clean degreaser and sponge it dry with a rag.**

**2** **Spray the sprocket side of the chain links, not the outside. Then take the bike for a spin. Centrifugal force will spin the lube deep into the links for complete lubrication.**

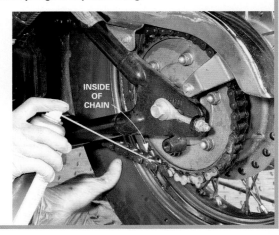

INSIDE OF CHAIN

## Lube clutch and brake cables

Cables last much longer with periodic lubrication. And with replacements costing $20 and up, regular lubrication is just plain smart. Lubricate the cables twice per season. It's easy to do, but you'll need this special lubrication tool for an effective job. Buy it (and a can of spray cable lube) at your dealer or online.

**Disconnect the stud end of the cable from the lever.** Then attach the cable luber. Insert the spray straw into the opening on the luber and inject the lube under pressure to force it into the cable.

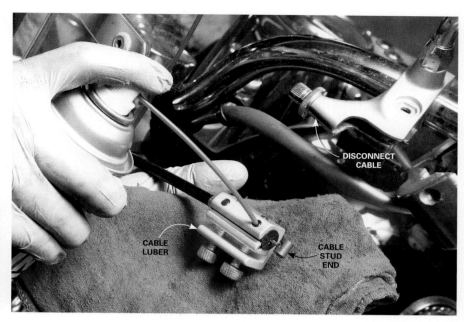

DISCONNECT CABLE

CABLE LUBER

CABLE STUD END

# See more road

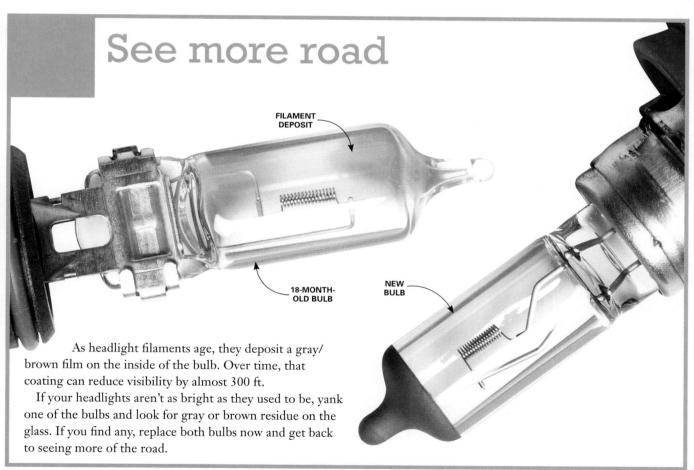

FILAMENT DEPOSIT

18-MONTH-OLD BULB

NEW BULB

As headlight filaments age, they deposit a gray/brown film on the inside of the bulb. Over time, that coating can reduce visibility by almost 300 ft.

If your headlights aren't as bright as they used to be, yank one of the bulbs and look for gray or brown residue on the glass. If you find any, replace both bulbs now and get back to seeing more of the road.

# The art of car cleaning

Detailing your own vehicle saves a lot of money and can even produce better results than a professional job. But let's not kid each other. You can't get pro results with just a bucket of suds, old rags and a bottle of wax. And you can't whip out a pro-level job in just a few hours—it's a full-day commitment. We'll share tips from the pros and steer you away from common mistakes. When you're done, you'll have a vehicle that sparkles inside and out—and you'll be the envy of the neighborhood.

## Wash first—with the right suds

Even though hand dishwashing liquid is a great degreaser, it's not the thing to use on your vehicle's finish. Yes, it removes dirt, grease and old wax. But it also sucks important oils right out of the paint's finish. Use it repeatedly and you shorten the life of your paint job. Instead of dish soap, use a cleaner formulated for vehicles (available at any auto parts store).

Once you've mixed the suds, go one step further—fill a second bucket with clean rinse water. Use it to rinse the wash mitt often (Photo 1). That'll remove most of the road grit from the mitt to prevent scratches. When you're finished, throw the mitt in the washing machine to get it completely clean.

## Pluck the finish

A car hurtling down the road at 60 mph becomes a dartboard for any crud in the air. Your vehicle's clear coat deflects some of it but can hold the sharper grit. Washing removes the surface dirt, but clay-barring is the only way to pluck out the embedded stuff. A clay bar kit includes a lubricating spray and several pieces of synthetic clay. It's time consuming, but trust me, pulling out all those "darts" helps you get a glass-like finish when you're done.

Buy a clay bar kit and prepare the clay (Photo 2). Then spray on the detailing spray lubricant from the kit and wipe the clay over a small section at a time (Photo 3).

**1 RINSE BEFORE YOU RELOAD**
Swish the wash mitt in clean water before you reload it with fresh suds. Dump and refill the rinse bucket with clean water before you start washing the opposite side of the vehicle.

**2 MAKE A CLAY PANCAKE.** Tear a piece of clay into four sections. Flatten one section into a small pancake in the palm of your hand and store the rest in a clean place until you need it.

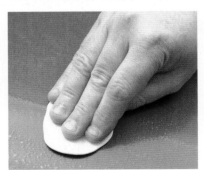

**3 WIPE AND KNEAD.** Rub the clay over the paint with a back-and-forth motion. Fold the clay against itself, knead it and reflatten until the clay turns gray. Then toss it and get a fresh piece.

## Polish the finish

Many car owners confuse polishing with waxing. But they're separate steps. Polishing removes small surface imperfections and scratches and buffs the finish to a shine. Waxing adds more gloss and protects the finish from the elements. Most DIYers skip polishing because they don't want to invest the money for a polisher or the elbow grease for a hand polish. But polishing your vehicle's finish is the key to getting the best gloss (pros would never skip it).

You can buy an entry-level variable-speed dual action (DA) polishing kit (machine and pads) at an auto parts store. Don't confuse these polishers with inexpensive high-speed rotary buffers, which will burn paint if you apply too much pressure or rest on one spot too long. DA polishers are easy to use, paint-friendly and do a great job. Apply a dollop of polish to the pad and wipe the pad across a 2 x 2-ft. area. Then run the polisher (Photo 4). Wipe off the final haze with a micro-fiber cloth.

**4** **POLISH WITH A LIGHT TOUCH. Run the polisher at a slow speed to spread the compound over the entire area. Then boost the speed and let the polisher do the work for you. Quit when there's just a light haze.**

## Get a mirror finish with synthetic wax

Some of you probably swear by carnauba wax. It produces a deep, warm shine. But we prefer the wet-gloss look of the newer synthetic polymer waxes (also known as paint sealant). We tried one of the newest synthetic waxes for this story. It's pricier than other synthetics, but it doesn't leave a white film on plastic or trim—which is a real advantage. Plus, it's really easy to apply (Photo 5).

**5** **APPLY SYNTHETIC WAX. Apply the wax to the foam applicator and rub it into the finish with a swirling motion. Then wipe off the haze with a microfiber towel. Swap in a clean towel as soon as the first one loads up.**

## Move to the interior

Most DIYers start cleaning the interior by shampooing the carpet. That's a mistake—you'll just get it dirty again as you clean the upper surfaces. Instead, start at the top and work your way down. Vacuum the headliner, dash, console and door panels. Then clean all the glass, and dust the nooks and crannies (Photo 6).

Once the dust is gone, clean all the plastic components (dash, console and door panels) with an automotive vinyl cleaner (household cleaners remove vinyl softening agents,

causing premature cracking). Then apply a vinyl protectant to condition the vinyl and protect against UV sun damage. Use a glossy spray if you prefer a wet look, but don't use it on the top portion of the dash (Photo 7).

Finish off the interior by vacuuming and shampooing the upholstery and carpet. But first, raise the nap (Photo 8). Then use spray shampoo and a brush, or rent an extractor machine. Whichever method you choose, don't overdo the soap. Soap residue actually attracts more dirt in the long run.

**6** **SUCK IT UP WHILE YOU DUST.** Sweep the dust out of the cracks with a detailing brush. Catch all that crud right away with your vacuum.

**7** **PROTECT WITHOUT REFLECTION.** Prevent glaring dashboard reflections in your windshield by using a matte-finish vinyl protectant. See the difference in this photo.

**8** **BRUSH AND VACUUM. Use a stiff brush to "raise" the matted carpet and upholstery fibers. That will loosen trapped dirt so you can vacuum it away.**

## De-stink the interior

The two most common car smells are tobacco smoke and that gym-socks "aroma" coming from your A/C ducts. We've got the fixes for both offenders.

To neutralize smoke, buy an aerosol can of automotive smoke odor eliminator (available online). Holding the can 12 to 14 in. away from fabrics, lightly spray the headliner (don't soak it), seats, door panels and carpet. Then spray the rest of the can into the heating system (Photo 9). Leave the windows closed for at least one hour. Your vehicle will smell like baby powder for a while, but that'll go away.

To kill off mold and mildew in your A/C system, buy a can of automotive air conditioner cleaner (sold online). Find the rubber drain tube from the evaporator coil (usually located under the dash) and remove it from the evaporator housing.

Following the product directions, shoot the entire can into the evaporator housing (Photo 10). The foam expands to coat the evaporator coil,

**9** **SPRAY SMOKE NEUTRALIZER. Turn the fan to high and switch the system to recirculate mode ("max. A/C" if you don't have that option). Find the intake opening by holding a tissue near the blower motor. Then spray the mist into the opening.**

killing the stinky culprits. After 15 minutes, turn the blower fan to low and let it run for five minutes. Bye-bye, locker room smell.

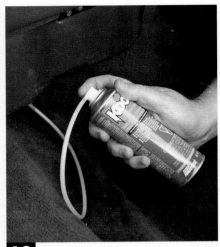

**10** **INJECT MOLD-KILLING FOAM. Thread the plastic hose into your A/C evaporator case. Then shake the can and depress the valve until the can is empty. Replace the drain hose and any other parts you removed.**

## Leather care

This may sound extreme, but if you've got leather upholstery, buy a leather-cleaning kit and keep it in the vehicle. Because if you clean the oops right away, you really increase your chances of a complete cleanup. If you wait, lipstick, ink and dye transfers from clothing (and plastic shopping bags) can set permanently in as little as 24 hours.

Pretreat the leather with a conditioner before you start the stain removal process. Then remove the stain (photo at left).

**11** **APPLY INK REMOVER RIGHT AWAY. Wipe the ink lifter directly on the pretreated leather and rub it in. Let it sit for 30 seconds and wipe it with a clean cloth. Then apply leather cleaner and the leather protection cream.**

## Replace the wiper blades

It's easy to tell when your blades need replacing. Simply press the washer button and see if your blades wipe clean. If they streak, they're toast. The auto parts store will have lots of economy blades, but go with a name brand instead (ANCO, Trico or Bosch). They cost more than economy blades, but their higher-quality rubber wipes better, has better UV protection and lasts longer.

Follow the installation instructions on the package. Be sure you have a firm grip on the wiper arm once you remove the old blade. If it gets away from you, it can hit the windshield with enough force to crack it.

# Selecting the right ball mount

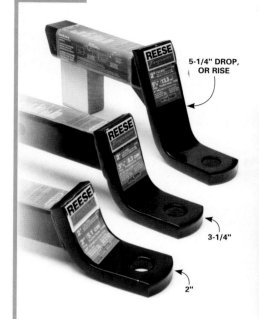

**5-1/4" DROP, OR RISE**

**3-1/4"**

**2"**

Buying the right ball mount for receiver hitches is critical to the safe operation of your trailer. If you install the wrong mount, the weight imbalance may break either the ball mount or the trailer coupling, causing a huge accident that could easily kill people. Follow the measuring instructions below to find the right "drop" or "rise" height.

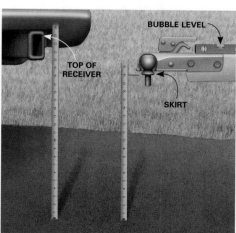

**BUBBLE LEVEL**

**TOP OF RECEIVER**

**SKIRT**

Park the vehicle and the trailer on level ground. Drop the trailer jack and level the tongue with a bubble level. Then lock the proper-size trailer ball into the trailer coupling. Measure from the ground to the skirt of the ball. Then measure from the ground to the top of the vehicle hitch receiver. The difference between the two measurements is the "drop," or "rise." Find the ball mount that's closest.

# Ask the mechanic: Downshifting vs. braking

**Q** **I always downshift as I approach a stop. My buddy says I'm causing extra wear on my engine and clutch. I say I'm saving the brakes. What do you say?**

**A** We say you're a dope. The only time you should downshift to slow down is when you're descending a long hill. Keeping the vehicle in a lower gear slows the vehicle so you brake less often and that prevents brake pad overheating. Aside from that, it's just plain stupid to downshift—period. You're doubling the wear on your clutch. And, since every downshift forces the engine to spin faster, you're causing extra wear on the engine. Brake jobs cost far less than clutch jobs. And the amount of extra brake pad life saved by downshifting is minuscule.

# Buying the right coolant

Most DIYers buy coolant at the auto parts store because the label says it's "universal," meaning it works in all cars. The carmakers disagree. Over the past several years, they've issued service bulletins warning that "universal" coolants are often incompatible with the newer metal alloys and gaskets and seals used in their vehicles. The carmakers aren't saying that just to increase sales of their proprietary coolants; they're seeing real (and expensive) damage caused by these coolants.

If you use the wrong coolant, you won't see the damage for a few years. But when you do, it'll cost you a bundle. So heed the manufacturer's warnings and buy coolant right from the dealer. It'll cost more per gallon (most vehicles only need 2 gallons), but the peace of mind is worth it.

## Figure A: Anatomy of a garage door opener

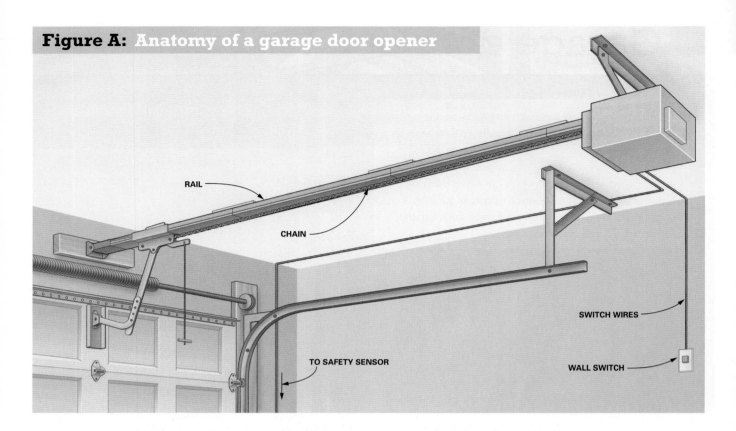

RAIL

CHAIN

SWITCH WIRES

TO SAFETY SENSOR

WALL SWITCH

## Figure B: Carriage assembly

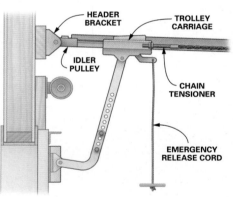

HEADER BRACKET

TROLLEY CARRIAGE

IDLER PULLEY

CHAIN TENSIONER

EMERGENCY RELEASE CORD

## Figure C: Power unit

SHAFT

CHAIN DRIVE GEAR

MAIN DRIVE SOCKET

LIGHT SOCKET

WORM GEAR

CIRCUIT BOARD

MOTOR

## Check your door first

With the door closed, pull the emergency release cord and lift the door to see if it opens and closes smoothly. If it doesn't, the problem is with your tracks, rollers or springs rather than your opener.

## And play it safe

Work with the door down. If the problem is a broken door spring and you pull the emergency release cord while the door is in the raised position, the door could come crashing down.

Unplug the opener. That way, you won't lose a finger if your unsuspecting wife hits the remote button while you're working. Even worse, you could electrocute yourself, in which case you wouldn't be able to blame your wife at all.

## Symptom: The remote works but the wall switch doesn't.

### Fix: Replace the wall switch and wires.

If the remote works but the wall switch doesn't, you may need to replace either the wall switch or the switch wires. To determine whether the switch or the wires are bad, first unscrew the switch from the wall and touch the two wires together (don't worry, the wires are low voltage and won't shock you). If the opener runs, you have a bad switch. If you have an older-model opener, a cheap doorbell button might work. If you have a newer opener that has a light and a locking option on the switch, buy the one designed for your model.

If the opener doesn't run when you touch the wires at the opener, use a small wire and jump those same two wires at the opener terminal. If the opener runs, the wire that connects the opener to the switch is bad. Sometimes the staples that hold the wire to the wall pinch the wire, causing a short. Install 18- to 22-gauge wire.

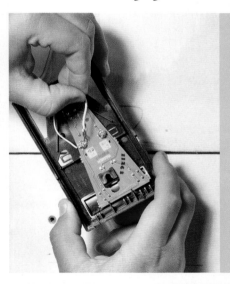

**TEST THE WALL SWITCH.** Unscrew one wire and touch the other terminal with it. If the opener runs, replace the switch.

**TEST THE WIRES.** Jump the two terminals on the back of the opener with a short wire. If the opener runs, replace the wiring.

## Symptom: The wall switch works but the remote doesn't.

### Fix: Replace batteries or buy a new remote or receiver.

If the wall switch works but one of the remotes doesn't, check the batteries first. Still nothing? You may need a new remote. Home centers carry a few models, and you can find a wide selection online.

If you can't find one for your opener model, you can try a universal remote or you can install a new receiver. A receiver replaces the radio frequency the opener uses with its own. A bonus of a new receiver is that it will automatically update older openers to the new rolling code technology, which stops the bad guys from stealing your code. Just plug the new receiver into an outlet close to the opener and run the two wires provided to the same terminals the wall switch is connected to.

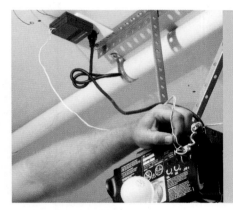

**INSTALL A NEW RECEIVER.** Plug your new receiver into an outlet and run two wires to the opener.

### Where to buy your parts

Go to an authorized online parts dealer or call your local garage door company. Home centers carry some parts, such as photo eye sensors, lubricants and remotes.

## Symptom: The door goes up, but it only goes down when you hold down the wall switch.

### Fix: Align or replace the safety sensor.

If the door goes up but goes down only when you hold down the wall switch, check to see whether the safety sensors are in alignment. The small light on each sensor should be lit up when nothing is between them. Door sensors do go bad, so if no light is showing at all, you may need to replace them. You can save yourself some time by using the existing wires. Also, direct sunlight shining on sensor eyes can make them misbehave.

**WHEN SENSORS GO BAD.** Sensors are brand-specific; buy new ones made for your opener.

## Symptom: You have power to the outlet, but there's no sound or no lights when you push the wall switch and remotes.

### Fix: Replace the circuit board.

If the outlet has power, but there's no sound or no lights when you push the wall switch and remotes, you probably have a bad circuit board. Lightning strikes are the most frequent reason for the demise of a circuit board. The circuit board consists of the entire plastic housing that holds the lightbulb and wire terminals. The part number should be on the board itself.

Replacing a circuit board sounds scary, but it's really quite easy. It will take 10 minutes tops and only requires a 1/4-in. nut driver. Just follow these steps: Remove the light cover, take out the lightbulb, disconnect the switch and safety sensor wires, remove a few screws, unplug the board and you're done. Circuit boards are expensive, so make sure you protect your new one with a surge protector. You can buy an individual outlet surge protector at a home center.

## Symptom: Everything works fine except the lights

### Fix: Replace the light socket.

If the bulbs are OK but don't light up, you probably have a bad light socket. To replace the socket, you'll need to remove the circuit board to get at it. Use the same steps as in "Replace the Circuit Board" (below) to accomplish this.

Once the circuit board is removed, pop out the old socket by depressing the clip that holds it in place. Remove the two wire connections and install the new socket.

Be sure to use a bulb of the correct wattage. Using lightbulbs with a higher wattage than the socket is rated for will cause a socket to fail. Not only is this bad for the socket, but it can also be a fire hazard. If your light cover has turned yellow from heat, you're probably using too strong a bulb.

**REMOVE THE OLD SOCKET.** Remove the circuit board housing to access the light socket. Then unclip the old socket and snap in the new one.

**REMOVE THE CIRCUIT BOARD.** Removing the circuit board is as easy as unscrewing a few screws and disconnecting a couple of plugs.

## Symptom: The trolley carriage moves but the door doesn't open

### Fix: Replace the trolley carriage.

If the trolley carriage moves but the door doesn't open, the culprit is probably a broken trolley carriage. Before you pull the old one off, clamp down the chain to the rail. This will help maintain the location of the chain on the sprocket and speed up reassembly.

Once the chain is secure, separate it from both sides of the trolley. Disconnect the rail from the header bracket and move the rail off to one side. Slide off the old trolley, and slide on the new one. Reattach the chain and adjust the chain tension. Replacing the trolley on a belt drive and replacing it on a screw drive are similar procedures.

**SLIDE ON THE NEW CARRIAGE TROLLEY.**
Leave the rail attached to the opener, and install the new trolley from the other side. Clamp down the chain to make reassembly easier.

**MARK THE CHAIN AND SPROCKET.**
If you have to remove the chain for any reason, mark its location on the sprocket with a marker or wax pencil. The opener will require less adjusting when you put it back together.

## Symptom: The opener makes a grinding noise and the door doesn't move

### Fix: Replace the main drive gear.

**1 PULL OUT THE OLD GEAR.**
The shaft, sprocket and main drive gear should all come out as one piece. This procedure is best performed on a benchtop.

If the opener makes a grinding noise and the door doesn't move, your main drive gear is probably toast. The main drive gear is the plastic gear that comes in direct contact with the worm drive gear on the motor. The main drive gear is the most common component to fail on most openers.

Replacing it is a bit more complicated than the other repairs in this article but still well within the wheelhouse of the average DIYer. There are several components that need to be removed before getting at the gear.

Once you get the gear out, you can remove it from the shaft with a punch, or you can buy a kit that comes with a new shaft. Make sure you lube it all up when you're done. You can buy the gear alone or a complete kit that comes with the shaft.

**2 REMOVE THE GEAR FROM THE SHAFT.**
Support the shaft on a 2x4 and use a punch to drive out the pin that holds the gear in place.

PUNCH

MAIN DRIVE GEAR

2x4

**This heavy-duty aluminum pull-down ladder is a little spendy but worth it for the extra strength and longevity.**

## The simplest way to the attic

Adding a pull-down attic ladder is one of the cheapest, easiest garage upgrades. You're more likely to take advantage of the storage space in your garage if there's an easy way to get up there. Most attic ladders fit between 24-in. on-center trusses so you can install them without any structural changes. Search online for "attic ladder" to see what's available. Wood ladders are cheaper, but aluminum models are sturdier.

## Weekend mechanics love warm floors

Looking for a DIY-friendly heating system for your new garage? Install a PEX radiant in-floor heating system.

PEX tubing carries warm water through the slab, where it releases heat, warming the floor and garage. Since the floor is warm, you can keep the heat set at a lower level and still feel comfortable. Materials for a DIY in-floor heat system cost about $2 to $3 per square foot. A professionally installed system costs about twice this much. And you don't need a boiler. You can use a conventional water heater or an on-demand water heater as a heat source.

To insulate the tubing and prevent heat loss through the slab, install sheets of rigid insulation board under the

## Tall doors prevent Great Goofs

Every month we receive at least one Great Goofs letter from a reader who strapped something to his roof and wrecked the garage door. To avoid that problem, install an 8-ft.-tall garage door rather than the more common 7-ft. size.

If you decide to install an 8-ft. door, you'll have to build the walls at least 9 ft. tall to accommodate it. But tall walls are better anyway. They allow you more room to maneuver 4 x 8-ft. sheets of plywood and 8-ft.-long boards without hitting the ceiling or breaking lightbulbs.

**Install an 8-ft. door if you build a new garage so you can drive in with a load on top without worrying about taking out the garage door.**

tubing and around the edges of the slab. And of course you'll want to insulate the garage walls, ceiling and overhead door, and pay close attention to sealing air leaks around all the doors and windows too. For information on installing and purchasing in-floor heat supplies, consult a PEX supplier.

**Install a PEX in-floor heating system to keep the garage comfortable in cold weather.**

## Make your garage a drive-through

If you have the space, add a second garage door in back so you can park the boat trailer out of sight in the backyard. Plus, there are other benefits to a big back door. For dusty woodworking operations, you can't beat the flow-through ventilation provided by two big garage doors. And if you're planning a backyard get-together, you can open the back garage door and turn your garage into party central.

**Park the boat and trailer out of sight behind the garage with a back door.**

**Plan ahead and frame the opening for the air conditioner sleeve and a dedicated outlet while building the garage.**

**Avoid problems with height restrictions by building shed dormers to make a partial second floor.**

## Shed dormers add second-floor headroom

Local building codes may restrict the height of the roof, but by carefully planning the size of the dormers, you can meet code requirements and still get plenty of headroom on the second floor. Incorporating shed dormers in your plan allows you to gain some of the benefits of a second floor—more headroom and extra windows—without the added hassle of a full second floor. Unfortunately, you can't just throw up trusses. Consult an architect or structural engineer to help work out the framing details. You'll probably end up hand-framing the roof, but don't worry. It's not that hard, and you'll gain a real sense of satisfaction from building it yourself.

## Don't forget the A/C

A through-the-wall A/C unit is a good choice since it doesn't block a window and you can put it wherever you want.

Air conditioning in a garage may seem like a luxury, but there are a lot of advantages. The A/C reduces humidity, which helps keep tools dry and rust-free. Use the dimensions provided with the unit to build the opening in the wall. Add a header over the opening, just as you would if you were putting in a window. Also add a separate 20-amp circuit for power to the A/C.

from heater to objects below. Most infrared heaters are installed at the back of a garage pointed toward the garage door, then aimed downward at a 45-degree angle. They can also be installed between car bays if the garage door opener rail allows and you don't have a tall vehicle.

With a forced-air heater, the installation details aren't as exacting. Most are placed in a corner, near a gas line and an electrical outlet (needed to power the blower). The instructions will indicate the exact spacing required between the unit and the sidewalls or ceiling.

How many Btu you need depends on variables such as the garage size, your climate zone and the temperature you want to work in. A basic rule of thumb for forced-air heaters is 45,000 Btu to heat a two- to 2-1/2- car garage, and 60,000 for a three-car garage. The makers of low-intensity infrared tube heaters say that 30,000 Btu can heat a two- to 2-1/2-car garage, and suggest 50,000 for a three-car garage. Check with a local heating pro or the heater manufacturer for a specific recommendation to fit your needs.

Both heater types need to be vented if powered by natural gas or LP gas. Check the instructions for specific vent pipe sizes and lengths (some models include a vent kit, or you can purchase components separately). Most can be routed either through sidewalls or through the attic and roof.

One other option, if venting or gas-powered heat isn't what you want, is an electric infrared heater. Granted, electric heat may cost you more to run, but check with your local electrical utility to see if it offers any type of rebate or off-peak rates that would make this option more cost-efficient.

INFRARED TUBE HEATER

## Forced-air heater

### PROS
- Less expensive initial cost (50 percent less than comparable infrared heater)

### CONS
- Noisy
- Loses heat quickly if garage door is opened (longer recovery time)
- Heat rises and stratifies (the air is warmer at ceiling, cooler near floor), but you won't notice it with a 7- or 8-ft. ceiling
- Air movement tends to blow airborne dust around (woodworkers will have to shut down unit before staining and finishing projects)

## Low-intensity infrared tube heater

### PROS
- Little noise
- No air movement (dust settles)
- Lower cost to operate
- More uniform heat distribution (no stratification)
- Quicker heat recovery if door is opened/closed (floor and objects retain heat)

### CONS
- Higher initial cost (50 percent more than forced-air)
- Correct location of heater is critical (minimum 7 ft. from floor, 3 ft. from objects). Adequate headroom is also critical, because you can overheat if you're working near the unit.

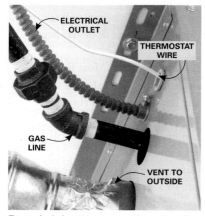

**Forced-air heater connections (rear)**

ELECTRICAL OUTLET
THERMOSTAT WIRE
GAS LINE
VENT TO OUTSIDE

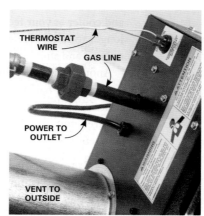

**Infrared heater connections (rear)**

THERMOSTAT WIRE
GAS LINE
POWER TO OUTLET
VENT TO OUTSIDE

# What's the quietest garage door opener?

A belt-drive opener is the quietest. The lifting mechanism is a rubber belt, often steel reinforced, which makes a heck of a lot less noise than a chain drive. It also tends to cost more (but not that much more) than other options. Next quietest is a screw-drive opener, which has few moving parts and requires little maintenance. It's slightly cheaper and slightly easier to install than a belt-drive unit (but both are fairly straightforward for a skilled DIYer). Chain-drive openers are the noisiest and also the least expensive type of opener.

SCREW DRIVE  BELT DRIVE  CHAIN DRIVE

PHOTOS: GENIE

# Cool off your garage

Unvented garages get hot in the summer, and you need to get fresh air movement through the garage to flush out the hot air. The problem is common to virtually every unvented space that gets direct sun exposure. The sun heats the roof, which in turn heats the air inside. But with no outlet for it, the heat simply builds up. There are two good solutions that don't require an open garage door. First, ventilate the roof so the hot air can find an escape route. Begin by (1) cutting in a series of individual vents near the ridge or (2) installing a continuous ridge vent. Couple these with soffit vents (or in some situations, vents along the base of exterior walls) to create a natural airflow where cooler air enters through the low vents and hot air flows out through the high vents. This combination will alleviate much of the heat, especially on breezy days.

The second method—electric-powered blowers or vent fans (3)—is more reliable. This approach guarantees a steady airflow and is the only good solution if your garage has a ceiling (no access to the roof for venting).

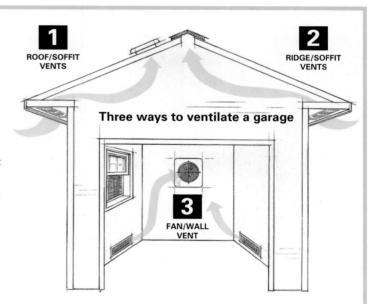

Blowers and vent fans don't have to run all the time. You can control them with a timer that you preset.

Another interesting type is a solar-powered roof vent (available online or at home centers). The fan is powered by a photovoltaic panel. You install this unit near the roof ridge. It'll only work while the sun shines, which is when your garage heats up the most.

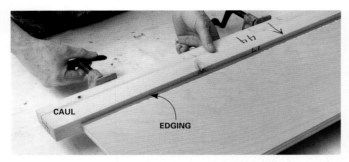

CAUL
EDGING

## One caul instead of many clamps

Thin, flexible parts require lots of clamps to create a consistently tight fit. Or you can use a caul. This solid-wood edging on plywood, for example, would have required a clamp every few inches. But with a stiff caul to spread the clamping force, I was able to use fewer clamps, spaced far apart.

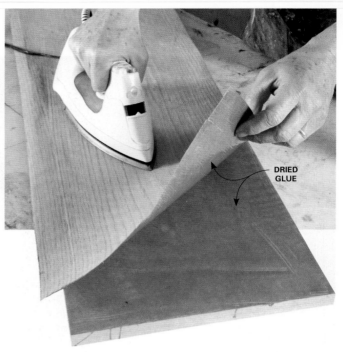

DRIED
GLUE

### Overhead hold-down

Sometimes a 2x4 wedged against overhead joists is better than a clamp. When routing a tabletop, for example, I can rout all the way around without stopping and shifting clamps. This trick is also handy when I need to apply pressure where clamps won't reach: gluing down bubbled veneer in the middle of a large tabletop, for example.

## Iron out veneer-clamping problems

Gluing down veneer is tough. You have to apply flat, even pressure over every square inch. There are fancy tools for this, but for small veneer jobs, try this nifty trick: Apply a thin coat of wood glue to the substrate and the back of your veneer. Let the glue dry. Then position the veneer and use a hot iron (no steam) to reactivate the glue and press it into place. The bond is almost instant and very strong. I love it.

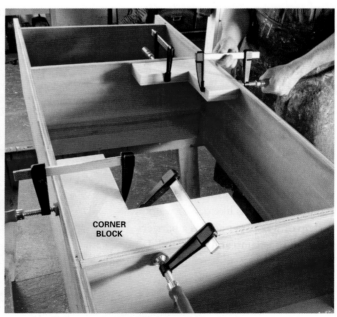

CORNER
BLOCK

## Hold it square

When you're clamping cabinets together, getting a square assembly is half the battle. These simple blocks, made from three layers of 1/2-in. plywood, pull the cabinet into square and keep it there. After the squaring blocks are in place, I use pipe clamps to squeeze the joints tightly together.

## Magnetic clamp pads

Instant on and instant off: You can't beat the convenience of these wooden clamp pads. Best of all, they don't leave oily stains like the plastic ones do. To make mine, I drilled shallow holes in 3/8-in.-thick blocks of softwood. Then I dropped in dabs of epoxy and inserted rare earth magnets. My magnets were 1/2 in. diameter and 1/8 in. thick. Make sure the magnet is flush or slightly below the pad surface.

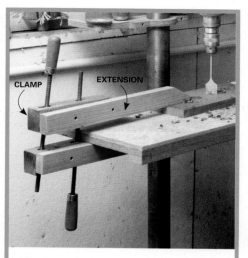

CLAMP    EXTENSION

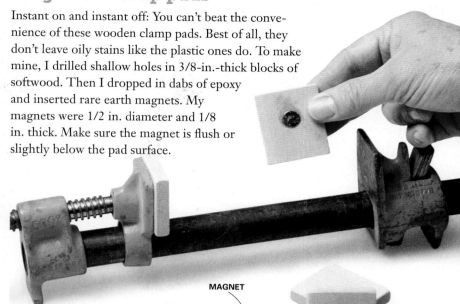

MAGNET

## Long-jaw hand screw

Extend the reach of your hand screw clamps with a couple of lengths of scrap wood. Screw the jaw extensions to the side of your hand screw and away you go. Works great and couldn't be easier.

## Tape those hard-to-clamp jobs

Every woodworker I know occasionally uses masking tape in place of clamps. But I prefer electrical tape because it's stretchy and lets me put the pressure exactly where I need it.

## Slow down

Glue-ups can be a frenzied, nerve-jangling activity. So why not slow things down a bit? Take the edge off your glue-ups with a slow-setting glue such as Titebond's Extend. The extra 10 minutes of open time can be a real lifesaver and nerve-calmer.

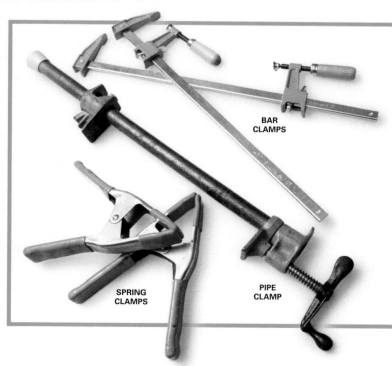

BAR
CLAMPS

SPRING
CLAMPS

PIPE
CLAMP

## Essential clamps for beginning woodworkers (and everyone else)

**Pipe clamps:** Pipe clamps are the everyday, high-pressure workhorses of woodworking. Because you can quickly screw the clamps onto different lengths of pipe, one set of pipe clamps does the same work as several lengths of bar clamps. Buy pipes in 2-, 3- and 4-ft. lengths and you're ready for most situations.
**Bar clamps:** Quicker and easier to use than pipe clamps, light-duty bar clamps are perfect when you need a long reach and moderate pressure.
**Spring clamps:** These are the fastest helpers for holding your work in place or doing light-pressure clamping. They're cheap, too.

## Anti-slip tip

Wet glue is like grease, allowing parts to slide around while you're trying to clamp them. But a few strategically placed brads or pins prevent that frustration. I like to use my 23-gauge pinner because the heads are almost invisible. But a standard brad nailer works, too.

## A dry run is a must-do

Every time I skip this step, I end up regretting my impatience. Don't make the same mistake. Take the time to rehearse your glue-up. That way you'll know all the clamps you need are at hand and there won't be any nasty, unexpected misfits in your joinery to ruin your glue-up and your day.

## Convertible pipe clamps

When you buy pipe for your pipe clamps, also pick up some couplers. That way, you can join pipes to make longer clamps.

COUPLER

## Put the pinch on miter joints

A pair of notched "pinch blocks" puts clamp pressure right on the miter joint. This approach is especially good for picture frames because it lets you deal with one joint at a time rather than all four at once. Position the blocks shy of the mitered ends so you can see how the joint lines up.

45°
NOTCH

## T-stands for everything

I've made a bunch of these T-stands for my shop over the years. I use them on both my workbench and sawhorses for all sorts of things: I set my projects on them when I'm painting and staining, I use them as drying racks when I'm finishing trim boards, I rest cabinets on them when I'm clamping on a face frame, and I lay planks on them for gluing and clamping. They stack together neatly and don't take up a lot of precious shop space.

—*Ken Collier, editor in chief*

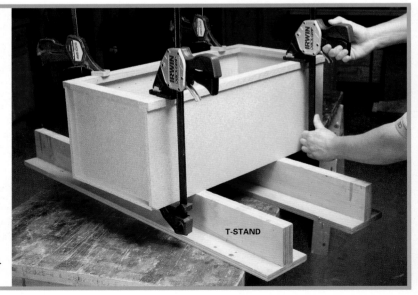

T-STAND

# What's the best wood glue for outdoor furniture?

**MEET THE PRO**

**Bob Behnke**, senior technical specialist at Franklin International, maker of Titebond glues and other products, is a chemist with 30 years of experience in adhesives, sealants and coatings.

According to adhesives expert Bob Behnke, the best all-around outdoor wood glue is a PVA-type glue with at least a Type II ANSI-HPVA rating (such as Titebond II or Gorilla Wood Glue). "A Type II ANSI rating on the label means it's a water-resistant product that can get wet and stay wet for a sustained period, such as a soaking rain, but it will dry out without losing strength."

ANSI ratings signify different levels of water resistance for plywood adhesive. A Type I rating means the bond is waterproof and won't weaken when submerged and exposed to high temperatures. A Type II rating means the bond is water resistant, which is fine for most outdoor projects. Behnke says that with so many glue choices, finding the right glue for a project can be confusing. "Always consider two things: the substrate you're holding together and what the glue needs to do after it's dry."

For example, if you're making a wooden cutting board that's going to go through a dishwasher, you'll need a glue that can not only handle getting wet but can also stand up to the high heat of a dishwasher. In this case, Behnke says, you need a glue with a Type I ANSI rating (such as Titebond III or original Gorilla Glue).

Another consideration is open time (how long you have before the adhesive sets up). Wood glues have distinct differences in open and assembly times, so choose an adhesive based on the project and your working style. If you're confused about which adhesive to use for your project, Behnke suggests you check the technical data sheets or call the manufacturer's hotline and ask an expert.

# Cut narrow strips with a sliding jig

To make a series of identical narrow strips for shelf edging, you don't need to remove the blade guard or move the fence for every cut. Just attach a short strip of wood slightly thinner than the width of the rip cut to the end of a 4-ft. 1x6. Then hold the board against it and push the jig through. The jig keeps your hands well away from the blade, and you can rip as many pieces as you need without ever moving the fence.

To make the jig, attach a 5-in.-long strip of wood, 1/16 in. narrower than the width of the desired rip, to the end of a 1x6 as shown. Basically you're creating a horizontal push stick. Add a handle near the end of the jig to give yourself better control as you run the jig through the saw.

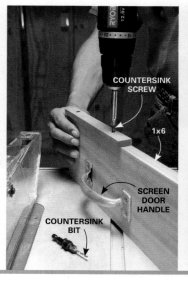

COUNTERSINK SCREW

1x6

SCREEN DOOR HANDLE

COUNTERSINK BIT

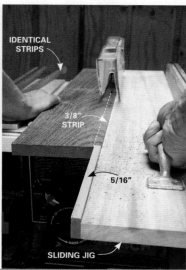

IDENTICAL STRIPS

3/8" STRIP

5/16"

SLIDING JIG

# Replace missing wood with epoxy

If you discover missing veneer, chipped wood or a damaged molding, you can fix it easily with epoxy putty. Kevin showed us the process he uses, and the resulting repair is so realistic that it's hard to spot.

When it's hardened, the epoxy is light-colored and about the density of wood. You can shape, sand and stain it like wood too, so it blends right in. You'll find it at home centers and specialty woodworking stores.

To use this type of epoxy, you slice off a piece with a razor blade or utility knife and knead it in your gloved hand. When the two parts are completely blended to a consistent color and the epoxy putty starts to get sticky, it's ready to use. You'll have about five or 10 minutes to apply the epoxy to the repair before it starts to harden. That's why you should only slice off as much as you can use quickly.

Photo 1 shows how to replace missing veneer. Here are a few things you can do before the putty starts to harden to reduce the amount of sanding and shaping later. First, smooth and shape the epoxy with your finger (Photo 2). Wet it with water first to prevent the epoxy from sticking. Then use the edge of a straightedge razor to scrape the surface almost level with the surrounding veneer. If you're repairing wood with an open grain, like oak, add grain details by making little slices with a razor while the epoxy is soft (Photo 3).

After the epoxy hardens completely, which usually takes a few hours, you can sand and stain the repair. Kevin sticks self-adhesive sandpaper to tongue depressors or craft sticks to make precision sanding blocks (Photo 4) . You can also use spray adhesive or even plain wood glue to attach the sandpaper.

Blend the repair into the surrounding veneer by painting on gel stain to match the color and pattern of the existing grain. You could use stain touch-up markers, but Kevin prefers gel stain because it's thick enough to act like paint, and can be wiped off with a rag dampened in mineral spirits if you goof up or want to start over.

Choose two colors of stain that match the light and dark areas of the wood. Put a dab of both on a scrap of wood and create a range of colors by blending a bit of the two. Now you can use an artist's brush to create the grain (Photo 5). If the sheen of the patch doesn't match the rest of the wood when the stain dries, you can recoat the entire surface with wipe-on finish to even it out.

**1** FILL THE DAMAGE WITH EPOXY. When the epoxy putty is thoroughly mixed, press it into the area to be repaired.

**2** SMOOTH THE PUTTY. Use your wetted finger to smooth the putty. Press the putty until it's level with the surrounding veneer.

**3** ADD WOOD GRAIN. On open-grain wood like this oak, use a razor blade to add grain marks.

**4** SAND THE EPOXY. Sand carefully to avoid removing the surrounding finish. Make a detail sander by gluing sandpaper to a thin strip of wood.

**5** STAIN THE EPOXY TO MATCH. Stain the patch with gel stain to match the color and pattern of the grain. Match the stain color to the light and dark areas of the wood.

## Get rid of dents

You can often get rid of small dents by wetting them. The moisture swells the crushed wood fibers back to their original shape. (You can't fix cuts or gouges this way, though.)

Moisture must penetrate the wood for this to work. Finishes prevent water from penetrating, so Kevin suggests making a bunch of tiny slits with a razor blade to allow the water to penetrate. Use the corner of the blade, and keep the blade parallel to the grain direction. Next, fill the dent with water and wait until it dries. If the dent is less deep but still visible, you can repeat the process. As with most of the repairs we talk about here, the repaired surface may need a coat of wipe-on finish to look its best.

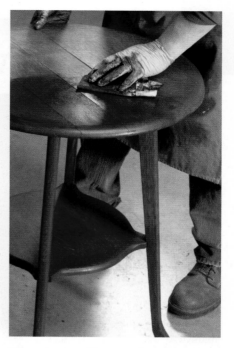

## Fill small cracks

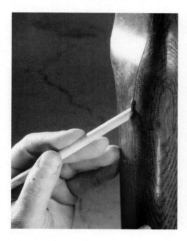

If you find nail holes or tiny cracks after applying the final finish, fill them with colored wax fill sticks, wax repair sticks or fill pencils, found at home centers and paint stores.

The directions tell you to rub the stick over the defect. But Kevin recommends breaking off a chunk and warming it up in your hands. Then shape it to fit the flaw and press it in with a smooth tool. He uses a 3/8-in. dowel with an angle on the end. For cracks, make a thin wafer, slide it into the crack and then work the wax in both directions to fill the crack. Buff with a soft cloth.

## Renew the luster with wipe-on finish

The final step in your restoration project is to wipe on a coat of finish. After you clean your furniture piece and do any necessary repairs and stain touch-up, wiping on a coat of finish will restore the sheen and protect the surface. Any wipe-on finish will work, but Kevin prefers a wipe-on gel urethane (sold at woodworking stores or online). It's thick, so it's easy to put on with a rag. One coat is usually all you need to rejuvenate an existing finish.

To apply wipe-on finish, first put some on a clean rag. Apply it in a swirling motion as you would with car wax. Then wipe off excess finish, going in the direction of the grain. Let the finish dry overnight and you'll be ready to proudly display your furniture restoration project.

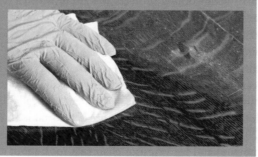

## Restore the color with gel stain

It's amazing what a coat of gel stain can do to restore a tired-looking piece of furniture. The cool part is that you don't need to strip the old finish for this to work. Kevin demonstrated the tip on this round oak table. The finish was worn and faded. He loaded a soft cloth with dark gel stain and worked it into the surface. Then he wiped if off with a clean cloth. It was a surprising transformation. Of course, gel stain won't eliminate dark water stains or cover bad defects, but it will hide fine scratches and color in areas where the finish has worn away.

There are other products, but Kevin prefers gel stain because he finds it easier to control the color and leave a thicker coat if necessary. Also, since it doesn't soak in quite as readily as thinner stains, gel stain is somewhat reversible. Before it dries, you can remove it with mineral spirits if you don't like the results. Gel stains offer some protection, but for a more durable finish or to even out the sheen, let the stain dry overnight and then apply a coat of wipe-on finish as shown above.

My favorite bench plane is my No. 4-1/2 smooth plane. It cost several hundred dollars, but it's worth it.

**BENCH PLANE**

**MEET THE PRO**

**Tom Caspar** started making furniture right out of college in a friend's farm outbuilding, with no electricity. His first love is hand tools. He has a side gig, the Unplugged Workshop, instructing wannabe hand-tool users.

## I love premier hand planes

When a top-quality bench plane is in my hands and I hear the shavings shearing away, then feel the ultra-smooth surface left behind, I'm in shop heaven. I'm connected with the wood in a way no power tool could ever deliver.

Of course, I didn't figure out how to use a plane overnight. It took a long time to learn how to tune the tool, sharpen its blade and push it the right way. Using a plane requires skill earned the hard way, but that's also part of its appeal. When I pick it up, I feel like a pro baseball player going up to bat. The crowd is cheering, the bases are loaded and I'm swinging for the fences.

## My 4 beloved router bits

I have almost 100 router bits of every size and shape. But if NASA allowed me to take only four to a lunar woodworking shop, these are the ones I'd pick.       —*Gary Wentz, senior editor*

### 3/8-in. round-over bit

The 3/8-in. version has the most versatility. Create a simple rounded edge or set the bit a little deeper for a "beaded" edge. The 3/8-in. radius is perfect for forming a "bullnose" on 3/4-in.-thick stock. But since the bearing won't have a flat edge to ride on for the second edge, you'll need a router table.

### Rabbet bit and bearing set

Lots of projects require rabbets, and usually the fastest, simplest way to cut them is with a rabbet bit. Add a set of bearings in assorted sizes and you can cut rabbets of various widths. If you do a lot of woodworking, you'll find other uses for your bearing collection, too.

### 1/16-in. round-over bit

Sharp edges on wood are easy to dent and create a weak spot in finishes like paint or polyurethane. So whatever the project, I like to round edges slightly. A scrap of sandpaper will do the job, but this little bit does it faster and more consistently.

### Pattern bit

When you're cutting shapes, no band saw or jigsaw can match the goof-proof accuracy of a pattern bit; just make a template from MDF and let the bearing guide the bit. Or run the bearing along a straight-edge to clean up a crooked cut on plywood or solid wood. I also have bits with bearings at the bottom, but I use the top-bearing version a lot more.

# Shop tips from a pro

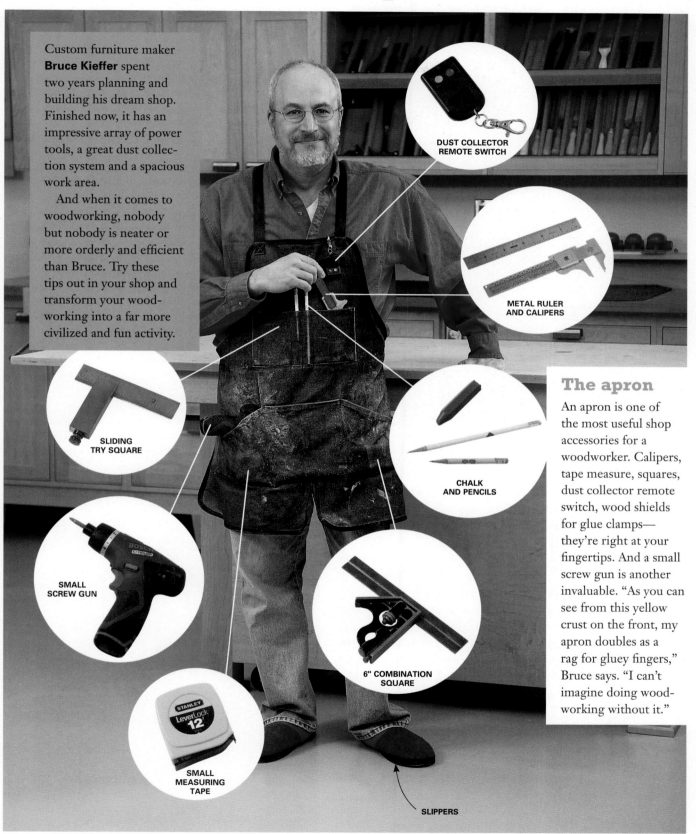

Custom furniture maker **Bruce Kieffer** spent two years planning and building his dream shop. Finished now, it has an impressive array of power tools, a great dust collection system and a spacious work area.

And when it comes to woodworking, nobody but nobody is neater or more orderly and efficient than Bruce. Try these tips out in your shop and transform your woodworking into a far more civilized and fun activity.

**DUST COLLECTOR REMOTE SWITCH**

**METAL RULER AND CALIPERS**

**SLIDING TRY SQUARE**

**SMALL SCREW GUN**

**SMALL MEASURING TAPE**

**6" COMBINATION SQUARE**

**CHALK AND PENCILS**

**SLIPPERS**

## The apron

An apron is one of the most useful shop accessories for a woodworker. Calipers, tape measure, squares, dust collector remote switch, wood shields for glue clamps—they're right at your fingertips. And a small screw gun is another invaluable. "As you can see from this yellow crust on the front, my apron doubles as a rag for gluey fingers," Bruce says. "I can't imagine doing woodworking without it."

## Poly squirter

Want to know how to avoid drips and messes when you apply polyurethane varnish to large surfaces or multiple pieces of trim? Bruce grabs his "high-tech glue bottle poly applicator" (an ordinary squeeze bottle) and squirts narrow beads of finish onto the boards, then rolls them out. The poly flows neatly onto the wood and rarely drips onto the floor. "After practicing a few beads, you can squirt out just the right amount for each board."

## Stay-flat plywood spacers

We were puzzled by the little belted-together blocks that were stuck between pieces of plywood alongside Bruce's lumber rack, and received eye-opening instruction.

"Plywood or other sheet stock can warp, especially if it's stored surface to surface. The blocks separate the sheets so air can circulate on both sides. Flat sheets from the lumberyard says flat this way, no matter how long they're stored," Bruce said. The leather is flexible, so you can use them on any combination of thicknesses of sheet goods.

The blocks are a snap to make from scrap wood and leather. Cut two 1-in.-wide strips of leather (or vinyl or heavy cloth) and space and screw 2-in. x 3/4-in. x 1-in. blocks along the strap. "The air space also keeps them a lot easier to grab when you need to pull one out. For full sheets, use three sets of spacers, one at each end and one in the middle."

— SPACERS

**WEATHER STRIPPING**

## Find-anything hardware drawer

Nothing has a chance to randomly accumulate in Bruce's shop—not in apron pockets, on cabinet shelves, not even in a drawer. There is truly a place for everything, everything goes in its place and no usable area remains empty. One of his hardware drawers is a sublime example.

In this drawer, movable partitions are held in place by strips of foam weather stripping at the front and back. The 44-plus boxes rest on edge, labels up, for easy grabbing and stowing. "I key the labels in on the computer and print them out on sticky labels." Think of never having to wonder where to find a 1-in. drywall screw or a 3/8-in. washer!

Shop for boxes at craft, tackle, office or dollar stores, or online.

## Stay-put driver bits

The only seemingly random—but in fact truly ingenious—setup we spotted during our tour was this: a few magnets stuck to shelf standards inside cabinets with assorted driver bits attached. "They're right there when I need them, and those babies stay *magnetized*!"

**MAGNET**

## High-and-dry plywood

Walking through the garage connected to Bruce's shop, we noticed some riser blocks supporting a few sheets of plywood. "I just cut some 2-in.-wide plywood scraps and screwed them together to form T-blocks and store the plywood over them. If snow, slush or rain sneaks in on the car tires and gets the floor wet, the wood is safe."

**RISER BLOCK**

**6.5-AMP
RECIP SAW**

**LITHIUM-ION CORDLESS
RECIP SAW WITH BATTERY
AND CHARGER**

## Don't write off corded tools

You can't argue with the convenience of cordless tools. But in most cases, the batteries will die long before you've worn out the tool. And in the case of tools requiring heavy power, like circular saws and recip saws, using corded tools delivers more. They'll last forever and cost less.

## Six tips to make your lithium-ion battery last

A lithium-ion battery is expensive. Follow these tips to get the most charge for your ka-ching.

**1 Don't discharge it completely**

Running a lithium-ion battery until it's fully discharged can lead to an early death. Try not to discharge it lower than 20 percent before recharging it. Recharge it when you notice even the slightest drop in performance. Don't wait until your tool has stopped working.

**2 Charge it frequently**

You might have heard that it's best to charge batteries only when they need it. Not true. Frequent charging is good for them, even when they're only partially discharged.

**3 Charge it at the right temperature**

The optimum temperature range for charging lithium-ion batteries is 40 to 85 degrees F. Charging them at extreme temperatures (below 32 degrees F and above 105 degrees F) disturbs the chemical reaction taking place in the cells and can result in a permanent loss of run-time. Keep your charger indoors or in the shade.

**4 Store it partially charged where it's cool (but not freezing)**

Lithium-ion batteries generally last three to five years if stored properly. Extreme temperatures shorten their life span, so don't store them in your truck, garage or freezer. Store them in a cool place, like your basement or refrigerator, at about 40 percent charge. This partial charge keeps the battery and its protection circuit operating during storage.

**5 Buy fresh batteries**

Lithium-ion batteries have a finite life span. They start to slowly degrade right after they're manufactured, so it's important to buy the freshest batteries possible. Check the date code on the battery or packaging to make sure you're buying a fresh battery (instead of one that's been sitting on a distributor's shelf for a year).

**6 Use your batteries frequently**

Don't buy an extra battery and store it for long periods. The battery will degrade more rapidly if it's not used at least every couple of months. If you have two, be sure to use them both.

# Shop for a system, not just a tool

You may be drawn to a drill, but think about future tools before you choose. If the batteries and charger from your first tool can power other tools, you can buy "bare" tools in the future and save a lot of money. Most manufacturers offer a wide variety of tools that accommodate the same battery type. Eighteen-volt tools in particular have a broad range of options.

**Sticking with one voltage size** from a single brand means you'll always have charged batteries and enough chargers.

RYOBI (5)

# Save money with bare tools

Several manufacturers offer bare tools (the tool only), and what you see at home centers is often just a fraction of what's available. Check online for the widest selection.

PORTER-CABLE

# Two batteries are better than one

Buy a kit with two batteries. It's almost always cheaper than buying a cordless tool with one battery and buying a second battery separately.

**Kyle Beria** is a Field Editor and contractor in San Marcos, CA.

## Goes where other tools don't

I use my oscillating tool no less than three times a week, often in tight situations where no other tool will fit. I've used it to cut pipe in cramped quarters, to section out dry rot in a beam where a router or saw couldn't reach, to remove termite-damaged rafter tails my recip saw couldn't reach…. Oscillating tools are *amazing*. After friends borrow mine, they go right out and buy one for themselves.

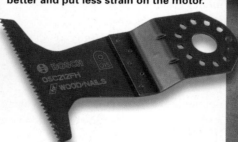

## Extra-wide blades

**Extra-wide blades like this 2-1/2-in. version are perfect for cutting round stuff like pipe because they don't slip off a curved surface the way narrow blades do. For other jobs, narrower blades are usually best; they plunge-cut better and put less strain on the motor.**

## Scraper blades

**Scraper blades come in lots of styles: stiff or flexible, sharp or blunt, straight or offset. The long, thin version shown above is for digging caulk out of joints.**

## Don't burn up the blade

Heat kills blades. Occasionally swing the blade back and forth out of the kerf to clean out dust. And don't press so hard.

## Scrape away gunk

I had stubborn patches of dried construction adhesive on my shop floor. I could have spent a couple of hours on my knees picking away at it with a putty knife. But my oscillating tool— equipped with a scraper blade—sliced it off in no time.

**Charles Crocker** is a Field Editor from Sherman, TX.

## Bring it along—you'll need it

Here's my best oscillating tool tip: No matter what the job, bring it along. When I recently offered to replace a toilet for a friend, I couldn't imagine any need to bring an oscillating tool, but I threw it in my pickup anyway. Glad I did.

Cutting off the corroded hold-down bolts was a lot faster than trying to unscrew them. Ditto for the bolts that fastened the tank to the bowl. The bowl was caulked firmly to the floor, and when I began to lift it, the flooring began to come up too. So I switched to a scraper blade and carefully sliced the caulk joint. Not a bad day's work for a tool I thought I wouldn't need.

**Gary Wentz** is a Senior Editor at *The Family Handyman*.

# What's the best chalk color for outdoor projects?

**MEET THE PRO**

**Lisa Hunter** is the Irwin Tools product manager for marking and layout tools, including chalk, reels, levels and squares.

"Choose your marking chalk color based on two things," says Lisa Hunter of Irwin Tools. "First, think about what sort of permanency you need. How long will the chalk lines be exposed to the elements? Second, decide what color will give the best contrast on the surface."

Marking chalk permanency ratings run on a scale of 0 to 4 (look for the rating on the chalk container). Carpenters who work on a variety of projects generally carry two colors—red and blue—in separate chalk boxes. (It's a bad idea to mix chalks.) They use blue when they need a chalk line that will disappear, such as when they're shingling. The blue chalk will wash right off after the first rain. Red, on the other hand, is pretty permanent. Use it on a roof and it might take years for it to disappear. But if you're laying out walls and you want the lines to stay there even if it rains, red is the way to go.

Indoors, if you're snapping lines on a blue painted wall, consider using violet or white chalk. The chalk will stand out and then dust right off the wall with no residue.

**Permanency ratings**
Marking chalk permanency ratings range from 0 to 4 (look for the rating on the chalk container).

**Permanency ratings**

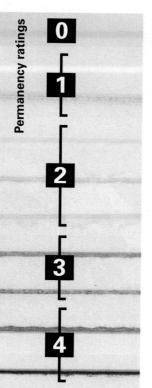

**0: Light violet.** This "dust-off" chalk is good for interior finish work (great for trim carpenters) and on composite decking because it won't stain and wipes off easily. Also good when white is hard to see and as an alternative to blue, which can bleed through indoor paint.

**1: White and blue.** These two are good for general-purpose interior marking and on roofs, siding and paneling when moisture is not an issue.

**2: Fluorescent green, yellow and orange.** These high-visibility chalks can last in wet conditions for two weeks and work well for outdoor rough framing.

**3: Red and black.** These will last for about two months in wet conditions and are often used outdoors for roofing and concrete work.

**4: Indigo blue (not shown), crimson red and midnight black.** These permanent chalks can last forever, even in high-moisture areas.

---

**Cut a recess on the underside of cracked furniture parts. Force glue into the crack, clamp it together and glue plywood into the recess to strengthen the repair.**

to span the recess (see Editor's note, p. 246).

**STRAIGHT BIT**

## Flatten a bowed surface

Whether it's a cupped

## Cut perfect arcs and circles

Often, you can create a curve that's "good enough" using a jigsaw followed by a belt sander. But when an arc or a circle has to be flawless, a router is the perfect tool. Some careful setup is required, but the results are worth it. Mount an oversized base plate on your router (see Editor's note, p. 246) so you can screw it to a 1x4 trammel. Before you start cutting the arc, raise the bit just above the wood. Then position it at the top of the arc and at both ends to make sure the cutting path is correct. When you cut, make shallow passes no more than 1/4 in. deep. Keep the router moving to avoid burn marks. You can use a 1/2-in. or smaller straight bit or a spiral bit to cut arcs. Spiral bits cut faster with less chipping, but they cost about twice as much as standard straight bits. Don't use a spiral bit that's smaller than 3/8 in. diameter. Small spiral bits break easily when you're making deep cuts.

SPIRAL
BIT

PIVOT POINT

TRAMMEL

BASE PLATE

**Connect your router to a trammel and screw the trammel to a block. Cut the arc by making repeated shallow passes with a straight or spiral bit.**

**Round sharp wood edges with a small round-over bit. Run a 1/8-in. round-over bit along door bottoms to prevent splinters and snags on carpet.**

## Ease sharp edges with a round-over bit

Whether you're building furniture or installing trim, avoid leaving sharp edges on wood. They're more likely to chip, splinter or dent with everyday use. Sharp edges also create weak spots in paint and other finishes, leading to cracking and peeling, especially outdoors. Fussy carpenters often ease sharp edges with sandpaper or a file. But a 1/16- or 1/8-in. round-over bit does the job more consistently and neatly. These small-profile bits are difficult to set at the correct cutting depth, so always test the cut on scrap wood first.

1/16"
ROUND-OVER
BIT

1/16"

# Circular saw jigs for table saw-quality cuts

If you have a full-size table saw, you're all set for making plywood cuts. And if you have a portable table saw, you can use it for smaller ripping jobs like making shelving and drawer parts. But you can also do a fine job with only a circular saw fitted with a cabinet-grade, smooth-cutting blade and a couple of simple screw-together jigs made from cheap melamine closet shelving stock.

## Ripping jig

Use an 8-ft. length of 16-in.-wide shelving to build the ripping jig. Draw a line 3 in. from the edge and cut along it with the circular saw. Screw this piece to the larger piece about 3 in. away from one edge, with the factory edge facing the widest section of shelving as shown. Then use that edge as a guide to cut off the melamine. Now it's just a matter of lining up that edge with marks on plywood stock and clamping it to make perfect cuts up to 8 ft. long on any piece of plywood.

3"
3"
FACTORY EDGE
6"

STOP
4"
FACTORY EDGE

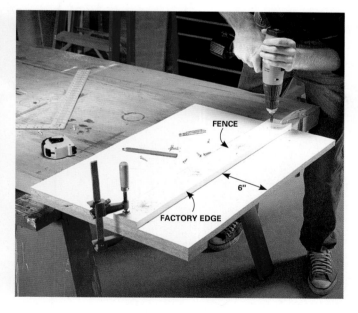

FENCE
6"
FACTORY EDGE

## Crosscutting jig

You can use the ripping jig for crosscutting, too, but this crosscutting jig has the advantage of a stop on the bottom. Push the stop against the plywood, align it with the cutting mark and clamp for quick, accurate crosscuts. Make it from a 4-ft. length of 24-in.-wide melamine shelving (or plywood if wide shelving isn't available). Cut a 4-in.-wide strip for the stop from one end and another 4-in.-wide strip from one edge for the fence. Align the factory edge of the short piece with the factory edge at the other end of the shelving to make the stop. Then clamp and screw the two pieces together while checking alignment with a carpenter's square. Flip the jig over and measure from the long factory edge 6 in. to position and screw the long saw guide as shown. The key with both jigs is to use the straight factory edges for guiding the saw.

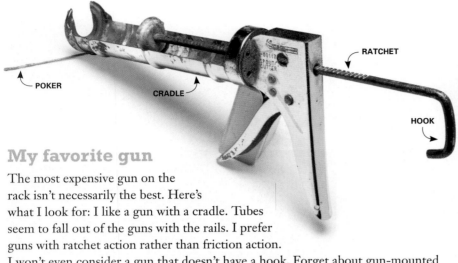

POKER · CRADLE · RATCHET · HOOK

## My favorite gun

The most expensive gun on the rack isn't necessarily the best. Here's what I look for: I like a gun with a cradle. Tubes seem to fall out of the guns with the rails. I prefer guns with ratchet action rather than friction action. I won't even consider a gun that doesn't have a hook. Forget about gun-mounted tube cutters—I've yet to see one of them do a good job. I use a utility knife. And if all other things are equal, buy the gun with the longer tube poker. Some aren't long enough to work on every kind of tube.

## Mark's tooling tips

I'm not a huge fan of tooling. I try to get the bead right the first time. But sometimes it's a necessary evil. Elastomeric and polyurethanes don't tool well—a finger dipped in soapy water is your best bet. Latex is easily tooled, and even if you screw it up, you can wipe it off with a wet rag and start over. The only time I tape off an area is when I'm using a silicone product, and the only time I use a tool other than my finger is when I'm working with tape.

Tooling kits like the one shown above are available at home centers. If you get your bead close to the way you want it, my best advice is to leave it alone. It seems the more I mess with a bead, the uglier it gets.

## Ride the smooth side

When one of the surfaces I'm caulking is rougher than the other, I always try to ride the tip on the smoother surface (the brick mold in this case). If you ride the middle or the rough surface (siding), the caulking will duplicate the bumps, sometimes in an exaggerated way.

## The after-mess

Some tubes have air in them and "burp" at the worst possible moment. Some continue to run after you set them aside. The bottom line: There's going to be cleanup. Use mineral spirits to clean up elastomeric and polyurethane. Latex cleans up great with just a wet rag. Silicone is another story, it seems to get on everything. My only tip for cleaning up silicone is that when it does get all over your gloves (and it will), just consider the waterproofing it provides as a bonus.

## Don't use your wrists

Every golfer knows that the best way to keep a putter moving in a straight line and at a consistent speed is to control it with the upper body. It's the same with caulking. Use your upper body, or even your legs, to move the tube along, not your wrists.

## Salvage a wet tube

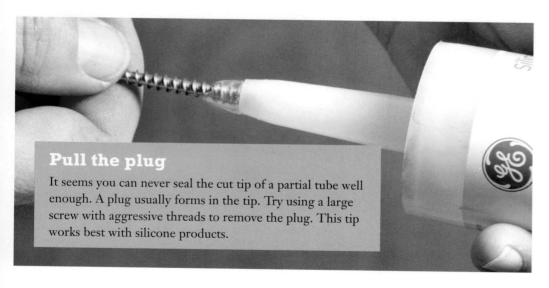

The new guy (it's always the new guy) left the case of caulking out in the rain again. Those soggy tubes are now going to split open under pressure. Before that happens, wrap some duct tape around the tube. I've also salvaged tubes with house-wrap tape, masking tape, stretch wrap, shipping tape—it all works. Just use whatever's handy.

## Pull the plug

It seems you can never seal the cut tip of a partial tube well enough. A plug usually forms in the tip. Try using a large screw with aggressive threads to remove the plug. This tip works best with silicone products.

## Meet in the middle

When you have a long bead to run and you can't get it done in one shot, don't start again where you left off. Instead, start at the other end and meet in the middle. It's hard to continue a bead once you've stopped without creating a glob. I also try to keep the meeting place somewhere other than eye level.

# Three-penny crosscut sled

The best tool for making perfectly square crosscuts isn't a miter saw—it's a table saw. That's why table saws come with a miter gauge. But the truth is, if you want to make perfectly square cuts, you're better off leaving the miter gauge in the rack and building a crosscut sled.

A table saw equipped with a crosscut sled is more accurate and allows you to crosscut material up to 2 ft. wide depending on the size of your saw's table. This sled design is the world's easiest and fastest to build. It's made with scraps you probably have lying around the shop and three pennies you'll find under your sofa cushions!

You'll need a 2 x 2-ft. scrap of 3/4-in. plywood; any type, as long as it's flat. Dig up a 2-ft.-long chunk of super-straight hardwood 1x3. That's it for the wood, but you'll need double-faced tape and 3/4-in. No. 8 flathead screws as well. It's best to have two adjacent factory edges on the plywood so you know you're working with a square corner (see Photo 2). Remove the guard and unplug the saw to build the sled.

## Cut the runner first

Most miter gauge slots on full-size saws are 3/4 in. wide and 3/8 in. deep. Rip a 5/16-in.-thick, 24-in.-long strip off the 1x3 and test the fit in the slot. The strip should slide smoothly with very little play and be slightly below the surface of the saw table. If the strip's too wide, you'll have to hand-sand the edge a bit until you get it to glide smoothly. If you have a surface planer, use that to get perfect dimensions. It's worth spending time on the strip since it's the key to smooth, accurate cuts with the sled. Some saws have slots of different dimensions, and you'll have to custom-make a runner that fits.

## Assemble the parts

Apply double-faced tape to the runner (Photo 1). Keeping one end of the runner even with the saw table edge, set the fence to 23 in. and lower the plywood onto the runner. Keep the plywood tight against the fence and even with the edge

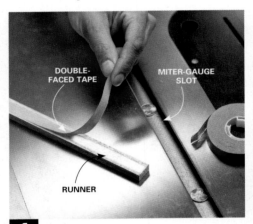

**1** Stick double-faced tape to the runner. Three pennies in the slot will keep the runner slightly above the saw table so it'll stick to the sled's underbelly.

**2** Lower the plywood onto the runner. Be sure to keep the plywood even with the saw table edge and tight against the fence as you lower it into place. If there are any gaps at the fence, your new sled won't give you square cuts.

## Tip

To find wide spots in the runner, rub the slot sides with a pencil. Slide the sled through a few times and the graphite will show you where to file or sand more.

of the table as you lower it into place (Photo 2). Flip the plywood over and then drill four evenly spaced 1/8-in. countersunk pilot holes. Add the screws but don't overtighten them (Photo 3). That will make the runner bulge at the screws and cause binding. Move aside the fence and give the sled a test slide. If the action is a little tight or sticky, hand-sand the runner edges until the action is smooth.

Rip the leftover hardwood down to 2 in. for the sled's fence. Glue and nail the fence to the plywood with 1-1/4-in. brads (Photo 4). If your saw table has a sharp corner at the infeed edge, prop the fence up with the pennies before fastening so it won't catch during sled operation. Run the sled through the blade to true up the outside edge and cut off the excess fence. You're now ready to make perfect crosscuts. But never use the fence while you're using the sled. That's dangerous because even with a sled, a workpiece can get pinched between the blade and the fence and kick back at you.

**3** Screw the runner onto the underside. Don't overtighten the screws—that can cause the runner to bulge and bind in the slot.

**4** Glue and nail the fence to the edge of the plywood. Keep the right edge even with the plywood and don't worry about the left side.

**5** Push the sled through the saw to cut everything square and true. You're ready for business!

## Use a push sled for repetitive cuts of thin strips

One of the big benefits of a table saw is that it can be used to crank out perfectly even strips, safely and easily. Here's how:

Make repetitive cuts of thin strips using a 3/4-in.-thick push sled with an extended end screwed to the back edge. You won't have to remeasure and reset the fence for each cut. Set the saw fence to the width of the sled plus the width of the strips you want to cut. After each pass, slide the workpiece against the sled, and cut again to the same width.

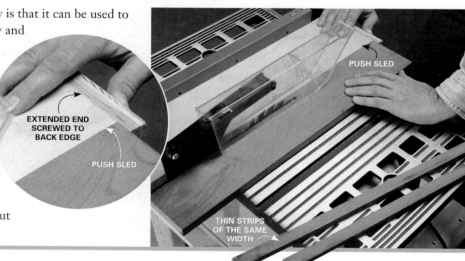

EXTENDED END SCREWED TO BACK EDGE

PUSH SLED

PUSH SLED

THIN STRIPS OF THE SAME WIDTH

# A veteran trimmer reveals his secret weapons

Jerome Worm makes even experienced carpenters feel like beginners. He manages to combine speed and perfection in a way few carpenters can match. That's why we asked for his advice on trim tools. Here's what he told us...

**MEET THE PRO**

**Jerome Worm** has been a trim carpenter for more than 25 years. He has installed thousands of doors and many miles of base and casing, and shows no fear when faced with a curved stair rail or an ornate fireplace surround.

## Match the gun to the trim

### Brad nailer

A brad nailer is a small, lightweight tool that shoots skinny 18-gauge brad nails that are ideal for thin trim. Before you buy, check the maximum brad length. Many models shoot brads ranging from 5/8 in. to 2 in. long, but some max out at 1-1/4 in.

**Easy jam removal**
Whether you're using a finish or a brad nailer, you'll occasionally hit something hard (like a drywall screw) that will cause the gun to jam. This gun lets you clear jams just by opening the magazine. Others have a quick-release nosepiece. Without these options, you have to disassemble the nosepiece.

**Handle exhaust**
Some models exhaust through the handle, away from walls and trim, to avoid staining.

**Don't forget the coupling**
Before you leave the store, check to see if the gun comes with a coupling. Many don't. If it comes with a swivel coupling, buy a non-swivel version. Jerome says he's never met a swivel coupling that didn't leak.

### Finish nailer

For trim that's 3/4 in. thick or more, you need a 15- or 16-gauge finish nailer, which shoots fatter, longer nails (up to 2-1/2 in.). A finish nailer is also good for hanging doors and installing windows and jamb extensions. Before you buy a gun, make sure the nails it requires are widely available—not just at one store at the other end of town.

**Adjustable exhaust**
A gun with a fixed exhaust port can leave oily stains on the wall. An adjustable port lets you aim the exhaust away from the wall.

**Easy depth adjustment**
The gun should countersink nails without driving them so deep that they split the trim or blast right through. The crude way to control depth is to adjust pressure at the compressor. A better way is to get a gun with a depth dial on the nosepiece.

**Angled magazine**
Finish nailers come in two shapes. On some, the magazine is parallel to the handle. On others, it's angled. Angled is the way to go. It's easier to get into tight spots.

POLYURETHANE

## Almost perfect air hose

Polyurethane air hoses are just plain better than rubber or PVC ones. They're just as tough but much lighter (especially nice when you're working from a ladder). Plus, they don't leave those nasty skid marks on walls when you yank them around a corner. The downside is that hoses can be gangly, tangly and hard to roll up.

### Tip

If you buy a small compressor, keep the box and molded foam packaging. You can toss the compressor (and accessories) into your truck bed or back seat and it won't tip over on those hairpin turns.

## Small compressors are big enough

For most trim jobs, there's no reason to lug around a compressor that weighs 40 or 50 lbs. There are lots of options in the 20- to 25-lb. range. And that's big enough to keep up with a one-man trim crew. A little compressor can even power a big framing nailer if you give the compressor a few seconds to catch up after three to five shots.

### Odd-job solution

You'll never know how badly you need an oscillating tool until you try one. It's handy for a litany of projects, including trim. The blade slips nicely behind trim to cut stubborn nails so you can remove trim without splitting it. It also lets you neatly trim shims—none of the slipping or cracking you sometimes get with the utility knife method. Jerome likes to hang a bunch of doors and then run around trimming them off. It's almost fun. The sanding pad is good for trim work, too, especially inside corners and around balusters.

## Pry bar

There are a hundred kinds of pry bars out there, but this is the only one in Jerome's tool pouch. What makes it unique is that the bend at the claw is less than 90 degrees. With that gentle bend, Jerome can slip the claw behind base trim from below and pry off trim without damaging the wall above the trim. This pry bar is also a favorite of painters, so you'll find it at paint stores as well as hardware stores.

260 TOOLS, MATERIALS AND SUPPLIES

## Terrific trim ladder

A 3-ft. ladder is perfect for trim work. That height puts you right where you need to be for crown molding or provides a perfect work surface for jobs like coping. This sturdy aluminum model is a whopping 30 in. wide, so it also makes a great sawhorse or supports scaffold planks. Plus, it has steps on both sides. Find it at tool stores or online.

## Spot sander

Trim carpentry produces sharp edges and splinters that need to be smoothed out one way or another. Some guys like sanding sponges, but Jerome prefers a 100-grit adhesive-backed sanding disc folded in half. It's tougher than regular sandpaper, doesn't eat up valuable tool pouch space and doesn't tear on sharp edges the way sponges do. It's cheap, too.

### What's with the gunk?

It's wood glue that has built up over the years. Jerome closes the bottle by pushing the cap against his pouch. Gross, but efficient.

## Nail sets—it takes two

Jerome always carries a nail set with a small tip. It's good for setting nails with large heads and makes a good center punch to create starter holes for hinge screws. But a small nail set slips off the heads of brads, so Jerome also carries a larger nail set, one with a concave tip that locks onto tiny brad heads. Rubber-coated nail sets give you a better grip and—more important—the bright colors are easy to spot when you leave them lying around.

CONCAVE TIP

# What's the best router bit to buy—A 1/4-in. or 1/2-in.?

If your router takes both shank sizes, go with the beefier 1/2-in. bit. It's not much more expensive, and because it's a thicker, stronger bit (more than four times the mass of a 1/4-in. bit), it will be less prone to breaking, wobbling or vibrating. A more solid bit means a cleaner cut. And the additional mass will also do a better job of dissipating heat and lessen the chance of burning a profile.

If you have a 1/4-in. router that doesn't come with an optional 1/2-in. collet (the part that receives the bit), you may be tempted to buy an adapter so it can take a bigger bit. Don't. It doesn't have the same power and torque to run 1/2-in. bits. Save your 1/4-in. router for light stuff such as profiling edges and laminate work. Buy a router designed to accept 1/2-in. bits for heavier work.

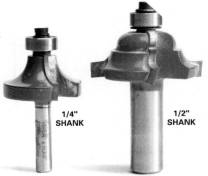

1/4" SHANK   1/2" SHANK

# Trim crooked boards with a plywood straightedge

The prettiest pieces of wood at the lumberyard aren't always straight and smooth. But cleaning up those rough edges isn't difficult. To straighten out a crooked board (with minimum waste), simply screw it solidly to a straight strip of plywood. Then run the board through the saw with the plywood against the fence. Your board will now have a straight, smooth side to hold against the fence when you're ripping it to width.

Plywood straightedges are also handy for ripping tapers. Simply mark the desired taper on your board, align it with the edge of the plywood, screw it in place, and cut.

Make the sliding plywood straightedge from a 1-ft. x 8-ft. strip of 3/4-in. plywood. Attach the rough board to the plywood with screws driven (predrilled) through a waste section. If there's not enough waste area, screw up through the plywood into the rough board and fill the small

WASTE

3/4" x 12" x 96" PLYWOOD

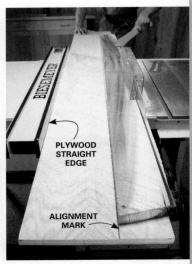

PLYWOOD STRAIGHT EDGE

ALIGNMENT MARK

holes later. Or consider using special surface-mounted hold-down clamps, available from woodworking stores.

# A word about table saw blade guards

Get together with any group of woodworkers and carpenters, and invariably you'll hear gruesome stories about table saw injuries. All the accidents have one thing in common: The blade guard was removed. There is a persistent myth in the carpentry world that blade guards are difficult to work with, but in our experience, it's simply not true. They slide up easily as the wood goes through, and the blade is clearly visible through the plastic. And they save fingers.

# Cut your sanding time in half!

On the list of favorite DIY activities, sanding would be near the bottom, just above dealing with a plugged toilet. But there are ways to speed up this boring chore. In many situations, you can get it over with in half the time—if you know a few tricks.

## Grab a second sander

With two sanders, you can put both hands to work and, well, sand twice as fast—duh! Keep the sanders close together and think of them as a single machine. If your hands wander apart into separate territories, you'll oversand some spots and miss others.

—*Gary Wentz, senior editor*

## Sand faster with suction

Connecting to a vacuum doesn't just cut down on dust. It actually allows your random orbit sander to work faster. Even with the sander's built-in dust collection system, the sander rides on a thin cushion of dust that prevents full contact between the grit and the wood. So by increasing dust removal, a vacuum improves sander efficiency. On some sanders, hooking up to a vacuum doubles the sanding speed.

### Know when to stop

How smooth is smooth enough? We put that question to professional woodworkers—and couldn't get a straight answer. (Woodworkers are notoriously noncommittal.) "It depends ..." was the typical response. Here's what that means:

"Open-grain" woods like oak and walnut have coarse grain lines and a rough texture, so sanding to very fine grits is a waste of time. "Closed-grain" woods like maple and cherry have a smoother, more uniform texture, so they need to be sanded with higher grits before the sanding scratches will disappear.

The finish matters, too. For thick coatings like polyurethane, varnish or lacquer, most of the guys we talked to stop at 150 grit on open-grain woods, 180 on closed. For oil finishes, which don't create much buildup, higher is better; 220 on open grain, 240 on closed.

### Skip a grit

You don't have to use every single grit as you sand your way from coarse to fine. Instead, use every other grit; 80-120-180 or 100-150-220, for example.

## Stop the swirls

For faster hand sanding, you just press harder and move faster. But with a random orbit sander, that strategy will actually slow you down. Too much pressure or speed creates tiny swirling scratches that you'll have to sand out sooner or later (often later, after stain makes them visible). A light touch and patience are the key to avoiding those swirls. Just rest your hand on the sander; don't press. The weight of your arm provides enough pressure. Move at a snail's pace—no more than 1 in. per second. Going that slow feels unnatural and takes some self-discipline. So try this: Stretch out a tape measure along your project and watch the second hand on a clock while you sand. After about 30 seconds (or 30 in.), you'll get used to the right speed.

## Bigger is better*

A 5-in. random orbit sander (left) is the essential sanding tool for any DIYer. If you're a serious woodworker, you'll also love a 6-in. version (right). An extra inch may not seem like it would produce a big jump in sanding speed, but it means almost 45 percent more sandpaper surface, plus a more powerful motor. Sanding faster comes at a price, of course: Six-inch sanders start at about $150 (vs. about $50 for 5-in.), and the larger sanders are a little harder to control, especially on vertical or narrow parts.

### *Sometimes

## Pre-sand your stock

Before cutting up boards for your next project, sand them all with 80 or 100 grit. You might waste a little time sanding areas that will end up as scraps, but you'll come out ahead in the long run. The initial sanding—removing scratches, dents and milling marks—is the heaviest sanding. And if you sand boards before cutting or assembly, you can use the tool that does deep sanding fastest: a belt sander. Sanding whole boards also eliminates the repetition of stopping, starting and setup for individual parts.

## Save your sanity

"Sanding syndrome" is a psychological disorder caused by fussy attention to detail combined with brain-rotting boredom. Symptoms include drooling on the project, hearing voices in the whine of a belt sander and seeing cartoon characters in wood grain patterns. There's no sure way to prevent sanding syndrome, but a little entertainment helps. Earmuffs or earplugs with built-in speakers block out power-tool noise while reducing boredom. Search online for "stereo earmuffs" or "noise isolating earbuds" to browse a huge selection.

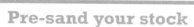

## Stack 'em and sand 'em

"Gang sanding" with a random orbit or belt sander lets you smooth a bunch of edges in one pass. As a bonus, the wider surface prevents the sander from grinding too deep in one spot or tilting and rounding over the edges. This trick also makes sanding a self-correcting process; all the parts will end up exactly the same.

## Sand across the grain

The first commandment of sanding: Sand with the grain. But when you have a lot of wood to grind off, break that rule and run your belt sander diagonally across the grain (at about 45 degrees). Instead of scratching away at the wood fibers, the belt will rip them out. It's incredibly fast—and dangerous. Be careful not to gouge too deep, and expect to follow up with some heavy sanding to smooth the "plow marks" left behind.

## Premium paper works faster

Better sandpaper has sharper particles of grit, which bite into wood faster. And not just a little faster—a lot faster. Premium paper removes wood at two or three times the rate of standard paper. It costs a bit more, but the grit stays sharp much longer, so you actually save money, whether you're using sheets, discs or belts. Norton 3X, 3M SandBlaster and Gator Ultra Power are three common lines.

## Prevent glue spots

Glue spots are cruel. When you think all the tedious sanding is done and you apply stain or even varnish, they'll appear like bleached smudges. Getting rid of them means more sanding. On a flat surface, glue drips aren't a big deal. You'll remove them automatically as you run through the normal sanding process. But in hard-to-sand spots like inside corners, prevention is the best strategy, and a little masking tape will save you a lot of hassle.

# Cutting curves

If you grab your jigsaw whenever there's a curve to cut, next time try your circular saw instead. It'll do a sterling job for long, gradual curves in a fraction of the time a jigsaw will. Plus, you'll get a much smoother cut. If you're cutting plywood, set the saw to cut just deep enough to cut through the wood. The deeper the blade, the harder it'll be to make the cut because it'll get bound in the kerf. If you're cutting thicker material, cut halfway through on the first pass and then make a second, deeper final cut following the original cut. This trick isn't for super-tight curves, though. If it's too hard to push the saw through the cut, you'll just have to go with the jigsaw—sorry.

## Bump and shave

**Bump ...**

**... then shave**

When you need to trim just a smidgen off a board or molding, try this: Lower the blade of your miter saw and press the end of the workpiece against it. Then raise the blade, pull the trigger and cut. Depending on how hard you pushed against the blade, you'll shave off from 1/16 to 1/32 in. Once you get the feel of it, you'll be able to adjust the pressure and the width of the shave.

## Use a half-fence for complicated grain

Wood with knots or wavy grain and wood that has been dried unevenly will often warp badly as you rip it. If the halves bend outward, one will push against the fence and cause burn marks, a kickback or an uneven cut. If this begins to happen, clamp a smooth, straight length of 3/4-in. wood against the fence, ending at the center of the saw blade. This half-fence gives the trapped

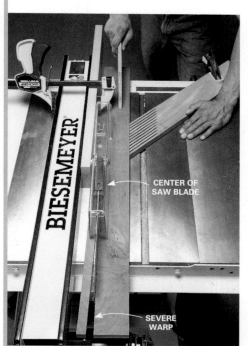

CENTER OF SAW BLADE

SEVERE WARP

piece (the section between the blade and the fence) room to bend without pushing back against the blade. Keep several push sticks on hand so you can work around the clamps and complete the cut smoothly.

If the two halves bend toward each other as they're being cut—pinching the splitter at the end of the blade guard—turn the saw off and wedge a shim between the two pieces. Then complete the cut.

## Chapter Sixteen

# DOORS, WINDOWS, BASEBOARD AND TRIM

# Perfect window trim

## You don't even need a tape measure!

Like most veteran carpenters, I've trimmed hundreds—maybe even thousands—of windows. So trimming out a window is second nature to me. But when I see windows that were trimmed by a rookie or watched rookies trim a window, I realize it's not quite as easy for others.

The truth is, most carpenters don't even use a tape measure. Nope, it's all done by eye, using a sharp pencil, a miter saw and an 18-gauge nailer. I'll show you how to pull off a window trim job that'll look every bit as good as a trim guy's—without hours of frustration. We're working with standard trim, between 3/8 and1/2 in. thick—the types you'll find at any home center.

—*Travis Larson, senior editor*

## 1 Mark the length

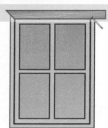

Cut a 45-degree angle on one end of the trim and hold it so the short end of the angle overhangs halfway, or 3/8 in., onto the jamb. Then mark the other end flush with the inside of the jamb. That'll give you a 3/16-in. reveal.

## 2 Get the spacing right

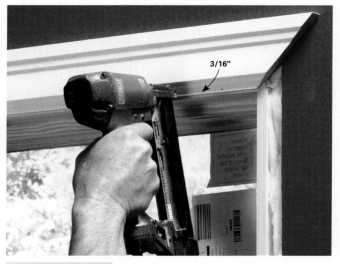

Hold the trim 3/16 in. away from the jamb at both ends and along the base of the trim. Nail the trim to the jamb with 1-in. brads spaced about every 6 in. Nail the thick part of the trim to the framing with 2-in. brads.

## 3 Check the fit, then cut to length

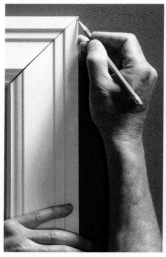

Cut a 45-degree miter on one end of the trim board. Adjust the miter as needed for a perfect fit. Then scribe the cut length 3/16 in. past the bottom of the jamb. Nail the trim onto the jamb first and then to the framing, as you did with the top piece.

## 4 Glue and pin for a solid miter

Glue and pin together the miter from both directions with 1-in. brads. Wipe the glue squeeze-out with a damp rag right away.

## 5  Trim the other side

Repeat all the same steps on the other side of the window, fitting first the top miter, and then marking and cutting the bottom one. Nail the trim into place.

## 6  Fit the first bottom miter

Cut an overly long piece of trim and cut a miter on one end. Overlap the far end to check the fit. Mark and recut the miter as needed for a perfect fit.

## 7  Fit the opposite miter

Cut a test miter on the other end and check the fit. Adjust the miter as necessary until you're satisfied with the joint.

## 8  Scribe for length

With the saw still set for the previous miter, flip the trim over and scribe the length for the end that has that miter. Transfer the mark to the front side and make the cut.

# Dealing with problem drywall

If you have drywall that's "proud" (sticking out past the jamb) or recessed behind the jamb, you have to deal with it before trimming or the trim won't lie flat. Here's what to do:

**If the drywall projects past the jamb 1/8 in. or less,** and is close to the window jamb, just chamfer the edge with a utility knife. Check to see if you've pared off enough drywall by holding a chunk of trim against the drywall and jamb. If it rocks and won't sit flush against both surfaces, carve out some more.

**If the drywall's recessed behind the jamb,** don't nail the trim to the framing at first. Only nail it to the jamb and pin the mitered corners together. After the window is trimmed, slide shims behind each nail location to hold out the trim while nailing, then cut off the shims. Caulk the perimeter of the trim to eliminate gaps before painting.

**If the drywall projects more than 1/8 in.,** crush in the drywall with a hammer. Just be sure the crushed area will be covered by trim. In this situation, your miters won't be 45 degrees. You may need to go as low as 44 degrees to get a tight miter.

## Avoiding trim-induced headaches

Here are a few tips to help you avoid a few trim hassles:

- Whenever you can, cut with the thick side of the trim against the miter saw fence. You'll be less likely to tear out the narrow tapered edge that way.

- Cutting right up to the pencil mark almost always leaves pieces too long, so remove the pencil line with the blade. You'll most likely still have to shave off more.
- Sneak up on cuts by starting long and dipping

the saw blade into the wood while you work your way to the cutoff mark.
- Trim out the biggest windows first. That way, you can reuse miscuts for the smaller windows and not run out of material.

- When nailing 3/4-in.-thick trim, use 15-gauge 2-1/2-in. nails for the framing and 18-gauge 2-in. brads for nailing to the jamb.
- To prevent splitting, avoid nailing closer than 2 in. from the ends.

# Real-world tips for hanging doors

You already know the standard approach to hanging a door: Set it in the rough opening, then level, shim and nail it. This traditional approach works fine in a perfect world where walls are always plumb, floors are level and you have plenty of time to fuss with the fit. But in the real world, some nonstandard tricks can help you finish the job faster and better.

SHIMS

HINGE LOCATION MARK

## Shim before the door goes in

The usual method of holding the door frame in place while you shim behind the hinge side is awkward. It's a lot easier to shim the hinge side of the rough opening before you put in the door frame. After that, it's a simple job to set the frame in place, screw or nail it to the shims, and then shim the strike side. Measure the width of the rough opening before you start shimming to see how much shim space is available. Usually the rough opening allows for about 1/2 in. of shimming on each side of the frame. If the rough opening is extra-wide, you can use fewer shims by tacking scraps of 1/2-in. plywood at the hinge locations first and then add shims to plumb the jamb.

**SHIM THE EASY WAY.** Mark the location of the hinges on the drywall alongside the opening so you'll know where to place the shims. Place shims at the top and bottom hinge locations using a long level or a straight board and a short level. Then add the center shims.

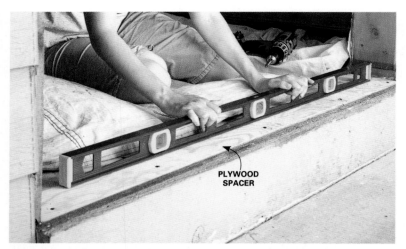

**AVOID CLEARANCE PROBLEMS.** Screw a strip of plywood to the bottom of the rough opening to raise the door and prevent it from rubbing on the floor inside.

PLYWOOD SPACER

## Make sure your exterior door clears the rug

Most of the time, you can simply set your new exterior door frame directly on the subfloor and the door will easily clear carpeting or a throw rug. But if you're replacing an old door with a thick sill, or if the floor will be built up with tile, thick carpet or an extra layer of wood, you could have a problem. And there's no easy solution after the door is installed. You can't simply trim the bottom, because then the door won't seal against the sill. To avoid this problem, add a spacer under the door before you install it. The key is to determine where the top of the tile, carpet or throw rug will be, and then raise the door frame to leave about a 1/2-in. space under the door (photo left).

## Set interior jambs on spacers

If you set the doorjambs directly on the subfloor, there's a good chance the door will rub against the carpet later. Of course, you can cut off the bottom of the doors, but it's easy to avoid this extra work by planning ahead. Find out the thickness of the finish floor and then calculate where the bottom of the door will be. Plan the installation so there will be about 1/2 to 3/4 in. of space under the door. Usually setting the doorjambs on scraps of 3/8- to 1/2-in.-thick trim will put the door at the correct height.

**HIDE THE SCREWS.** Pull back or remove the weather strip on the latch side of the door frame and drive screws where they'll be hidden.

WEATHER STRIP

3" SCREW

EXTERIOR DOOR-JAMB

SPACER

SIDE JAMB

**AVOID TRIMMING DOOR BOTTOMS.** Raise doorjambs with scraps of trim to make sure the door will clear the carpeting.

## Hidden screws make exterior doors stronger

There are many benefits to using screws rather than nails to install exterior doors. They can be adjusted and won't easily pull out or loosen. But you don't want to leave the painter with the task of filling big, ugly screw holes. The trick is to hide the screws under the weather stripping on the latch side. On the hinge side, you can simply replace one screw in each hinge with a matching 3-in.-long screw. Always start by drilling a clearance hole that allows the screw to slide freely in and out of the hole. This ensures the screw will pull the jamb tight to the shims, and allows for adjustment if needed. Don't let the spinning screw rub against the weather strip—it will slice right through. I know this from bitter experience.

NOT PLUMB

## Tune up the rough opening

Twisted or out-of-plumb rough openings wreak havoc with door installations. If you install the jambs to follow the walls, the door is likely to swing open or shut on its own. On the other hand, if you plumb the jambs against the out-of-plumb rough opening, the trim will be hard to install.

As long as the bottom of the wall isn't held in place by flooring, there's a simple solution. Just move the studs on both sides of the opening back to plumb. Don't think you can do this with your trim hammer, though. You'll need a maul or a sledgehammer.

**1 CHECK FOR PLUMB.**
Check both sides of the door opening. If they're more than 1/4 in. out of plumb, adjust them before you install the door.

**2 NUDGE THE WALL.**
Protect the wall with a 2x4 scrap while you move the bottom of the wall over with a sledgehammer. When the wall is plumb, toe-screw the bottom plate to the floor to hold it in place.

## How one pro installs a door in four easy steps

**John Schumacher,** owner of Millwork Specialties Ltd. in Minnesota, has been installing doors and millwork for more than 20 years. He's learned to avoid callbacks by doing the job right the first time. Here's his door installation method in a nutshell.

**1. Plumb the hinge jamb.** The hinge side of the door has to be plumb or the door will swing open or closed on its own. Start by shimming the hinge side of the rough opening. First make marks to indicate the centers of the hinges. Then use a long level or a long, straight board along with a short level to plumb the shims. Tack a pair of tapered shims at the top hinge. Then install the bottom shims and finally fill in the middle.

**2. Screw the hinge-side jamb to the stud.** Remove the door from the frame and set it aside. Remove the hinge leaves from the jamb. Set the door frame in the opening with the jamb resting on the finished floor or on a spacer. Drive 3-in. screws through the jamb where they'll be hidden by the screws.

**3. Adjust the gap along the top.** Slide shims between the floor and the latch-side jamb until the head jamb is level. Now reinstall the door hinges and the door. Adjust the shims under the latch-side jamb until the gap between the top of the door and the top jamb is even.

**4. Shim and nail the latch-side jamb.** Shim behind the latch-side jamb to make an even gap between the door and the jamb. Usually three or four sets of shims, evenly spaced along the jamb, are plenty. Drive two finish nails into each set of shims to hold the jamb in place. Cut off the protruding shims with an oscillating tool or a utility knife.

## Trim the bottom to level the top

Old houses are notorious for having sloping floors. Even some newer houses settle in unexpected ways. If you don't cut the jamb to compensate for the out-of-level floor, you could have a problem getting an even space between the top of the door and the head jamb. This is critical if you're installing a door over existing flooring where the jambs have to fit tightly to the floor. Photos 1 and 2 show how to trim the jambs to fit a sloping floor.

**1** **CHECK WITH A LEVEL.**
**Level across the opening and shim up one side until the bubble is centered. The distance between the level and the floor tells you how much to cut off the jamb.**

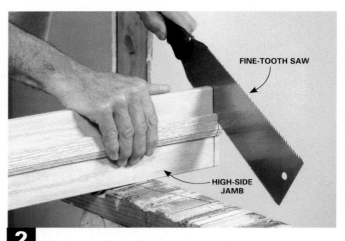

FINE-TOOTH SAW

HIGH-SIDE JAMB

**2** **CUT THE HIGH-SIDE JAMB.**
**Trim the jamb with a fine-tooth saw. A "Japanese"-style pull saw cuts fast and leaves a clean cut.**

## Hide screws behind the hinges

Screws are better for securing the hinge jamb because nails can work loose. You can easily replace one of the short hinge screws with a long screw, but it can be difficult to find a strong screw that matches the other screws. Here's a trick we learned: Hide the screw behind the hinge. It only takes a minute or two to remove all the hinges and gain access to this area. Then you can drive a self-drilling screw through the jamb with ease. Make sure the jamb is straight and plumb before you reinstall the hinges.

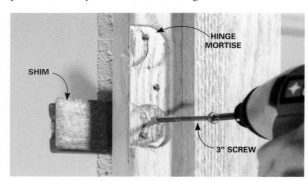

HINGE MORTISE

SHIM

3" SCREW

**USE SCREWS, NOT NAILS.**
**Screw through the jamb in the hinge mortise. The screws will hold better than nails and will be hidden by the hinges.**

### Troubleshooting tips

**Door won't latch**
Out-of-plumb jambs or a warped door can cause this. If the door won't latch because it's hitting the latch-side stop on the top or bottom, the fix is to move the stop. If it only needs a little adjustment, you can just tap it over with a hammer and a block of wood. Otherwise, pry it off carefully, and with the door closed and latched, reinstall it against the door.

**Door binds and resists closing**
If the door isn't rubbing against the jamb, but there's tension when you try to close it, then it's binding on the hinge jamb. Usually this means you haven't shimmed correctly and the jamb isn't at a right angle to the wall. Fix this problem by adjusting the hinge-side shims to twist the jamb back to a right angle with the wall.

# Tight miters

There are perfect miters—and then there are miters that have been tweaked to look perfect. You can learn how to do both with the right tools, a few pro tips and a good dose of patience.

## Make sure your blade is sharp

Choosing the right blade for your miter saw, and making sure it's sharp, are crucial for cutting tight-fitting miters. You can't cut perfect miters with a dull blade, one with too few teeth or one that's designed for ripping. Check your blade for sharpness by cutting a 45-degree miter on a 1x3 or larger piece of oak or other hardwood (photo at right). If the blade cuts smoothly with very little pressure and leaves a clean, almost shiny cut with no burn marks, it's sharp enough to cut good miters. When you check your blade or shop for a new one, here's what to look for.

**TEAR-OUT**

**DULL BLADE CUT**

**SHARP BLADE CUT**

**If the cut end of the miter looks scorched, rough or chipped, have the blade sharpened or buy a new one.**

**SHARP BLADE**

**DULL BLADE**

First, it should be labeled as a "trim" or "fine crosscutting" blade. A 10-in. blade should have at least 40 teeth, a 12-in. blade at least 60. If the blade is for a sliding miter saw, be sure the teeth have a hook angle of zero to negative five degrees. Teeth with a neutral or negative hook angle are less aggressive and safer for sliding miter saws. Expect to spend a little more money for a carbide-tipped blade that'll perform well and last.

## Tweak the cut

Even on perfectly square corners, 45-degree angles won't always yield perfect miters. Wall corners can be built up with corner bead and compound, and window and door frames can slightly protrude or be recessed behind surrounding drywall. That's when you have to start fiddling with the angles to get a tight fit.

In most cases, you'll be making adjustments as small as a quarter of a degree. If the gap is small (about 1/16 in.), recut one side of the miter (Photo 2). If the gap is larger, you'll have to recut both boards or the trim profiles won't line up.

**1** Cut the moldings at a 45-degree angle. Hold the miter together to see how it fits. If there's a gap, estimate how much you'll have to trim off to close the gap and make a mark where the moldings touch.

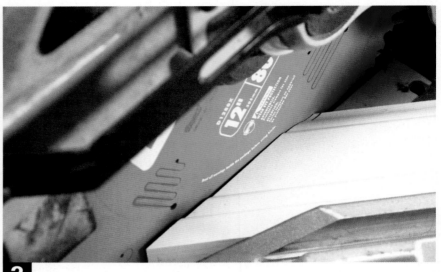

**2** Push the trim tight to the blade and adjust the angle of the saw until the gap equals the amount you need to trim off the miter.

## Glue and sand for a seamless fit

Here's a trick to make miters look great, but it only works if you're installing raw trim that will get finished after installation. It's easy. Glue the joint, then sand it smooth.

The sawdust from sanding will mix with the glue to fill any small gaps. Sanding the miter will also even out any slight level differences and make the job look more professional. Don't

try to fill large gaps, especially in trim that'll be stained. Glue-filled gaps absorb stain differently than the surrounding wood and will stick out like a sore thumb.

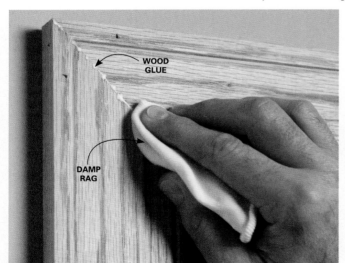

WOOD GLUE

DAMP RAG

**1** Apply a thin layer of wood glue to the end grain of each piece before you assemble them. Use a damp (not wet) cloth to remove excess glue from the joint.

120-GRIT SANDPAPER

**2** Sand over the miter with a small piece of 120-grit sandpaper. Sand across the joint and finish up by carefully sanding out any cross-grain sanding marks by moving the paper with the grain from both directions.

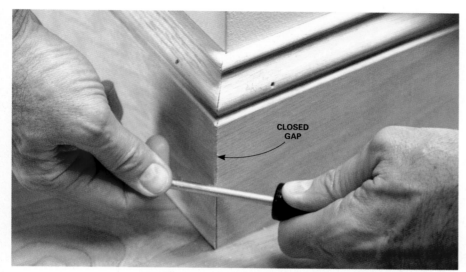

Hide a slight gap in an outside corner miter by rubbing it with the shank of a screwdriver or nail set. This will bend the wood fibers in and slightly round the corner.

## Burnish the corner

You can make less-than-perfect miters on outside corners look their best with this tip. If your baseboard or crown molding has a slight gap in the outside corner miter, you can hide it by rubbing the tip of the miter with the shank of a screwdriver or nail set. The bent fibers will disguise the gap, and the slightly rounded corner will be less likely to get chipped or damaged.

The best way to prevent this problem is to cut your outside corner miters about 1 degree sharper than the actual angle so the tips of the miters touch. This will leave a tiny gap at the back of the miter where it's barely noticeable.

## Fit one miter at a time

Whether you're edge-banding a tabletop as shown here, trimming out a window or door, or installing baseboard, it's always best to fit one miter at a time whenever possible. Start with a scrap of molding with a miter cut on it as a test piece. When you have the first miter fitting perfectly, mark the next one. Then cut and fit the adjoining miter before you nail either piece. For edge banding, work your way around the project using the same process for each edge piece.

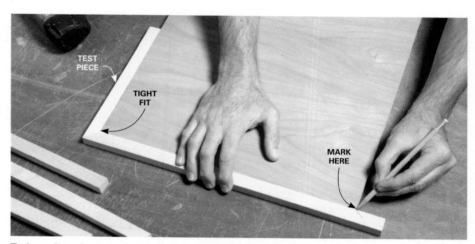

Tack a mitered scrap of edging to one side. Use it to hold the first edging piece in position. Hold the mitered end tight to the mitered scrap while you mark for the opposite miter.

Cut test pieces to check the angle of the miter.

## Guess and test

There are all kinds of ways to find odd angles (see p. 259 for one method), but most carpenters simply make a guess and then cut a pair of test pieces to see how lucky they are. The angle of these two walls looks to be about 30 degrees. Divide 30 by two to arrive at the miter angle, and cut a couple of scraps at 15 degrees. Here there's a gap in front, so increase the angle slightly and recut the scraps at 16 degrees. When you've zeroed in on the correct angle, the scraps will fit perfectly, and you can then cut the actual moldings.

# Coping tight joints

Because inside corners are rarely square, simply butting two mitered pieces into the corner almost always looks lousy. The only foolproof method for great-looking inside corners is cutting a coped joint. This age-old carpenter's trick involves cutting the profile on the end of one molding and fitting it against another like pieces of a puzzle. The resulting joint is easy to file and sand for a perfect fit, even on out-of-square corners. It looks difficult, but don't worry—with a coping saw, a few special techniques and a little practice, you'll be cutting perfect copes in no time.

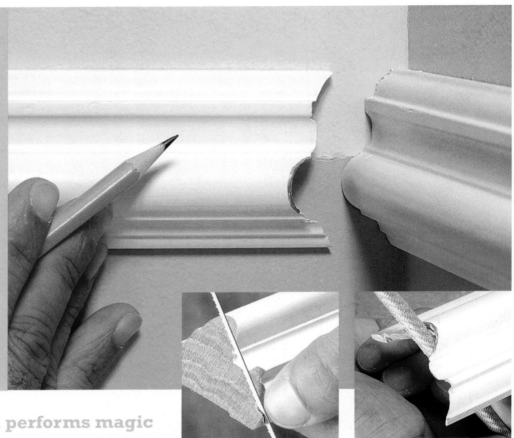

## A simple hand tool performs magic

Copes are sawed with—you guessed it—a coping saw. You don't need to spend a lot of money on one, however. The basic version available at hardware stores, home centers and lumberyards works great. Pick up an assortment of blades. Use fine-tooth blades for thin material and intricate cuts. A blade with 20 teeth per inch works well for most copes. Some carpenters prefer to cut copes with a jigsaw. If you own a jigsaw, install a fine-tooth blade (the narrow type used for cutting curves) and give it a try.

A coping saw is designed to cut on the pull stroke (with the blade's teeth facing the handle). But many carpenters prefer to mount the blade with the teeth facing away from the handle so the saw cuts on the push stroke. Try it both ways and decide for yourself which method you prefer.

**COPING SAW**

## Cut a 45-degree bevel to mark the profile

The first step in coping is to establish the cutting line. Cutting a 45-degree bevel (Photo 1) is the easiest method if the two moldings you're joining have the same profile. The molding shown has a complex profile, making for a challenging coping job. Most of the moldings you'll encounter will be considerably easier. Crown and cove moldings that

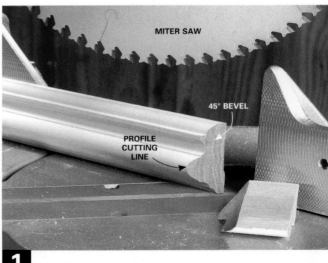

MITER SAW

45° BEVEL

PROFILE CUTTING LINE

**1** Bevel the end of the molding to be coped at a 45-degree angle to reveal the profile.

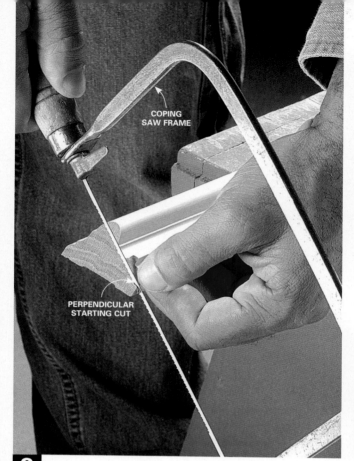

**COPING SAW FRAME**

**PERPENDICULAR STARTING CUT**

**2** Guide the blade with your thumbnail to start the cut accurately. If your molding has a little flat spot on top, start the cut with the blade of the coping saw held perpendicular to the molding to make a square starting cut.

rest at an angle against the wall and ceiling require a slightly different beveling technique to reveal the profile for coping. Photo 7 shows you how to position a crown molding in your miter box to cut this bevel.

## The fine blade reaches the tiniest corners

Photo 2 shows you how to start the cope. The technique varies slightly depending on the profile of the molding. Moldings like this with flat spots on the top require a square starting cut. If you start angling the cut too soon, you'll see a little triangular gap on the top of the moldings when you join them. Cut a practice cope on a scrap to confirm your starting angle.

Clamp the molding to a sawhorse or hold it in place with your knee while you saw. Don't force the blade. If the blade starts to leave the cutting line, back up a little and restart the cut. On steep curves, the frame of the saw may hit the molding. If this happens, back the saw out of the cut and saw in from the opposite direction. You may be able to complete some simple copes with one long cut, but in most cases you'll have to approach them from two or three different angles to finish the job (Photos 3 and 4).

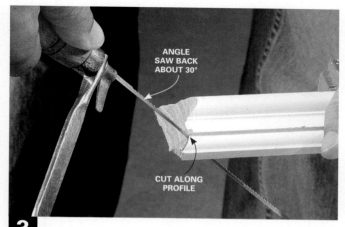

**ANGLE SAW BACK ABOUT 30°**

**CUT ALONG PROFILE**

**3** Angle the coping saw about 30 degrees to remove more wood from the back of the molding than the front. Then slowly and carefully saw along the profile. Concentrate on staying just outside the line. You can always sand or file away extra material.

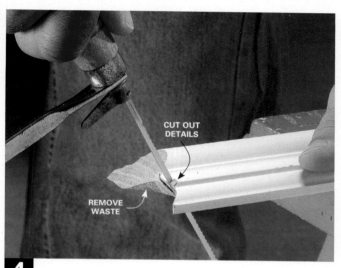

**CUT OUT DETAILS**

**REMOVE WASTE**

**4** Restart the cut to saw around sharp curves or to cut out notches. Complex shapes like this may require three or four approaches at different angles.

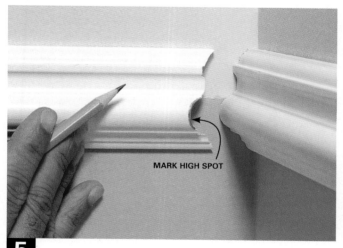

**MARK HIGH SPOT**

**5** Check the fit of the coped joint. Use a sharp pencil to mark spots that have to be sanded or filed.

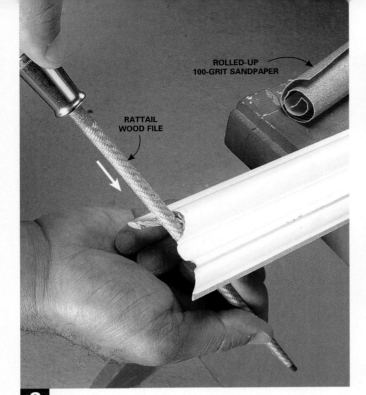

**6** File or sand off high spots. Use rolled-up sandpaper or a rattail file to fine-tune curved sections. Continue checking the fit, then filing or sanding until the joint fits tight.

After a few minutes of sawing, the cut will be complete; now it's time to test-fit the cope on a matching piece of trim. Some copes fit perfectly on the first try. Others require several more minutes of filing and sanding before you get a good fit (Photo 6). If the joint is close to fitting, you'll only need to touch up the high spots with 100-grit sandpaper. Use files to remove larger amounts of material.

## Crown and cove moldings are a little trickier

Photo 7 shows you how to position the crown molding upside down in your miter box for cutting the bevel. Attach a wood stop to the extension table to hold the molding at the correct angle.

Sawing copes on crowns, especially large ones, requires more effort because the angle of the cut has to be about 50 degrees—much steeper than for a baseboard cope. Even experienced carpenters cut this angle too shallow once in a while. Usually one or two areas will hit in the back and you'll have to remove more material (Photo 8).

Switch to a blade with fewer teeth for cutting thick materials like crown moldings. Then expect to spend 10 or 15 minutes on each joint to get a perfect fit.

Before you tackle crown molding copes, practice on smaller moldings like base shoe or simple baseboards to gain confidence. Once you've mastered coping you'll never miter an inside corner again.

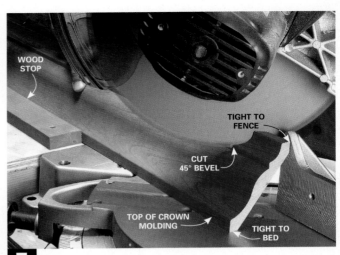

**7** Position your crown molding upside down in the miter box at the angle it will rest on the wall (flat spots tight to the bed and fence). Screw or clamp a stop to the extension table to support the crown molding at the correct angle.

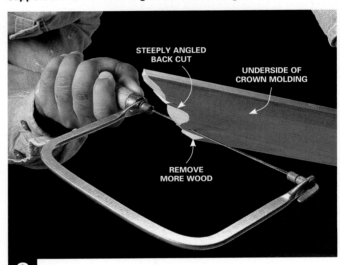

**8** Cope crowns at a sharper angle. Recut areas that are hitting in the back. It's common to have to remove large amounts of material in some areas to get a tight fit.

**9** Measure and cut the end of the first crown molding square. Butt it into the corner. Don't nail within 16 in. of the corner. Cope the second piece of crown molding and file and sand it for a perfect fit.

# Hide the nail heads

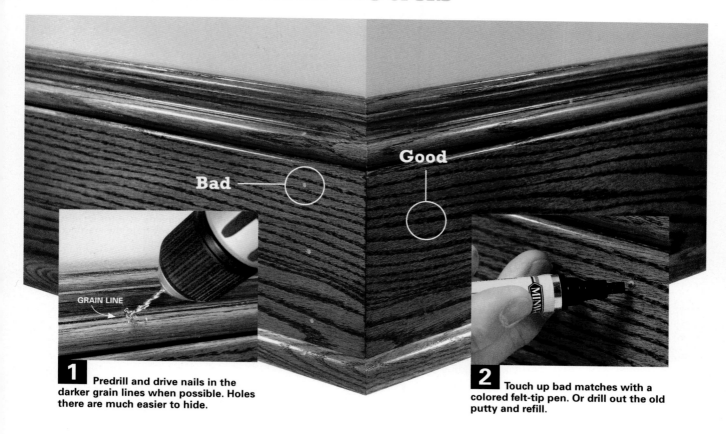

**Bad**

**Good**

GRAIN LINE

**1** Predrill and drive nails in the darker grain lines when possible. Holes there are much easier to hide.

**2** Touch up bad matches with a colored felt-tip pen. Or drill out the old putty and refill.

If you want your trim work to have a rustic, distressed look, go ahead and make the nail holes stand out. But if you're seeking a smooth, furniture-like finish, you have to make those nail holes disappear. Hiding nail holes takes a little more time and patience, but you'll get the fine, flawless appearance you want.

Begin by staining and sealing the trim before you put it up. Then buy colored putties to closely match the stain colors on the wood (Photo 3). (The other option, filling the holes with stainable filler before staining, is tricky unless you have a lot of experience.) Prestaining also makes the darker grain lines of the wood stand out. Position your nails there for the least visibility.

Buy several putty colors and mix them to match the wood color. Wood tone is rarely uniform, even when the wood is stained, so you can't rely on only one color to fill every hole (Photo 3). Fine-tune your blends and set your test piece alongside the trim to check the visibility of the nail holes under real light conditions. Lighting can significantly affect whether the filler blends or stands out.

Keep in mind that you can correct old mistakes or fix a situation where the wood has darkened after a year or two (with cherry, for example). Simply buy wood-tone felt-tip pens and touch up the filler (Photo 2). Or lightly drill out the

most unsightly old filler holes with a small drill bit and refill them. Colored putties and touch-up pens are available at most hardware stores, paint stores and home centers.

COLORED PUTTY

**3** Blend putty colors to more closely match the finished wood colors. One color won't do it all.

TEST PIECE

# Tips for replacing window and door screen

It's easy to replace the screen fabric in an aluminum frame. What's hard is figuring out which diameter spline to buy and how tight the fabric should be stretched. No problem—here's how to conquer both of those issues.

## Spline replacement

Let's start with spline basics. Don't reuse the old spline unless it's fairly new. It's probably dried and brittle, so install new spline when you install new fabric. New spline is more pliable and will slip into the channel easier and hold the fabric tighter. Besides, it's cheap.

There are nine different sizes of spline (yikes!), but most home centers only carry the four most common sizes. Forget about measuring the spline channel width. Just bring a small section of the old spline with you and visually match it to the new spline. If none of the options are dead-on, buy the two closest sizes. Then test-fit each one using a small patch of new screen. The spline should take just a bit of effort to snap into the frame. If you have to use a lot of muscle, the spline is too large.

## Installing the screen

You may be tempted to buy aluminum fabric. Don't. It's harder to install and is overkill for residential applications. Instead, take your old screen fabric with you to find new screen that matches the color and mesh size. That way it'll match your other screens. Then buy a concave spline roller and a roll of screen fabric.

Cut the screen 1 in. larger than the opening. Then clip off a corner of the fabric and place it over a corner of the aluminum frame. Press the spline and fabric into the channel and continue rolling it into the long edge of the screen (Photo 1). Round the corner (don't cut the spline at the corners), and use the same technique along the second edge of the screen frame. Next, place a heavy object in the center of the screen fabric (Photo 2) and finish installing the screen. Note: Don't overstretch the screen trying to get it "banjo"-tight. That'll bend the frame. Finish the job by trimming off the excess screen (Photo 3).

**CONCAVE ROLLER**

**1** Roll in the screen and spline. Align the screen squarely to the frame along the longest edge. Lay the spline directly over the channel ahead of the roller. Lightly stretch the screen away from the starting corner as you roll the spline into place.

**2** Depress the center with a heavy object. Load a brick in the center of the screen to create the proper amount of slack. Then continue installing the fabric along the third and fourth sides of the screen frame. Remove the brick.

**3** Cut off the excess screen. Use a brand-new utility blade and position the knife at a steep angle against the frame. Then trim off the excess screen.

# Adjust bypass closet doors

TILT TOWARD JAMB

LOCK IN PLACE

There's no reason to put up with sticking bypass closet doors or doors that have uneven gaps against the jambs—especially since they're so easy to fix. Usually the mounting bracket screws have loosened up, making the door sag and rub against the carpet or floor.

To fix it, you'll have to work from inside the closet, so get a flashlight and screwdrivers. Start by pushing one door closed against the jamb. Hold it against the jamb while you adjust the brackets as shown. Do the same on the other door. If the screw holes are stripped, just move the bracket over a few inches and remount it.

**1** **SQUARE THE DOOR.** Push the door against the jamb and lock it in place with shims at both corners.

ADJUSTING SCREW

PIVOT SCREW

LOCKING SCREW

**2** **TIGHTEN SCREWS.** Remount in new screw holes if necessary. Then test the door to make sure it rolls smoothly.

# Top 7 window cleaning tips

**MEET THE PRO**

**Brad Bolt,** owner of Clearly Professional Window Cleaning, Maricopa, AZ

Brad Bolt is a Field Editor and a pro window cleaner. Here are some of his favorite DIY tips.

**1** Use two different scrubbers—one for inside and one for outside—so you don't carry pollutants and bird excrement inside.

**2** Any kitchen dish liquid cleans dirt and grease and leaves the glass slippery so your squeegee glides well. A 100 percent biodegradable soap will protect sensitive plants outside. Inside it will protect toddlers and pets who put their mouth on the windows or sills.

**3** Magic Erasers remove silicone caulk and water drips.

**4** A paint-can opener is perfect for popping out window screens.

**5** A 12- to 14-in. squeegee is a good size for most situations. Put in a new rubber blade after each cleaning to prevent streaks.

**6** A razor blade removes paint overspray and gunk. Keep the glass wet and use a new blade each time. Microscopic rust particles on the blade can scratch the glass.

**7** Carry two detailing rags—one for dirty jobs like sills and the other for detailing the edges of the glass.

# Index

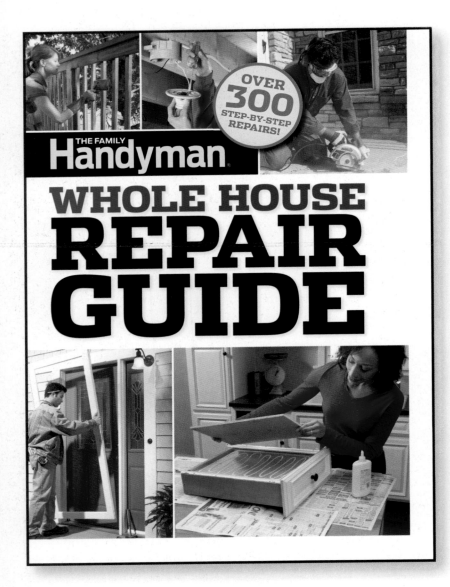